The Old Vic

THE OLD VIC

The Story of a Great Theatre
from Kean to Olivier to Spacey

TERRY COLEMAN

FABER & FABER

First published in Great Britain in 2014
by Faber & Faber Limited
Bloomsbury House
74–77 Great Russell Street
London WC1B 3DA

Typeset by Faber & Faber Limited
Printed in the UK by CPI Group (UK) Ltd, Croydon, CR0 4YY

The right of Terry Coleman to be identified as author of this work has
been asserted in accordance with Section 77 of the Copyright, Designs
and Patents Act 1988

A CIP record for this book is available from the British Library

ISBN: 978–0–571–31125–5

2 4 6 8 10 9 7 5 3 1

For V, without whom . . .

Contents

CONTENTS

Introduction

I welcome this lively history of the lively Old Vic. I've been lucky enough to perform in some wonderful theatres, but from the moment I stepped on to the Old Vic stage back in 1988 I immediately knew what Laurence Olivier meant when he said it enjoyed the most powerful actor–audience relationship in the world, and I'd say that comes through in this book.

I'd also say that over my eleven years as artistic director I've got to know this theatre well – its historic stage, the splendour of its auditorium and the less than splendour of its historic dressing rooms. But I didn't know the many fascinating aspects of its history that Terry Coleman's book uncovers.

Our priority now is to restore the building and raise an endowment fund to ensure that the next generation of actors and audiences will continue to enjoy the theatre as so many generations before have done, from 1818 on. I hope that this book will help connect people to the Old Vic's glorious history, so that they may be convinced of its importance for the future.

KEVIN SPACEY

PART ONE

1818–1880

Royal Coburg to Palace of Varieties

1

The Royal Coburg Theatre

The Old Vic owes its existence to Waterloo Bridge. At the beginning of the nineteenth century there was no bridge across the Thames between Westminster and Blackfriars. But during the last years of the Napoleonic wars a grand new bridge, said to be the finest in the world, was being built to make a crossing from the Strand. At the same time two promoters, Jones and Dunn, were running the Surrey Theatre, about a mile south of the river on the Blackfriars Road. The owner of that theatre's bricks and mortar, seeing that the bridge would encourage a new audience to stream across the river, modestly proposed to increase the rent sevenfold, from £600 a year to £4,200. At which Jones and Dunn, with a new partner called John Serres, resolved in 1816 to raise the money to build a new theatre a few hundred yards from the southern point of the new bridge, and to strip the old Surrey by taking away all the sets and costumes and lights, and practically all the interior fittings, which, as the lessees, they owned.

It happened that Serres was marine painter to the King. He used his royal connections to secure the patronage of His Serene Highness Leopold, Prince of Saxe-Coburg, and his wife Princess Charlotte. The theatre was to be called the Royal Coburg. Coburg is not a name which means much now, and Leopold was an impoverished and obscure German prince who had served as a cavalry officer in the Russian army, but his wife Charlotte was a royal princess of England, a handsome, self-willed, loud-voiced, and spirited girl who loved the theatre and was herself adored by the public, one of the few royals who was. And she was moreover the Prince Regent's only child and therefore heir presumptive to the throne of Britain. Her husband was obscure. The name of Coburg was obscure. Charlotte was not. It was an astonishing coup to secure her patronage.

On 14 September 1816 the theatre's foundation stone was laid, opposite the Pear Tree pub in Lambeth Marsh, with the royal standard, flags, and music, and before a large crowd who had come in the expectation that the princess herself, or at least her Coburg consort, would lay the stone. 'Although', as the *Observer* reported, 'application had been made to the illustrious couple', neither appeared, and the work was done by their proxy, Alderman Samuel Goodbehere, a master needle-maker and former sheriff of the City of London. He laid on mortar with a trowel, gave a grand dinner for the grandees and a cold collation to 140 workmen, and work began on the theatre designed by Rudolph Cabanel of Aix-la-Chapelle, said to be architect to the restored Louis XVIII of France.

In the following year, 1817, the bridge was completed, named Waterloo after the battle in which the Duke of Wellington had defeated Napoleon two years before, and opened with grand ceremony when the Duke and the Prince Regent walked side by side across it. But the theatre was already in trouble. The ground was swampy and foundation stones had to be brought across the Thames from the fourteenth-century Savoy Palace, the last remnants of which were being demolished. Then, in the grandest of theatre traditions, the money ran out. The projected cost of £4,000 became £12,000. The 140 workmen went on strike and even removed the scaffolding. An appeal for more investors failed. The project was rescued only by a Soho tallow-chandler called Francis Glossop, whose son Joseph had theatrical leanings, and by the Waterloo Bridge Company which had an interest in encouraging audiences to cross its bridge and pay the toll. The auditorium of the Coburg was a grand horseshoe, and Mr Serres had created a marine saloon running the width of the theatre. On its walls were painted a panorama of the Royal Navy's bombardment of Algiers in 1816 and a view of Venice exhibiting upwards of five hundred figures. Through this saloon the grander patrons passed to their boxes, which were painted fawn with gilded wreaths of flowers. At last, in May 1818, the theatre opened. The builders had still been at work the day before.

Evenings at the theatre were long in those days. The first night started at half past six and ran for four hours. The programme offered first a melodrama, *Trial by Battle*, the abduction of a village beauty by a wicked baron; then a fairy pantomime; and then *Midnight Revelry*, a harlequinade based in part on Milton's *Comus*, the clown to be played by the celebrated Mr Norman. Only it didn't happen that way. Mr Norman wanted to go on first so that he would have time to get to Covent Garden, where he was double-booked. So when at the beginning of the evening Mr Munro, the baron–villain, appeared on stage to give the Coburg's opening address, Mr Norman appeared through the curtain too, and put his case to the customers. They took his side, pelted the objecting management with apple cores and orange peel, and so it was decided. The harlequinade came first.

A print was sold showing the auditorium on that first night, and much too elegant it looks with all the women, down to the orange-seller in the pit, in high-waisted Regency dresses and the men in wigs or silk hats. Now it is true that an Old Vic audience today sits between Cabanel's same walls of 1818, and beneath his same roof, but everything else is different. In 1818 the best seats were in two tiers of boxes where the dress circle is now. There were no stalls, only a pit with backless wooden benches, and then the gods, the gallery, approached precipitously by a separate stone staircase. Boxes were four shillings and three shillings per person, the pit two shillings, and the gallery a shilling. Lighting was by oil lamp. The theatre, the same size as today and in the same space between the same walls, held, and this was the management's figure, 3,800 – 1,230 in the boxes, 1,090 in the pit, and 1,512 in the gallery. The whole house today holds 1,067. Outside, Waterloo Road was unpaved and half completed, and Waterloo Station thirty years in the future. The approach to the theatre was across a badly lit bridge and then through Lambeth Marsh, a happy den of thieves.

In spite of everything that first season was a success. The Coburg was intended as a summer theatre, and from May to October twenty-four dramas, ballets, and burlettas (farces with music) were given. Then William Barrymore, as actor-manager, thanking the public at the last October performance for its bounteous liberality and kind indulgence, announced a three-week closure for the re-embellishment of the house and then an unexpected winter season – with 'the introduction of fires to render the temperature of the air warm and comfortable'. He meant stoves, not open fires. The Coburg, he said, would smile at difficulty and gain a name worthy of its princely patronage. All the avenues to the theatre would be well lighted, and extra patrols, in the pay of the theatre, would afford ample security. Above all, Barrymore the showman promised to his discerning patrons 'a constant supply of novelty'.

The Coburg had always done novelty well. Serres had

added to his marine saloon a view of Moscow before the con-
flagration of 1812. Then there was the famous looking-glass
curtain, lowered so that the audience could see its own reflection. Joseph Glossop, the tallow-chandler's son who had by
then bought a controlling interest with his father's money, had
the idea from a Paris theatre. It was made of sixty-three mirrors assembled in a gilt frame but was all over fingermarks and
next to impossible to clean, weighed five tons, was suspended
from the roof, and soon had to be removed for fear of bringing
the house down. The first night it was lowered there was great
applause at its audacity, but after three or four minutes a voice
from the gallery called out: 'That's all very well. Now show us
summut else.'

From the beginning the audience *had* been shown something
else. The Coburg specialised in the spectacular. In *Wallace: Hero
of Scotland*, the set was an immense waterfall with bridge and
rocks, swarmed over by clansmen. In *The North Pole*, billed as a
celebration of British Intrepidity, an immense ship – the theatre
bills liked the word 'immense' – forced its way through islands
of ice, with her bowsprit projecting over the pit. An Indian
extravaganza gathered together on stage slaves, warriors, and
a rajah on a caparisoned elephant. The principal character of
Mazeppa was an impetuous wild horse galloping on stage. One
freely adapted version of *Richard III* starred the king's horse,
'White Surrey', rather than the actor playing the king.

The Coburg did however offer another *Richard III* without
a scene-stealing horse, and what seems to have been a play
loosely based on *Julius Caesar*. Both principal parts were played
by Junius Brutus Booth, who later emigrated to America where
he achieved great fame and founded a dynasty of actors, one
of whom, his son John Wilkes Booth, in 1865, achieved even
greater notoriety by assassinating Abraham Lincoln. Hazlitt,

the most fashionable critic of the day, often penetrating but sometimes plain highfaluting, saw Junius Brutus Booth and did not like him or the audience:

> The acting was bad, but that was nothing. The audience was low but that was nothing. It was the heartless indifference and contempt shown by the performers for their parts and by the audience for the players and the play, that disgusted us with all of them.

Hazlitt felt he was in a bridewell (a jail) or a brothel, among pickpockets and prostitutes, rather than in the precincts of Mount Parnassus or in the company of the Muses.

This was hard on the Coburg, but Glossop was no angel, and certainly not above a little piracy. In February 1821 the Drury Lane theatre put on a French melodrama called *Thérèse, or the Orphan of Geneva*. Glossop took a fancy to it, went to a performance with a professional copyist, and then the two sat up all night reconstructing the play. A week later it was presented at the Coburg. Drury Lane went to law and got an injunction, but this was overturned when Glossop somehow persuaded the court that his version was not plagiarised from Drury Lane but translated from the French original. The affair did not end there. Glossop had a talent for real-life melodrama and in May was back at Drury Lane, on which occasion he believed that the stage manager, James Winston, insultingly called a him a lamplighter, a reference to his father's trade of tallow-chandler. Glossop thereupon waited outside and then, witnessed by a pastry cook, a hatter, and as it happens a real lamplighter, horsewhipped Winston in the street. Winston brought an action for damages before the Lord Chief Justice. Glossop, through his counsel, who was no less than the Solicitor General, the second law officer of the Crown, submitted in mitigation that there was no substance in the *Thérèse* accusation, just some malignity towards Glossop on the part of Drury Lane, that he had been insulted, that he had been provoked by Winston's defending himself with a walking stick, and that he had furthermore only chastised him with a lady's horsewhip. The jury found for Winston and awarded him damages of £150. This was half a good night's takings at the Coburg, but it was all hilarious publicity for Glossop.

The Coburg's great night of 1821 was the visit of Queen Caroline. Poor mad George III had died, the Prince Regent had succeeded as George IV, and his wife Caroline, whether he liked it or not, became Queen. He would have preferred not. In 1795 he had become engaged to her sight-unseen; when he first set eyes on her he asked for a glass of brandy, and they had remained together only long enough to beget a daughter. By 1821 they had been separated for years, and she returned to England only to claim her place at the Coronation. The Prince Regent had done his utmost to malign her but had failed to divorce her by Act of Parliament, and she in consequence was most popular with the Press and the people. On 26 June she went to the Coburg. The performance was at six-thirty. By just after two the theatre was already crowded and thousands waited outside. The Queen drove up in a coach and four, was met with ceremony and lighted torches and conducted by Serres through the marine saloon to the royal box fitted for the occasion with crimson velvet and bouquets of flowers. She saw a classic triple bill – a one-act comic sketch; a new musical piece called *Marguerite; or the Deserted Mother*; and a melodrama called *The Carib Chief and the Irish Witch*. To all this was added an acrobatic act by Il Diavolo Antonio. Throughout the evening there were cries of 'God bless your majesty' and 'The

Queen for ever'. Glossop was delighted. That night the takings amounted to £317. A month later the Queen was barred from the Coronation in Westminster Abbey by prize fighters dressed as pages, and a month after that she died, saying she was poisoned. Not even the Coburg could have outdone that for a plot.

Next year Grimaldi appeared and Glossop disappeared. Grimaldi, the clown whose make-up and dress and whole appearance have since been imitated by every clown, played for ten weeks, in spite of illness, once with his son in the pantomime *Disputes in China*. Glossop, after attempting to raise £10,000 to buy a share of his old enemy, Drury Lane, fell on hard times, got wind that a warrant was out for him accusing him of forgery, and left England in a hurry. But he absconded to some prosperity. For the next three years he had a share in running both La Scala, Milan and San Carlo, Naples, the biggest theatres in Italy and indeed the whole of Europe.

By 1824 a new impresario, George Davidge, had taken over the lease, and the Coburg put on its greatest extravaganza yet. This was *George III: or the Father of His People*, a supposed tribute to the late king. In defiance of all precedent the late king was impersonated on stage, together with the reigning George IV, various nobles, William Wilberforce, and Charles James Fox. A series of scenes showed George III's life from early days at Windsor, a Hyde Park review, a speech from the throne abolishing the slave trade, and a Westminster Abbey oratorio with 120 singers; the entertainment ended with George III, in cocked hat and riding boots, ascending into heaven. The play was somehow not prohibited and ran for ten weeks, but then, when Davidge's licence came up for renewal, the magistrates told him they thought the representations 'injudicious if not improper, representing sacred characters and the highest persons in the realm'.

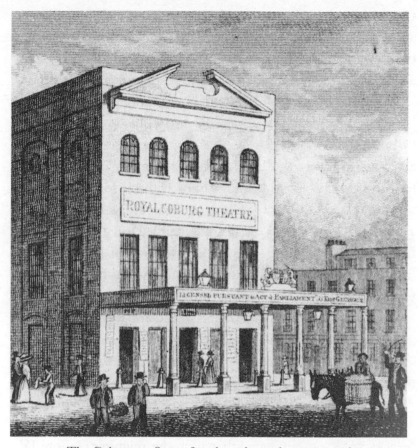

The Coburg, *c.*1824, after the colonnade was erected

Davidge also pushed his luck by presenting more Shakespeare – of a sort. In strict law only the so-called patent theatres of Covent Garden and Drury Lane, which held ancient royal licences, could present Shakespeare or any straight play. This was an historical accident, but the privilege it conferred was jealously guarded by the patent theatres. The others, the Coburg among them, were known as minor theatres, which had nothing to do with their size or capacity. At the Coburg, to get round the restrictions of the patent, *Richard III* had been presented with musical interludes, but this device had failed and cost Davidge a fine of fifty pounds. So he became more and more ingenious. A sort of *Merchant of Venice* was put on as *The Three Caskets*; *Lear* became *The King and His Three Daughters*; and a *Hamlet* was commissioned, supposedly based on a celebrated French tragedy-pantomime, in which neither Hamlet nor Ophelia died and the play ended with their marriage and coronation.

Davidge became yet more emboldened and in 1831 retained the great and wild Edmund Kean, who had played all the great Shakespearean parts. For six nights, at the vast fee of fifty pounds a night, he played Richard III, Lear, and Othello. His appearance on 27 June has become legendary. Reports differ, but the most generally accepted has him playing Othello, being displeased at the greater applause given to Iago, drinking a great deal of brandy and water, and then defiantly coming forward, still blacked-up, to take a rowdy curtain call.

'What do you want?' he said.

'You, you.'

'Well then, I am here.'

More uproar.

'I have', Kean responded, 'acted in every theatre of the United Kingdom of Great Britain and Ireland. I have acted throughout the United States of America, but in my life I have never acted to such a set of ignorant, unmitigated brutes as I see before me.'

In 1832 Davidge appeared before a Commons Select Committee set up to enquire into the state of the theatre and in particular into the archaic distinction between patent and minor houses. The chairman was Edward Bulwer-Lytton, a young Member of Parliament and journalist who later wrote plays and other works, and is best remembered for his novel

The Last Days of Pompeii. The examination first established that the Coburg was a minor theatre, licensed by magistrates under Act of Parliament, and then question and answer went like this:

What is the nature of your licence? – Music and dancing.

What construction do you put upon music and dancing? – I generally apply the construction of the Act of Parliament itself, which says music, dancing, and other entertainments of the like kind.

Do you conform to that act by giving the public nothing but music and dancing? – Certainly not.

Then what construction do you put upon 'other entertainments'? – I conclude it is a very comprehensive question which has never yet been decided . . .

Do you include Shakespeare's plays? – I am aware that there is an Act of Parliament which declares that should not be the case, but it has gone on from management to management to represent plays of that description, and I have fallen into the same course which other managers have adopted before, without pretending to the legality of it.

You have given Shakespeare's plays on your stage? – Yes, repeatedly.

Do you find they attract as much as your musical and dancing entertainments? – Considerably more. I am induced to think that the style of entertainment given in the minor theatres some twenty or twenty-five years ago, and which was popular at that time, would not be tolerated by the play-going public now.

What description of representations were those? – Pantomime, and excessively loose rhymes to the jingle of a piano-forte; frequently recitative or the language spoken in rhyme; horrible doggrel or jingle, which the public now would scout.

So there it was. Shakespeare to be preferred to horrible doggerel. But Davidge was in trouble at the Coburg. He was famously tight-fisted and had made a bad mistake in refusing to offer decent terms to his resident playwright, Douglas Jerrold, for a melodrama called *Black Ey'd Susan*. Jerrold had taken it to the Surrey, where it immediately ran for 150 nights, and was then performed on and off for fifty years. All the original backers were gone. Serres was bankrupt and dead. In 1833 Davidge sold his lease of the Coburg to Daniel Egerton and William Abbott, who had run theatres in London, Dublin, and Paris.

2

The Royal Victoria Theatre

If they did nothing else, and the sad truth is that they did little, Egerton and Abbott did give the theatre its famous name. The Coburg connection, at first so glorious, had ceased to mean anything. It had once carried with it the patronage of Princess Charlotte, heir presumptive to the crown. But she, a strong and lively woman, had given birth to a stillborn son one day in 1817 and died the next. She was twenty-one, had been the most popular of the royal family, and was sincerely mourned. As her bereft husband, Leopold, said: 'Two generations gone in a moment.' And it was so. Charlotte had been George III's heir, and her son had been her heir. Their death together left the throne with no heir in the direct line. The *Morning Post* said no occurrence in its recollection had ever produced such general, sincere, and deep affliction throughout the metropolis of the empire. The London theatres closed for two weeks.

Charlotte died before the Coburg theatre even opened. Her widower, Leopold of Saxe-Coburg, later visited it only twice, and by 1831 he had anyway left England to become the first King of the Belgians.

By 1833, when Egerton and Abbott took over, George III had been dead for thirteen years, George IV had died three years before, and Charlotte, if she had survived, would have been Queen. History would have been different. There would have been no Queen Victoria.

Back in 1817, when Charlotte died, the plot would have done for a Royal Coburg burletta. George III had six sons – the Prince Regent and five royal dukes – but they had not produced a single living legitimate child between them. So the begetting of a royal child was necessary to save the dynasty. The third son, the Duke of Clarence, had sired ten children by a mistress, Dorothea Jordan, who happened to be an actress, but they were illegitimate and did not count. However, one of the king's sons, Edward Duke of Kent, was not only unmarried but a good friend of the bereaved Leopold. Edward was the most travelled royal of his day, having served in the army in Germany, Gibraltar, Canada, and the West Indies. His friend Leopold had a widowed sister, a princess of Saxe-Coburg, who was known to be fertile because she had borne two children to her late husband. Leopold consequently recommended her to Edward as fit for the purposes of wife and mother. Edward set aside his French mistress of many years, married the princess, and within a year they produced a daughter. Edward then promptly caught cold in Salisbury Cathedral and died. The duchess was unfortunate with her husbands but she and their daughter survived him, and that daughter was Victoria. She became heir presumptive to the throne, and in 1837 succeeded her uncle William IV and became Queen.

Back in 1833, having taken over the Coburg, Egerton and Abbott searched for a new patron, approached the widowed Duchess of Kent, and then very respectfully announced to the public that Her Royal Highness had been graciously pleased to take the theatre under her immediate protection for the encouragement of native dramatic talent and to command that in future it should be called 'The Royal Victoria'.

They had their new patron and new name. But there is one small caveat, one last twist in the plot, which is that the Duchess of Kent's own Christian name was also Victoria, and she was after all the patron. But it would be uncivil not to assume, as the world has ever since, that the theatre was named not after the duchess but after her daughter the future queen.

The new lessees redecorated the auditorium and built a new stage, Waterloo Bridge was made toll-free to patrons, and horse omnibuses called Red Rover were put on to convey passengers from Westminster to the theatre. The only trouble was that there were not likely to be many from that direction. As the proprietors of both Covent Garden and the old Coburg had publicly remarked, it was becoming fashionable to dine later and later, as late as seven rather than at four, and with the theatres opening at six-thiry this late hour of dining had 'taken away, as it were, all the upper classes from the theatre'. Davidge, when he ran the Coburg, had been asked if the theatre could not adapt its hours to those of the fashionable world, and said it could not. That would have meant starting the performance at ten at night and sometimes going on until four in the morning. He said there would be loose scenes of every description and, when asked why, said: 'It might happen that gentlemen breaking up from convivial parties might fall in, and they would not be the best behaved people in the world.' And as Charles Kemble of Covent Garden also lamented: 'Religious prejudice is very much increased, evangelical feeling and so on; they take away a great number of persons from the theatre who used to frequent it.'

The result was, at the minor theatres anyway, a lowering of taste. Egerton and Abbott brought in *Black Ey'd Susan* which an earlier management had rejected, and put on a new farce called *The Spare Bed, or the Shower Bath*. The critic of *The Times*,

reviewing what he called a melodrama of caverns and cata-
combs, mysterious and magical appearances and disappear-
ances, goblins and demons in great variety, combats single and
general, ending in a grand explosion, said it was not necessary
to follow the plot since the virtue of the piece lay in the inven-
tion of the scene painters, dressers, and decorators, the scene
of the Colosseum in Rome by moonlight being particularly
impressive.

Victoria Theatre playbill, 1833, when *Othello* was supplemented
by the farce *The Spare Bed*

At any rate, Princess Victoria was pleased with what she saw when she visited the theatre with her mother on 28 November 1833. She wrote in her diary: 'It is a very clean and pretty little theatre, and the box we were in was very comfortable. The first performance was the opera of Guy Mannering in 3 acts, which is very pretty . . . Gustavus the Third was the next piece, a drama in two acts . . . In the last scene, the Masqued Ball, Mdlle. Rosier danced La Danse de Folie. She is a very plain person but dances very well. We came home at ¼ to 12. I was soon in bed and asleep.'

Perhaps she thought the theatre pretty because of its recent redecoration. It is odd she thought it little because it was as big as the then Drury Lane. The management had put on a better class of play than usual for her, though it is strange that she, as heir to the throne, should have been shown *Gustavus the Third*, in which the real assassination of a monarch, that of the King of Sweden in 1792, is enacted on stage. This is the same story as in Verdi's *Un Ballo in Maschera*, but that was not written until twenty-five years later.

That evening was the only time Victoria set foot in the Old Vic. She was fourteen at the time and heir apparent. She became Queen less than four years later on the death of her uncle William IV. Soon after her visit the theatre offered as part of its repertory an extravaganza called *Female Government, or the World Turned Upside Down. The Times* said it was very agreeable and received with peals of laughter.

Next summer the theatre pulled off a coup when it presented the violinist Niccolò Paganini, frequently said to be in league with the devil, to give a farewell concert at extra prices, seven shillings for the best boxes and upper boxes four shillings. Even so, it's difficult to see how this could have covered the fees he demanded, which were notoriously enormous. A little jingle ran:

> Who are these who pay five guineas
> To hear this tune of Paganini's?
> Echo answers, 'Pack of ninnies.'

He played pieces described on the bill as Larghetto Amoroso; the Dance of the Witches round the Walnut Tree of Benevento; and a Sonata composed expressly for Napoleon, as played before the emperor at Milan, on one string (the fourth). His fee that night went to Charlotte Watson, a seventeen-year-old singer, with whom, four days later, he eloped to France.

The Victoria did have what could almost have been called a house playwright in James Sheridan Knowles, who often acted in his own works which were as various as *The Blind Beggar of Bethnal Green* and *William Tell*. He also once acted Macbeth with Mrs Egerton as Lady Macbeth. His masterpiece was *Virginius*, and William Macready, a great tragedian, played the name part in a performance for the benefit of its author. He complained his dressing room was more ill-appointed than many provincial ones, and that the wings were choked with people. 'I was rather inclined to be out of temper with this but soon recollected myself and acted as well as I could – much of the character, Virginius, very well – really and with heart. My reception was most enthusiastic. At the end I was called for . . . Went on the stage, or rather was pulled on by Knowles – the applause was tumultuous. I bowed and retired.'

Abbott, he said, distressed him with importunities to engage for a few nights, but he firmly resisted and felt himself right to do so. Abbott was probably desperate. By then he was in sole charge. Egerton, thinking the partnership hopeless, had withdrawn, leaving Abbott complaining bitterly that his losses were much greater than Egerton's, and that one night the ballet had taken only thirteen pounds though it cost eighty to keep the house open. Egerton told the insolvency court that he had lost the entire earnings of a frugal, industrious life by his speculation at the Victoria. Having been declared bankrupt he took to his bed and died and was given a lonely funeral. The *Observer* reported that a plate on his coffin carried the inscription: 'Daniel Egerton, aged 65. Thy friends have forsaken thee.' No one from the Victoria was at the funeral. Then it was Abbott's turn. Only a month after the Macready night he too left the theatre, and escaped to America.

At this low point, Joseph Glossop reappeared. He had last been heard of thirteen years before when he had fled the country, but since then he had run La Scala, Milan. This, it was said, must have magnified rather than diminished his intentions of splendour since he was last in London. He took a lease of the Victoria and set about doing precisely what Egerton and Abbott had done before him – spending a fortune on yet again renovating the theatre. Cabanel, the original architect, was brought back, and so was the looking-glass curtain, put together from the sixty-three fragments stored in the building. It was all very grand. *Figaro in London*, a fashionable comic paper which was a forerunner of *Punch*, described the scene on the opening night:

> Immediately on the opening of the doors, the house was crammed in every part by persons who testified in phraseology as various as the prices their respective feelings at viewing the magnificence of the interior. The occupant of the dress circle, who had paid his *four* shillings, was struck with blank and perfectly silent astonishment, while the *sixpenny* tenant of the gallery vented his connoisseurship in loud exclamations of 'Crikey, Bill, an't this here magnificent?'

Against the taste of the time, the Victoria went determinedly upmarket. The first play was *Othello*. Then *Richard III* was given. Then *The Last Days of Pompeii* – piratically adapted from the novel without as much as acknowledging the author, Bulwer-Lytton – ran longer than either of the Shakespeares. A new leading actor called David Osbaldiston, who was later to play a large part in the history of the Old Vic, appeared in *Coriolanus*. But Glossop had borrowed up to the hilt, could not recoup what he had spent, and in March 1835 his creditors descended upon him, closed the theatre, and took costumes and scenery as well. *Figaro*, which had earlier been so admiring, changed its tune. 'Glossop's failure has caused a wide scattering of the pomp and pageantry of the Victoria Theatre. The singular villainy of this man deserved exposure. The various frauds, the mean unnecessary trickery – the shuffling – the base ingratitude to all who served and befriended him, the downright robbery of poor people by this double bankrupt, are unparalleled.' One of his unpaid debts was £900 of the £1,200 he had contracted to pay Abbott for the theatre lease. Glossop was next heard of as a boarding-house keeper in Brussels. In a year three men had failed. One was dead and two others had left the country. Running the Victoria was already as chancy a business as running the Coburg had been. The Duchess of Kent's royal patronage seems not to have survived all this. Up to August 1834 the theatre described itself in newspaper advertisements as the Royal Victoria. By the next year it was plain Victoria.

The theatre struggled on until it was closed in March 1836 by decree of a baron of the Court of Exchequer. It reopened after six months, in the hands of transient managements. One even installed a new chandelier, but the repertory descended into blood and thunder. The Victoria was where you went for a rowdy night out. One evening, as the *Observer* reported in December 1835, four masters of merchant ships at Wapping, on a spree, took a cab to the Victoria where they jumped on stage, insisted the actors should take a drink with them (great applause), were thrown out, and went to the nearest pub where they attacked anyone who approached them. Next morning in court they were discharged, no witnesses having come forward against them.

This was the theatre Dickens described in a piece called 'The Streets – Night'. He sees ragged boys sheltering from the rain under a shop-blind. 'Here they amuse themselves with theatrical converse, arising from their last half-price visit to the Victoria gallery, admire the terrific combat, which is nightly encored, and expatiate on the inimitable manner in which Bill Thompson can . . . go through the mysterious involutions of a sailor's hornpipe.'

Two hours later and Dickens describes the theatres emptying out.

> One o'clock! Parties returning from the different theatres foot it through the muddy streets; cabs, hackney-coaches, and theatre omnibuses, roll swiftly by; watermen with dim, dirty lanterns in their hands, and large brass plates upon their breasts, who have been shouting and rushing about for the last two hours, retire to their watering houses, to solace themselves with the creature comforts of pipes and purl [hot spiced beer]; the half-price pit and box frequenters of the theatres throng to the different houses of refreshment; and chops, kidneys, rabbits, oysters, stout, cigars, and 'goes' innumerable, are served up amidst a noise and confusion of smoking, running, knife-clattering, and waiter-chattering, quite indescribable.

By the end of the 1830s the Victoria had descended into out-and-out melodrama and animal shows. *The Black Legend of Rotherhithe* was followed by *The Smuggler's Gibbet*. Monkeys danced the tightrope in a pantomime. Frederick Tomlins, drama critic of the *Morning Advertiser*, and himself the author of a tragedy, reviewed the state of the London stage in 1840 and wrote:

> The Victoria Theatre has perhaps suffered more vicissitudes than any other. Its performances have been of every kind and every quality. Melodramas of the deepest dye and coarsest texture were once its staple commodity – when Turpin cut his horse's throat upon the stage and the fact was 'realised' by a quantity of red ochre. Here Kean has performed; as also his imitator Junius Brutus Booth; and Mr Sheridan Knowles in some of his own refined and genuine plays . . . It has been everything by turns but nothing long – ever aiming at novelty but never pursuing any course sufficiently steadily to raise a character or secure a continuous and respectable audience. Situated in one of the worst neighbourhoods, its audiences are of the lowest kind, and if the English emperor or empress should visit it, it would be necessary to imitate the Roman potentate by drenching the audience with rose-water to neutralise certain vile odours arising from gin and tobacco and bad ventilation. But even here . . . the universality of the power of dramatic genius, and the natural force of the mind and heart, is demonstrated by the attention and justice with which certainly one of the most uneducated audiences appreciate genuine pathos, and even genuine wit and poetry.

3

Osbaldiston and Miss Vincent

In 1841 David Osbaldiston took a lease on the Victoria, bringing with him Eliza Vincent, and together they revived the theatre. Between them they ran it for fifteen years, longer than anyone before Lilian Baylis. Osbaldiston was not just lessee but a thorough man of the theatre, an actor who had played the Ghost in *Hamlet* and the King in *Lear*. As a manager he had run Covent Garden for a while and then, for some years, the Surrey. There his leading lady was Miss Vincent, much admired, and with her he eloped and had a daughter, having left his wife and their son and two earlier daughters.

This gave the new manager and leading lady of the Victoria an attractively raffish air, and both were much disapproved of and written about. He was called Old Iron Jaws, condemned as mean, and said to have 'stolen the newsman's daughter'. Miss Vincent had in 1815 been born the daughter of a newspaper-seller in the Blackfriars Road. She had appeared as a child at Drury Lane as the Spirit of the Star in a Christmas piece, giving promise of talent and surpassing beauty which as a young woman she realised. She became a soubrette at Covent Garden. She appeared with Kean and Macready. When she went to the Victoria one publication called *The Daughters of Thespis*, promising to give what it called a peep behind the curtain at London's dramatic beauties, devoted its entire front page to a colour engraving of her, saying that at the Victoria she was 'announced in the largest of type in the largest of bills at the largest of the minor theatres, as the acknowledged heroine of domestic drama'. It also published a few lines of rather carping verse:

> Coquettish and lively is her air –
> Both studied, though both seem neglected;
> Careless is she with artful care,
> Affecting to seem unaffected.

In other words, she was an actress. And she obviously had that sexual presence without which an actress has little. She had, said *Daughters of Thespis*, been puffed into a sort of fame, the principal portion of which had been gained by exhibiting her person in tight buckskins and top-boots as the redoubted Dick Turpin, and singing an elegant ditty, coarse and vulgar even in a man, called 'Nix my dolly, fake away'.

It was a song full of thieves' cant. 'Fake away' begged to be sung suggestively, and no doubt she did just that. And she did get consistently good notices. The *Theatrical Times* said there was not an actress on the stage possessing greater versatility of talent, and then, hinting at another side to her, sweetly added: 'In private life, Miss Vincent's habits are of a most retiring nature – she is devotedly attached to botany, possesses a splendid collection of plants, and has gained several prizes from the Surrey Horticultural Society.'

She had played Dick Turpin in breeches and, the Victoria being the Victoria, it was the custom, when her noble steed's throat was cut, that copious stage blood should flow. But she had enjoyed her greatest success in domestic dramas, particularly in *Susan Hopley, or the Vicisssitudes of a Servant Girl*, a hit of

1842 which by 1849 had run for 343 performances. It was a melodrama, written by George Dibdin Pitt, the author of the greatest melodrama of all, *Sweeney Todd*, in which a barber cuts his customers' throats, tips them into the basement, and then sells them as meat pies. In *Susan Hopley* the servant girl of the title is seduced and betrayed, but then adored and rescued by an honest farmer. Osbaldiston advertised that the play started at six and ended at half past eight, so that servant girls wishing to see it would be able to get permission from their mistresses. Miss Vincent played the part so movingly that the audience would call out to warn her of the unseen villains lurking in the wild and dangerous scenery behind her.

And it was not an easy audience to move. A reporter from the *Morning Post* went to see the play.

> The sight is still before our eyes, the noise is still ringing in our ears. The boxes and the pit, the slips and the galleries, were crammed, and then the remaining multitude were heaped, displeased and discontented, in the saloons and the lobbies. Here chairs and tables were placed, fought for, and gained, and an uncertain and unsatisfactory sight was afforded through the aperture of the boxes. Men demanding the return of their money were huddled with women anxious for the safety of their bonnets, and children crying for a supply of oranges. The equilibrium of a table would now be disregarded, and then what shrieks, what squalls, what bumps, and what bruises. But why do we describe the scenes in the lobby when we went to describe the merits of the performance? For the best of reasons. We distinctly saw the one, and we could hardly catch a distant glimpse of the other. We peeped and peered over the shoulders and midst the

heads of the hundreds before and around us, and now there came a heroine in distress and presently a lover to relieve her, but our occasional view of the stage did not enable us to understand its incidents or its plot. But good or bad the audience were satisfied. They roared with delight at everything that was done and every word that was spoken, and the only dispute among them appeared to be which of the many there could shout the loudest.

Still, the reporter praised the spirit and energy of Osbaldiston for putting the play on, and the talent of Miss Vincent.

Osbaldiston knew he was on to a good thing, and why. 'Look around,' he adjured his audience in one playbill, 'and behold the moist tears of compassion, flowing from the overcharged heart. Who can restrain these, the best feelings of our nature, at the representation of such domestic woe, rendered still more poignantly acute by the reflection that the occurrence in real life is but too frequent and too fatal?' He then quoted Dr Johnson: 'What is nearest to the heart touches us most; the passions rise higher at Domestic than Imperial tragedies.'

Others put it less exaltedly.

> Memory of Susan Hopley
> Treated most impropl'y
> Then the Vic enjoyed monopl'y,
> Of such works it had the pick.

The Theatre Regulation Act of 1843 abolished the old distinction between patent and minor theatres. This meant that the Victoria no longer answered to the local magistrates but came like Covent Garden and Drury Lane under the authority of the Lord Chamberlain, and above all could freely put on stage plays, defined as 'every tragedy, comedy, farce, opera, burletta, interlude, melodrama, pantomime, or other entertainment of the stage'. The old restrictions had been evaded and for the most part unenforced, but now the Victoria could freely put on Shakespeare or any straight play without having to make a pretence of musical interludes and without the risk of a fifty-pound fine if a patent theatre felt its monopoly encroached upon. Osbaldiston announced his intention of producing what he called 'the Sterling Tragedies and Comedies of the British Stage on a Scale of Splendour and Effect hitherto unattempted'. In 1845 the Victoria did put on *Hamlet* and *Othello*, with Miss Vincent as Ophelia and Desdemona, but melodrama remained its bread and butter.

The railway was coming to Waterloo, being built on brick arches from the old Nine Elms station two miles to the west, and so did railway plays. In one a father was portrayed in anguished search of his son and his baggage in a railway waiting room. In another was presented a scene that predated a thousand silent films – the heroine tied across the line, the shrieking train approaching from a tunnel, and the girl untied and snatched away just in time as the express roars past. Osbaldiston's bills grew ever bolder, as they well might since this lessee–actor–manager was also his own printer, the Victoria having its own press. He boasted of 'powerful and increased talent', and of Miss Vincent 'supported by the strength of the company', which he claimed was the best in London north or south of the river.

In 1848 the Waterloo terminus was at last opened, among whose manifold advantages, he said, none could be greater than the 'opportunity they present of enabling Parties to witness the superior performances of the Victoria Theatre'. But it did not work that way. The station was only two hundred yards

away from the Victoria, but brought passengers who could just as well walk over the bridge to Drury Lane or Covent Garden. And by then the swamps and fields round Waterloo had been thoroughly built over, the local population had more than trebled since 1820, and that had become the Victoria's audience.

Piracy flourished. Dickens's stories and novels were looted, his *Christmas Carol* in 1844, and then *Martin Chuzzlewit*. Any best-selling novel was fair game. *Jane Eyre* was published in August 1847 and had run through several editions by December. Osbaldiston, never a man to let an opportunity slip, advertised that this wonderful work 'now cresting the sympathy and admiration of all the reading world of this vast metropolis' would be presented as an entirely new drama. By the end of January 1848, before its author was even known to be Charlotte Brontë, *Jane Eyre* was presented on stage at the Victoria, of course with Eliza Vincent. The dramatist, or adaptor, was not even credited.

That year, Miss Vincent played out in real life an episode that could have come straight from any Gothic novel. She was getting into her carriage at the stage door at eleven one night when a young woman, who had been lurking about for hours, rushed at her and attempted to strangle her. One of the company's actors, hearing cries of 'Murder', rescued his leading lady. The policeman who then arrested the assailant found she was carrying a quantity of stones and a sharp knife, and was exclaiming that she intended to murder Miss Vincent. The attacker, one Eliza Cole, otherwise known as Eliza White, was a prepossessing woman. Miss Vincent said she had known the girl as an actress years before but had nothing to do with her.

For her part the attacker claimed she had known Miss Vincent when she was with a Mr Shepperd (a former manager of

the Surrey, before Osbaldiston). She, Eliza Cole, had been a
ballet girl at the Haymarket with Miss Vincent, had fallen on
bad times, asked her for help, and been denied. She had been
waiting for some nights and seeing her getting into her carriage
thought it a 'good time to do for her'.

This was reported in garbled detail in the *Observer*. With
its murderous threats, and its hints of previous liaisons, it was
an everyday story of theatre folk. But the magistrate plainly
thought there was more to the affair than met the eye. First of
all he asked if the girl claimed relationship with Mr Osbaldiston, to which Miss Vincent replied not as far as she was aware.
Then the magistrate told the girl that if she had any complaint
to make she should make it in the proper way, and not with
violence. He then concluded that she did not appear to be in
a proper state, and that he would detain her until some of her
friends became answerable for her future conduct.

Three months later the girl was back in court again, charged
with threatening to murder Miss Vincent on a second occasion, and with attempting to extort money. It turned out that
she had spent three months in jail after her first appearance,
but as soon as she was let out she had gone to the Victoria,
rushed into the theatre lobby, demanded to see Miss Vincent,
and been refused. She had thereupon said she would have Miss
Vincent's life, and had been arrested. In court a second time,
Miss Vincent again said she knew nothing about her, the girl
said she was sorry, and the magistrate bound her over for six
months in her own recognisance to keep the peace. This was
lenient almost beyond belief, but the girl then said she could
not find bail and asked the magistrate to forgive her. At this
Miss Vincent said the girl had hovered round the theatre and
threatened to murder her, and she could not trust her. Only
then did the magistrate send the girl back to jail, probably on

remand since he had no jurisdiction to try her for threatened murder, and at this point she disappears.

Now this is all very suspicious, the more so when the names under which the ballet girl was charged are considered. At her first appearance she had been called Eliza Cole, otherwise known as Eliza White. When she appeared a second time it was as Harriet White, alias Cole. And it happened that Osbaldiston's deserted wife, whom he had left for Miss Vincent, was Harriet Coles, whom he had married in 1819. The ballet girl was young and so could not have been the wife, but some connection seems likely and that would explain the magistrate's leniency. Or perhaps the girl was mad, first calling herself Eliza after Osbaldiston's mistress and then Harriet after his wife. Whatever the truth, the publicity probably did little to harm Miss Vincent, that heroine of the domestic drama.

In 1849 and 1850 three writers of distinction described the Victoria and its audience – Charles Kingsley, author of *The Water Babies*; Henry Mayhew, a great reporter and author of *London Labour and the London Poor*; and, for the second time, Dickens.

The tone of Kingsley's account is perhaps heightened by his fervent Christian socialism, and in any case it was not a report but a passage in a novel, *Alton Locke*. He describes the crowd entering the theatre: '. . . and the beggary and rascality of London were pouring in to hear their low amusement, from the neighbouring gin palaces and thieves' cellars. A herd of ragged boys, vomiting forth slang, filth and blasphemy, pushed past us, compelling us to take good care of our pockets.'

Mayhew describes the New Cut and Waterloo as a well-known rookery of young thieves, who often stole from the market stalls from a love of mischief rather than from a desire for plunder. They stole apples, pears, oranges, or a few coppers, sometimes enough to pay for entrance to the Victoria gallery,

Rough trade outside the Victoria, 1851

which they delighted to frequent. He describes the 'almost awful' rush to the gallery, by way of its own side entrance, which started at three o'clock, this for a performance at six. Boys rushed in and perched on wooden balustrades three storeys up to get a good seat when the doors were opened. 'The girls shriek, men start, and a nervous fear is felt lest the massive staircase should fall in with the weight of the throng, as it lately did with the most terrible results.' That was on Boxing Day 1848, when four hundred boys crowded on the staircase and two were crushed to death.

Dickens, in his magazine *Household Words*, is more sympathetic. He describes Joe Whelks of the New Cut, who has few books and little inclination to read.

But put Joe in the gallery of the Victoria Theatre, show him doors and windows in the scene that will open and shut, and that people can get in and out of; tell him with these aids and by the help of living men and women dressed up, confiding to him their innermost secrets, in voices audible half a mile off; and Joe will unravel a story through all its entanglements, and sit there as long after midnight as you have anything left to show him.

This chimes in with the many accounts of rough and illiterate audiences following in silence the language of the plays of Shakespeare.

In December 1850 Osbaldiston and Miss Vincent played together in a play entitled *The Honeymoon*, but before Christmas he made his will and on 28 December he died. He was given what the press called a plain funeral, with a plain coffin, and an 'entire absence of the customary mournful paraphernalia'. Rain fell in torrents, yet at this plain funeral the mourners included his son George, his stage manager, his solicitor, and his doctor, and not only most of his own company at the Victoria but also other members of the 'profession'. The report in the *Era*, a newspaper which always gave a lot of space to the theatre, said Osbaldiston had departed this world much and deservedly respected, but added that his elopement with Miss Vincent was 'well known to all our readers and need not be repeated'. She was not listed among the mourners, but it was not then the general custom for women to attend funerals.

Osbaldiston's will showed that his personal property was something under £4,000. To Miss Vincent he left the lease of the Victoria, together with the entire scenery, machinery, costumes, properties, decorations, and general appointments of the theatre, with the proviso that his son George should remain as treasurer. To Miss Vincent he also left his villa at Brixton, with its furniture, plate, carriage, and horses. She was appointed sole executrix and residuary legatee. He left

34

nothing to any member of his company. But he did provide for his estranged wife, leaving her an insurance policy on his life for £1,000 and the balance at his banker's, about £180. The report in the *Era* which gave these details also mentioned that he had previously allowed his wife £300 a year, and that his two daughters by her had received a first-rate education which had been completed in Italy. As to his estate, Osbaldiston was said to have lost £2,000 on the Surrey Theatre (presumably before he came to the Victoria) and to have been unfortunate with gas-company shares. The report then concluded: 'The deceased lived in good style, and to this, coupled with the fact of his maintenance of two establishments, may be attributed the fact of his not leaving such an amount of property as was generally considered he had accumulated.'

Eliza Vincent took over the lease, but appeared on the stage less often. In 1852 she married Benjamin Crowther, an actor at Astley's Theatre, who soon afterwards went mad. It became the unkind rumour that his head was so turned by his good fortune in getting her that he was taken straight from the bridal party at the church doors to a lunatic asylum.

The Victoria continued, but with less ambition. In March 1853 one programme, advertised as the greatest novelty of the season but for one night only, included Matthews and Harrison with their celebrated dogs, Monsieur Plege's laughing gas, Herr Boom Stud's real horses, all finished off by living marionettes and southern minstrels. It sounds a bit desperate. Late that year Miss Vincent did make another appearance in *Susan Hopley*, but then she seemed to retire. From then on she was named on the bills as Directress but the theatre was managed by James Towers.

Then in November 1856 she caught cold and in a few days died, it was said of brain fever. She was forty-one. The London papers gave her the sort of send-off that would nowadays be given to the long-time heroine of a famous television soap opera, though her successor today would not have played Ophelia and Desdemona as well. The *Morning Chronicle* gave details of her career from the time when, at the age of six, she played a ruffian boy at the Surrey, and through her roles at half a dozen London theatres. It said her loss would be severely felt by the habitués of the Victoria, and that she had a just claim to the title awarded her – The Heroine of the Domestic Drama. The *Era* also sketched her career, recalling her Oberon in a version of Weber's opera of that name when she was only eleven. The writer attributed to her great force of expression and intensity of feeling, but felt he also had to say this: 'In early life she was remarkable for great personal attraction, to the possession of which must be ascribed the errors of her career.' The Victoria was closed the evening after her death.

The most affectionate notice was not in a London paper at all but in the *Manchester Examiner and Times*, whose interest was that Osbaldiston had come from Manchester. 'Miss Vincent, the once popular actress . . . died on Monday last very suddenly. Miss Vincent in her early career was one of the Vestris school, and by means of fine features, a clear voice, intelligence, and a piquant manner, possessed great power over a large audience.'

'Once popular' – sad, that. 'One of the Vestris school' – a high compliment, Lucy Vestris being famous for her operatic voice, her splendid legs in breeches parts like Macheath in *The Beggar's Opera*, and for having managed the Olympic theatre, off the Strand, for ten years. But, most of all, no actress could have wished for more than the last few phrases of that Manchester notice. Eliza Vincent had possessed great power over a large audience.

4

Catastrophe and Mrs Brown

Mr Towers had a bad time at the Victoria. He continued with domestic drama, though without a leading lady of Miss Vincent's appeal. He offered plays like *Hunger, or a Voice from the Streets*. At a time when the Lyceum across the river was presenting *The Iliad, or the Siege of Troy*, Towers put on *Love's Sacrifice, or the Wild Irish Girl*, which did have its charms. The leading lady was supposed to be Irish and could therefore dance jigs and sing about the Blarney stone, but in the action she became a Russian countess who married a French officer to save him from Siberia.

Still, the entertainment and the audience had got rougher. The gods in the gallery were famously raucous. John Hollingshead, founder of the Gaiety theatre in the Strand, has left a vivid account of the Victoria gallery of the time at a performance of Dickens's *Oliver Twist*. Fifteen hundred were packed in upstairs, the men sweating in shirtsleeves, the women with coloured bandanas round their shoulders. He likened them to the groundlings of Shakespeare's time and the 'swinish multitude' of his own. It was a thirsty audience, and the women's scarves were sometimes tied together to form a rope used to haul stone bottles of beer up from the pit.

The murder of Nancy was the great scene. Nancy was always dragged round the stage by her hair, and after this effort Sykes always looked up defiantly to the gallery as he was doubtless told to do in the marked prompt copy. He was always answered by one loud and fearful curse, yelled by the whole mass like a Handel festival chorus. The curse was answered by Sykes dragging Nancy twice round the stage and then, like Ajax, defying the lightning. The simultaneous yell became louder and more blasphemous. Finally when Sykes, working up to a well-rehearsed climax, smeared Nancy with red ochre, and taking her by the hair (a most powerful wig) seemed to dash her brains out on the stage, no explosion of dynamite invented by the modern anarchist, no language ever dreamt of in Bedlam, could equal the outburst. A thousand enraged voices, which sounded like ten thousand, with the roar of a dozen escaped menageries, filled the theatre and deafened the audience, and when the smiling ruffian came forward and bowed, their voices in thorough plain English expressed a determination to tear his sanguinary entrails from his sanguinary body.

Sykes, by the way, was most likely to have been acted at the Victoria by E. Faucit Saville, brother of Helen Faucit, an actress who later, by marrying a biographer of the Prince Consort, Sir Theodore Martin, became Lady Martin. It was fashionable at the time to condemn theatres which attracted such audiences as traps of temptation, pits of darkness, and hotbeds of crime, but the performance sounds wholehearted enough and the audience was thoroughly entertained. Of course there was some rough stuff. In November 1858 Henry Young, treasurer of the theatre, saw a young man in the gallery throwing objects into the pit. When he went up and tried to remonstrate, the man kicked him like a madman. When he tried to throw the man out he was, as he later told the magistrates, surrounded by ruffians who robbed him of his watch, chain, and hat. Next day the young man, described as dirty and ruffianly-looking, was jailed for fourteen days.

Then, that Boxing Day, Towers and the Victoria were overtaken by catastrophe. This was always one of the biggest days of the year, and two performances of the Christmas pantomime were on the bill. During the matinée there was an omen. An actor's wig caught fire and a second actor, trying to put it out, set fire to his own costume. It passed off. Neither actor was much more than singed. But while the afternoon performance continued the gallery audience for that evening was gathering in a crush on four flights of the gallery stairs, just as it had ten years before, also on a Boxing Day. This time the balustrade did not give way. But something else did. There is no coherent account. Some said that a gas burner on the gallery stairs went out and alarmed those near it who feared an explosion. Some said a gas burner did not go out but flared up. Some said a gas pipe was grasped at by a boy for support, and was ripped off the wall. Others said a boy in the gallery struck a fusee match to light a pipe and frightened the girls around him, who cried 'Fire'. At any rate, someone called 'Fire'. There was no fire to speak of in the auditorium, but at the alarm the audience fled. Those trying to escape from the gallery ran straight down into the crowd already gathered on the four storeys of the gallery staircase.

An early edition of the *Morning Chronicle* said:

The terror surged to a perfect ecstasy. The poor frantic creatures charged down the stairs, which are singularly steep, with a mad recklessness that could only lead to the

most fatal results. Those who thus precipitated themselves down the upper flights of the gallery – the scene
of this sad catastrophe – it is supposed had not the time
to regain their legs, far less anything like equilibrium,
before they were leaped upon by those behind them,
who were again in turn covered by others . . . The landing was crammed with a mass of suffering or insensible
victims of the accident to the depth of many feet.

The victims were pulled out, laid on the ground in The
Cut, or taken to chemists' shops. Some were badly trampled;
others had no sign of injury upon them but were lifeless. Sixteen were dead, all of them young boys, four of them aged
from nine to twelve, and all but one of the rest under twenty.
Most of the bodies were taken to Lambeth workhouse. The
evening performance was then given as if nothing had happened. The *Morning Post* said this might appear repulsive to
a proper sense of feeling, but that, given the circumstances,
with all the avenues of the house blocked up with an eager
and expectant crowd, it might be doubted whether any other
course could with safety have been pursued. ' Those', said the
Post, 'who have experienced the madness of an excited London crowd will appreciate the soundness of this observation.'
Towers evidently agreed, and chose to explain himself in a letter to the editor of *The Times*.

I assure you, sir, had I been able to consider my own
feelings I should certainly have closed the theatre after
so dire a calamity, but I found it impossible to do so, as
the gallery stairs were lined with people eager to witness the pantomime of the evening, and to attempt to
force a passage through them was out of the question,

and no doubt would have been attended with a more serious accident than even the tragedy of the morning. By inserting this you will greatly oblige and some way satisfy the public.

At the inquest there was still no agreement among the witnesses as to what had happened. One rumour had been that if the cause were a match, that match had not been struck in the ordinary way, but had somehow caught light in a man's pocket when he sat on it. It did become clear that however a match may have been ignited it was not in the gallery at all but in one of the boxes, in the best seats. John Croft of Walworth, a painter, said he had been in one of the back boxes in the dress circle, nearly in the centre. He had seen smoke arise some eight or ten seats in front of him and heard someone say, 'You're on fire. You're on fire,' to a man whose coat was said to be on fire. There was an immediate rush to the doors from the boxes. Against this, there was the evidence of Police Sergeant George Budd who said the gallery staircase had been on fire. He had seen a great light flaring out from a gas pipe on the first floor. In the rush he had seen many people shot down the stairs like sacks on to the first landing. Two persons had jumped over the balustrade from one flight on top of the people on another.

At the inquest the coroner said that if some evil-disposed person had raised the alarm, then it would be his duty to send him for trial on the charge of causing the death of those unfortunate boys. The jury, after a few minutes, brought in a verdict of accident, adding that the alarm had originated in the boxes. Towers claimed to have spent £300 strengthening the gallery stairs. He said he would pay for the funerals.

It was all a sad shambles, reported at length in the London papers. A correspondent of the *Observer* wrote that in thirty years at Palermo and Naples (where the theatres, incidentally, were larger than London's) he had never heard of any accident or elbowing at the doors. Anyone could buy a ticket from nine in the morning.

> All seats are numbered, consequently there is no need for elbowing one's way through the crowd . . . But the managers of the English theatres care more for their pockets, not wishing to have the seats numbered – in other words limited – and the inevitable consequence is that people have to wait for hours behind the doors of the theatre to secure, at the risk of their lives, the best places. Let an experiment be made in some of the theatres, and let them be conducted on the Italian system, the example will soon be followed by all the managers of the theatres in England.

Towers did not last much longer. He was succeeded by Frampton and Fenton, two optimistic and soon-forgotten showmen from Sadler's Wells who hoped to turn the Victoria into what they called a rescued temple of the drama. The nearest they approached to that was to engage Madame Celine Celeste to play *The Woman in Red*. Madame Celeste, who had begun as a French dancer, had toured America, was by then over fifty but still far from fluent in English, and was famous for the number of her farewell performances. (She soon after gave another at the Haymarket.) The appeal of the play can be gathered from the titles of its Acts – The Seal of Death, The Sorceress, and The Heart's Victory. The early 1860s were also the years of the American civil war. London audiences much favoured the anti-slavery northern states, so *Uncle Tom's Cabin* was pirated and adapted, and presented along with *Octoroon, or*

Life In Louisiana by Dion Boucicault, who is now best remembered not for slave dramas but for *The Colleen Bawn*.

By June 1867 Frampton and Fenton followed in the great tradition of the Victoria and petitioned for bankruptcy, owing £4,996 they could not pay and blaming 'depression of trade'. By August poor Frampton was reduced to taking out a four-line small ad in the *Era*, stating pitifully that he had thirty years' experience on the stage and asking for work: 'Tuition given and Ballet or single Dances arranged.' It is a dreadful warning to all actor-managers.

The audience in the temple of the drama that was the Victoria retained its reputation for rowdiness, and in 1867 a new lessee appeared who somehow acquired the reputation of

The Victoria from the stage in the 1850s or '60s,
an elegant auditorium for such a notoriously rowdy house

having set himself the improbable and perhaps unprofitable
task of quieting it. Mr J. Arnold Cave promised that any person whistling or making other disturbance would be expelled
by the police, and stated this in one playbill, though whether
the police would have obliged is another matter. He is even said
to have forbidden encores as causing unnecessary disturbance
to the artistes, but all this does not ring at all true if you look at
the way he was reported in the London papers. The *Daily News*
in September said he knew better than any other man in London how to manage such a house with advantage to himself
and the public. The *Era* said Mr Cave had issued an address
to playgoers remarking on the style of entertainment identified
with the Victoria and avowing his sensible intention of relying
on that in preference to any other. He had also promised first-
class scenery. And the *Era*, reviewing his first offering, *The Companions of the Chain*, said that in the very first scene the hero was
stabbed by a treacherous friend and made to write a deposition
in his own blood, and was later thrown down a trap as a meal
for water rats but escaped a second time. As to the heroine, she
was kidnapped, guarded by Fang, a baboon, pushed through
another trap door into the river, but saved by being fished up
in a net. 'It will be surely seen', said the critic, 'that the public
have no cause to complain of a scarcity of striking situations,
and Mr Cave could not have fixed upon a piece better cal-
culated to please and attract the playgoers in the immediate
vicinity of this theatre. There are several well-constructed sets
. . .' As well as water rats on stage, Cave had a plague of land
rats in his theatre. He brought in a cat to keep them down, but
this cat was joined by others until there were nearly twenty in
residence, and he had a plague of cats.

In March 1868 *Lloyd's Weekly* remarked that Cave continued to cater successfully for his patrons. His pieces always

presented a wholesome moral. No matter how unequal might be the forces engaged in the mimic battle of life on stage, virtue was sure to triumph over vice. 'The closely packed audiences watch these conflicts with almost breathless attention, and when the villains are worsted applaud with an earnestness that proves their sympathies are on the right side. The latest production here is a drama in four acts entitled *Quicksands and Whirlpools* . . .' By April the *Daily News* was moved to recollect the Victoria's classical productions of *Oliver Twist* and the dragging of Nancy round the stage by her hair, at which a thousand grimy men and women rose in one body in the gallery and cursed the murderer 'with all the energy and coarse language of an exalted multitude'.

And in another way Cave had seen a continuation of tradition. Over Christmas he had put up the prices for a pantomime about Nell Gwynne. The evening after Boxing Day a crowd at the top of the gallery stairs, being told by the money-taker that admission was sixpence not fourpence that night, refused to pay, turned back, tripped, and fell into those coming up behind. Peter Fleming, aged eleven, a butcher's son, was crushed and later died. In hospital he told his aunt he went to the Victoria because the pictures on the walls looked so beautiful and grand.

On stage, Cave knew very well what his patrons wanted, as was shown in one performance of March 1869. In between two plays, an address from the stage praised to the skies his qualities as manager since his arrival:

> He thoughtful saw the way to meet your wishes
> By serving solid and substantial dishes,
> No slight French cookery but British fare,
> Not rich perhaps, but nowadays too rare.

Cave then treated the audience to an entertainment of his own. Like quite a few managers of the time he had been an actor, and singer, and in his early days had even blacked up as an American negro minstrel and played the banjo. That night he sang 'Largo al factotum' (Make way for the factotum) from Rossini's *Barber of Seville*, the aria that goes 'Figaro here, Figaro there . . .' Then, breaking his own rule against encores, he sang a patter song called 'Bradshaw's Guide', which was the universal railway timetable.

It is a marvel of innuendo. A man meets a girl on a train. She does not know where she is going or what she wants.

A charming little creature was seated by my side,
She begged that I would lend her my Bradshaw's Guide,
And all the live long day then, both of us, we tried,
To find out what she wanted, in my Bradshaw's Guide.

They end up at an unknown hotel in an unknown town. 'Very satisfactory in every sense,' said the *Era*'s critic.

An impression of a night at the theatre in 1870 is given by George Rose – a High Anglican curate turned Roman Catholic priest and a former tutor to the Duke of Norfolk who turned journalist under the pen name of Arthur Sketchley. He invented a character called Mrs Brown, an illiterate Londoner, and published volumes of her recollections as she toured England and the world. She gave her opinion of the Scottish Highlands, the Nile, the Paris Exhibition, the Crystal Palace, South African Zulus, and, in a volume entitled *Mrs Brown at the Play*, the Victoria Theatre.

When her husband first suggests to her an evening at the Victoria she doesn't want to go to The Cut, but changes her mind when he assures her the tickets are for 'Queen Wictoria's

46

werry own theayter'. She says that's good enough for her. She's not going to look down on anything belonging to the Queen. So they make their way there through pawnbrokers' shops and pickled-eel stalls until they find the theatre. 'Well then,' she says, 'if I was Queen Wictioria, give me a better, for I considers it rather a ramshackle place for a queen to go constant.' Oh, says her husband, the outside is nothing; it's the inside as is awful grand. But Mrs Brown finds the entrance is like a passage into a cellar, with a gaslight on the wall flaring out so that it scorches her hair. They have to wait to get in, she leans against a wall, and gets whitewash and green paint on her Chinese shawl. Once inside, in the pit, she finds just forms all over the place to sit on, with nails sticking out that threaten to shred the black Norwich crepe dress she's wearing. The place is crowded. 'Do you think', she asks a woman next to her, holding a baby, 'as Queen Wictoria is a-comin' 'ere to 'er own theayter tonight, as I've always 'eard as there's crowds for to see 'er wherever she goes?' Mrs Brown learns that the Queen is not coming, and besides thinks the theatre not at all grand inside, rather a dingy hole. When the heroine onstage is pulled out of bed by the villain Mrs Brown enters into the spirit of the play by calling for the police, who instead of rescuing the heroine throw out Mrs Brown herself.

She is grievously disappointed. 'All as I've got to say is, 'owever Queen Wictoria can allow such shameful goin's on at her theayter puzzles me.'

The theatre Mrs Brown saw was fifty years old and had lived a hard life. Its elegance was long gone. Nails sticking out of benches tell the story. In August 1871 Cave announced that he intended to sell the Victoria to a limited company. It would be demolished and a magnificent new theatre built at a cost of £5,600. The Victoria's last night would be on 9 September.

The theatre was packed, in spite of increased prices. 'It could be seen at a glance,' said the *Daily News*, 'that the evening was one to be held in special fashion by the humble dwellers in the New Cut. A cherished institution, dear to them and their children, was doomed, and they had come to take a last fond look, and earn the right of narrating by the winter fire how they had seen the "Vic" proud in its glory and triumphant in its expiring moments.'

It was a packed programme. First there was *Rob Roy*, after Walter Scott, full of 'Auld Lang Syne' moments. Cave himself sang 'A Famous Man was Robin Hood', and then announced that in place of the Vic would arise a place of entertainment surpassing for magnitude and grandeur anything the kingdom of Great Britain and Ireland ever saw. It would present half melodrama and half music hall. At which a mournful-faced, bare-armed young man in the gallery called out: 'Ah, the poor old Wic. Pass the 'arf and 'arf, 'Arry.'

The evening was not finished. The last act of *Macbeth* was put on, and then the theatre closed by giving the piece it had opened with in 1818. *Trial by Battle*, by then archaic, was performed. The gallery showed its discontent by barracking this old piece of abduction by smugglers, but was shushed by other parts of the house and admonished by Cave who protested that it had not been introduced for larksome purposes but to give them a taste of ancient quality. When the evening was finally at an end, when the curtain fell and the theatre was cleared, there was a desolate look on the faces of the crowd that lingered outside which might, said the *Daily News*, have been caused by the paltry number of four deaths in the melodrama or by the fact that it was so late that the public houses were closed, or perhaps because they had seen the last of the 'Vic'.

Five days later the entire fittings of the Victoria were sold by public auction, from the stage, in the presence of a full house of curious spectators and more actors than had probably ever before been present at one time in the theatre. The place was to be stripped. The stage, with all its traps, fittings, barrels, and pulleys fetched twenty-five pounds. The great chandelier, which the auctioneer announced had just been repaired at a cost of £100, realised fifteen pounds. The vast gallery, with all its supports and railings, fetched three pounds ten shillings, and the eleven private boxes, with Corinthian pilasters and capitals, cornices and gilded plaster, two pounds ten shillings each. The scenery and properties went off in small lots but did not fetch a hundred pounds between them. Everything was to be removed straight away, so that the contractors could start immediately. Indeed, by the day of the auction demolition had begun and two spectators in the circle, not noticing that the floorboards had been removed, fell through into the pit.

5

Delatorre's Palace and the
Good Old Vic

To build a theatre now takes years. In the Waterloo Road in 1871, after the last show and the auction, the elegant but near-derelict Regency auditorium was torn down and, between the original side walls and under the original roof, a new theatre of great splendour, seating 2,300, was erected. It took twelve weeks.

But before the building could begin, and indeed while it was in progress, there were endless dealings with the Lord Chamberlain to be gone through. This grand official lived at St James's Palace and was in charge of the royal household and its ceremonials – weddings, funerals, the State Opening of Parliament, formal audiences, the care of royal swans on the Thames and of the Crown Jewels in the Tower, and all the ceremony of the Court. By an historical quirk he also licensed the thirty-four London theatres and many more in the provinces. He could censor plays, and retained this power until 1968. He could decide which plays should not be put on at all, and in 1870 had forbidden the performance of a play called *The Battle of Waterloo* at the Victoria. The French were being routed in the Franco-Prussian war and Viscount Sydney as Lord Chamberlain considered it was not fitting in such awful times to remind them of a former great defeat. His officials dealt with lesser matters. Cave had just stood up to Sydney's

chief clerk who was annoyed that when two of his friends, presenting his card, had turned up at the theatre one night they
had been given indifferent seats. To which Cave replied that it
had been a Saturday, the one night when there was likely to be
a full house. 'I trust to see these gentlemen again,' he replied,
'any night but Saturday, when it will afford me great pleasure
to give them the best Box in the house.'

But in 1871 the importance of the Lord Chamberlain to the
Victoria was that he had the great power to approve or reject
any plans for rebuilding. The new impresario, a man with the
splendid name of Romaine Delatorre, wanted a South Bank
music hall on the lines of the Alhambra in Leicester Square,
which was packing them in. But a music hall required space to
promenade, and here the Alhambra itself was already in trouble. Its manager had been summoned to St James's Palace and
told that a promenade had once again been established there
and that 'smoking and loose women were again in full swing'.
He was warned his licence might be cancelled.

Delatorre had already commissioned plans which showed
abundant space for promenading. He abandoned these and
turned to Jethro Thomas Robinson, an architect who was likely
to be safer, and who did indeed later become theatre adviser
to the Lord Chamberlain and to Lord's cricket ground. He
was a man in a great theatrical tradition. His son-in-law was
Frank Matcham, who went on to design more than 150 theatres, including the London Coliseum. In July 1871 Delatorre,
with Robinson's new plans, turned up at the Lord Chamberlain's office accompanied by Charles Hengler, a circus man all
his life, who was then running his Grand Cirque on the present site of the Palladium. Robinson's plans also showed some
space for promenading, though perhaps not for promenading
in full swing.

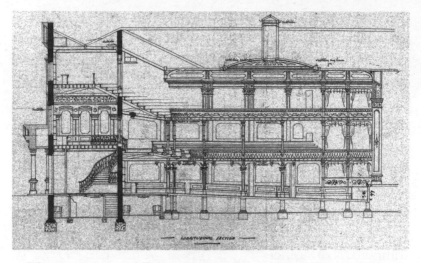

Western elevation of Delatorre's splendid new Royal Victoria Palace,
1871. This shows the auditorium substantially as it is today

Time was by then very short. On 7 September, only two
days before the last night of the old theatre, the Lord Chamberlain's report, complete with red wax seal, came back saying
there were no water closets or urinals for the pit, or for the first
tier (the best seats), or for the gallery. The report demanded
windows for ventilation on both sides of the first-tier saloon
and the gallery. On the plans, still in the Lord Chamberlain's
papers at the National Archives, it's plain that four lavatories,
two for the first tier and two for the pit, apparently the only
ones in the entire building, were then rapidly inked in, in what
is now the ground-floor foyer. Without any formal approval,
the work of tearing down the theatre went on. In November,
with the old theatre an empty shell, the Chamberlain's officials
were still concerned about smoking, and about the women
who might frequent the pit.

Still the work went on. And only on 18 December did
Cave write formally to Lord Sydney saying he had sold his
interest to Delatorre, was now 'merely stage manager of the

establishment for and on his behalf', and asked his lordship to be pleased to grant Delatorre a licence for dramatic entertainment on and after 23 December. It was cut that close. And only on 21 December, two nights before the opening, did the Lord Chamberlain's surveyor report that the plans as revised had been exactly carried out, that there were now abundant exits, and that 'the only comments were in the form of high approval'. But he then added: 'Mr Delatorre was again appraised that the gangways behind and beside Dress Circle and Pit must not be used as Promenades – and that drinking, smoking, and questionable company would not be permitted without risk of licence.'

One unfortunate man wrote to the Lord Chamberlain complaining that a private box he had bought years before in the old theatre had been destroyed in the recent alterations. He was referred to Delatorre. The opening night was a Saturday. On Friday workmen were still on the scaffolding. By next morning all was elegant and complete. The Royal Victoria Palace, as it was newly named, was ready to open.

And it was magnificent. The *Daily News* called it the most magnificent in the world. The *Era* said the dear old Vic had been turned into a thing of beauty. The *Observer* wrote that from beginning to end all was transformation. The façade was Italianate in the taste of the time. But Robinson's triumph was the auditorium, with its slender cast iron columns. There were three tiers in place of the old four, a central chandelier of 500 gas lights, twelve private boxes, stalls seats with padded armrests for 117, room for 560 in the pit behind the stalls, and 850 in the gallery. For its time it was a marvel. In London only the auditorium of Covent Garden predates it. How, then, did the theatre as it opened that night compare with the theatre as it is today? It was crowded in a way no modern theatre could be; 2,300 were packed into the same space today occupied by a thousand. The more than five hundred persons in the pit, on the ground floor where most of the stalls are today, sat on backless benches. The gallery had even narrower benches, was even more crammed, and was still approached only by a steep winding wooden staircase at the north-east corner. The audience entered through five separate doors. Those few in the twelve boxes came in through private entrances at the side of the theatre. Those in the stalls had a similar but separate entrance in the Waterloo Road. Those in the grand tier, now the dress circle, entered through the centre door in the façade and then mounted a sweeping double staircase to the first-floor saloon. Those in the pit entered by the two side doors at the front. So all that was different. But the structure of the auditorium was as it is today, down to the decoration, except that the tier fronts, now painted, were then gilded, and everything was new.

On the opening night the audience sang 'God Save the Queen', then 'God Save the Prince of Wales', and was entertained by an eastern pantomime, a harlequinade, a ballet, and by a scenic spectacle called *Hanging Gardens of the Moon*, the sets for which refused to descend or hang and held up the show for an hour. The audience was good-humoured but the infuriated designer, having threatened to shoot the master carpenter like a polecat, was sacked by Cave and later bound over by magistrates to keep the peace.

The strange thing is that it was only at this time, with the opening of a brand-new theatre, that the name of Old Vic was first used. There was nothing to call an old Vic before there was a new one. At the last performance in the old house that young man from the gallery had called out, 'Ah, the poor old Wic.' In print the theatre had been known as the Victoria and occasionally as the Vic. Then, with the coming of the new,

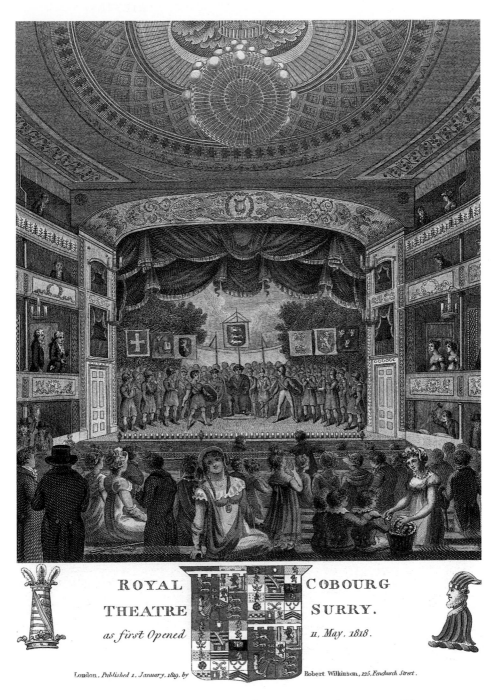

ROYAL COBOURG
THEATRE SURRY.
as first Opened 11. May. 1818.

London. Published 1. January. 1819. by Robert Wilkinson, 125, Fenchurch Street.

1 Opening night at the Royal Coburg, 1818. The play is *Trial by Battle*. The arms
are those of Princess Charlotte of Wales quartered with those of her husband Prince
Leopold of Saxe-Coburg. Note the orange seller, and the plain wooden benches

2 The Coburg by evening, *c*.1820, by Daniel Havell

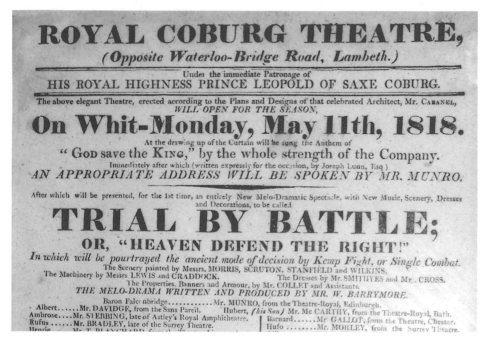

ROYAL COBURG THEATRE,
(Opposite Waterloo-Bridge Road, Lambeth.)

Under the immediate Patronage of
HIS ROYAL HIGHNESS PRINCE LEOPOLD OF SAXE COBURG.

The above elegant Theatre, erected according to the Plans and Designs of that celebrated Architect, Mr. CABANEL,
WILL OPEN FOR THE SEASON,

On Whit-Monday, May 11th, 1818.

At the drawing up of the Curtain will be sung the Anthem of
" GOD save the KING," by the whole strength of the Company.
Immediately after which (written expressly for the occasion, by Joseph Lunn, Esq)
AN APPROPRIATE ADDRESS WILL BE SPOKEN BY MR. MUNRO.

After which will be presented, for the 1st time, an entirely New Melo-Dramatic Spectacle, with New Music, Scenery, Dresses
and Decorations, to be called

TRIAL BY BATTLE;
OR, "HEAVEN DEFEND THE RIGHT!"
In which will be pourtrayed the ancient mode of decision by Kemp Fight, or Single Combat.

The Scenery painted by Messrs. MORRIS, SCRUTON, STANFIELD and WILKINS.
The Machinery by Messrs LEWIS and CRADDOCK.   The Dresses by Mr. SMITHYES and Mr. CROSS.
The Properties, Banners and Armour, by Mr. COLLET and Assistants.
THE MELO-DRAMA WRITTEN AND PRODUCED BY MR. W. BARRYMORE.

Baron Falconbridge............Mr. MUNRO, from the Theatre-Royal, Edinburgh.
Albert......Mr. DAVIDGE, from the Sans Pareil.   Hubert, *(his Son)* Mr. Mc CARTHY, from the Theatre-Royal, Bath.
Ambrose....Mr. STEBBING, late of Astley's Royal Amphitheatre. │ Barnard......Mr GALLOT, from the Theatre, Chester.
Rufus ......Mr. BRADLEY, late of the Surrey Theatre.   │ Hufo ....Mr. MORLEY, from the Surrey Theatre.
Henric ..... Mr. T. BLANCHARD

3 Playbill for the first night's melodrama, which lasted four hours, and at which the
management was heckled and pelted with apple cores and orange peel

Theatrical Reflection.
or a Peep at the Looking Glass Curtain at the Royal Coburg Theatre.

4 The Coburg's glass curtain, copied from a Paris theatre, in which members of the audience saw themselves reflected. It tended to mist over with the breath of two thousand spectators, and was almost impossible to clean. It also weighed five tons and threatened to bring the roof down, and was abandoned after a season

5 (*Right*) Junius Brutus Booth as Richard III, drawn by C. Shoosmith, 1817. Booth emigrated to America where in 1865 his son John Wilkes Booth achieved even greater fame by assassinating President Abraham Lincoln, in Ford's Theatre, Washington DC

6 (*Above*) Sarah Egerton, wife of the Victoria's manager in the 1830s, played Lady Macbeth but made her name playing, as here, parts like Madge Wildfire in Scott's *Heart of Midlothian*

7 (*Right*) Edmund Kean as Othello. After one such performance at the Victoria in 1831, when the audience howled for him, he responded by telling them he had never acted before such ignorant brutes

THEATRICAL TIMES

No. 41] SATURDAY, FEB. 13, 1847. [ONE PENNY

MISS VINCENT AS ADELINE, IN "THE BRIDE'S JOURNEY."

8 Eliza Vincent, leading lady and manager of the Victoria from 1841 to 1856, was connected with the theatre longer than anyone except Lilian Baylis. She was known as the Heroine of the Domestic Drama, and her most famous role was in the melodrama *Susan Hopley*, but she also played the classical roles of Ophelia and Desdemona

9 *The Sea*, a Victoria Theatre melodrama of the 1840s, with hurricanes, wild fights, and walkings of the plank. Here a mother with babe in arms, a survivor from the wreck in the background, is saved by a brave sailor who reaches down from the bowsprit of his own ship to rescue her from the menacing waves

10 T. P. Cooke as the innocent sailor William wrongly hanged by his captain in *Black Ey'd Susan*, one of the great melodramas of its day. The play is said to have inspired Melville's *Billy Budd* and even Benjamin Britten's opera

11 The Victoria Palace in the mid-1870s. The new owner tore down the old Regency façade and built the splendid auditorium that still survives. But the district went from bad to worse and the impresario went bankrupt

12 The hoped-for West Enders never came but as many as a thousand packed the gallery on Saturday nights. Engraving from *The Graphic*, October 1872, by Godefroy Durand, a French artist who covered wars in Europe, the Middle East, and China

13 (*Left*) Temperance menu offered by Miss Cons, with waiter, tea girl, customers with children in arms, policeman, and comical dog dancing on the stage

14 The Victoria Coffee House as Miss Cons built it, right across the front of the theatre, where the main entrance and foyers are now

the old theatre became the old Vic, and then the Old Vic with a capital O, and then that name was popularly adopted for the new theatre itself. The first time the name appeared in print in this form was probably at Christmas 1871 in the *Daily News*, two days after the opening, when the report began: 'Re-decorated, re-furbished, re-arranged, and as far as the interior is concerned almost rebuilt, the "Old Vic" once more takes its place amongst London theatres.'

For its first two years the Vic put on not so much melo-drama as romances – *The Lady of St Tropez, Flowers of the For-est*, and *Cinderella in Quite Another Pair of Shoes*. The newspapers reported, for the most part, humming, amused, and contented audiences. In 1872 *Scenes of New York Life and the Pacific Railway*, a 'marvellous great American sensation drama', was presented, ghastly and astonishing and transporting the audience right across the new continent. On Sundays, when the law allowed no performances, the theatre was even let for religious services, with singing, prayer, and sermon, which were attended by what the *Morning Post* described as 'the masses . . . the labouring population from the New Cut'. And no doubt, said the paper, as many came wanting to inspect the new building as wishing to listen to the devotions.

In July 1872 a sad paragraph appeared in the *Era*. Mr Charles Morton, for many years a favourite actor, was in the last stages of consumption. For fourteen weeks he had been incapable of following his profession and his means were now totally exhausted. Any little assistance would be gratefully received on his behalf by a friend at the Victoria Palace.

And by then the Palace was hardly thriving. Cave, having had enough of what he called servitude, left his job as stage manager and was given a rousing send-off and a presentation on stage. Thomas Snowdon, the builder of the splendid new theatre, went bankrupt, not having been paid for much of his work. The gallery at the Vic ceased to be enchanted. The gods, intent on a night out, talked, whistled, and heckled, 'and the little army of babies present assisted by making the din worse'. Delatorre had misjudged his audience. The gallery had got rougher and rougher as Waterloo Station brought more of the labouring poor to live and work in the area near The Cut. The carriage trade on which the Alhambra flourished had not crossed the river and come south to the Victoria.

From 1873 Delatorre's name was most frequently in the newspapers not as an impresario but as a debtor and a litigant. He was first made bankrupt. He appealed to the Court of Chancery where, in a suit attended by no fewer than four QCs, three Lords Justices heard the details of his ambitious speculations. Attracted by the notion of a southern Alhambra – this was directly stated in court – Delatorre had set out in glowing terms a prospectus inviting investors to buy and refurbish the Victoria at a cost of £12,000. The going concern would then be sold to a specially created company for £40,000, and the subscribers would treble their money. Such a company was formed in 1872, and it did buy the theatre, but only for £28,000. Much of that was paid in shares anyway, and in 1873 the new company itself was wound up and the shares became worthless. The subscribers were left protesting in vain. Lord Justice James said such appeals as theirs should not be encouraged. It is not known whether the four QCs received their fees.

For the second time in four years the theatre lease and contents were then sold at auction. It was a sale without reserve. The remaining lease was for twenty-four years with a yearly rental of £1,400. The first bid was £500. After a long pause the bids rose slowly in twenty-pound increments, sundry interruptions being made by Delatorre. The final bid was £820, by an upholsterer. The *Era* reported that the whole of the interior, including the fittings, decorations, and stage machinery, constructed two years before at a cost of £9,000, was included.

Delatorre emerges from the affair as the next thing to a crook. He had offices in the City and is sometimes referred to as a Parliamentary agent, a sort of lobbyist. He did not act fraudulently, or not quite. The prospectus for the Victoria Palace, forming a company which was not registered as a company, more a syndicate, proposed 'neither a speculation nor an investment but the purchase of a property on most advantageous terms, with certainty of sale at a very handsome profit'. As it was, he built his Alhambra in the wrong place, his builder went bankrupt, and the most his subscribers got was free tickets. But in the history of the Old Vic he is a hero. If he had not come along the Vic might, just might, have survived as a Regency theatre. That happened at Bristol with the Theatre Royal, and at Richmond, Yorkshire, but the original Victoria in London had lived a much harder life, and was by 1870 near-derelict. The spirit of the times was not to preserve but to tear down. Delatorre the chancer was not a safe man to know, and he probably cared nothing for the drama, but he was at least grand, and his grand ambitions, funded by other men's money, gave London a grand theatre, and one of its most distinctive.

The rest of the 1870s, after Delatorre's departure, is a sad story. William Frewer took a lease but went bankrupt within a year when he owed £500 and his only assets, in January 1875, were the bar takings and ticket sales for the current pantomime of *Jack and Jill*. Manager succeeded manager. John Aubrey, of the nearby Elephant and Castle Theatre, took the Victoria for a while as a vanity project, and put on his wife

Marie Henderson, who had played small parts for Delatorre, as Lady Macbeth. She did not impress, and Aubrey fell back on *Black Ey'd Susan*. By 1877 the Vic had given up presenting its own shows and was inviting offers from touring companies, but often remained dark for weeks at a time. In 1878 Cave returned as lessee, putting on anything from *Hamlet* to *Uncle Tom's Cabin*, from American banjo soloists to *Don Giovanni*. When he presented *Bluff King Hal*, in places an adaptation of *Henry V*, he played the bluff king himself.

Then early in 1880 Cave received an offer from a committee of benevolent gentlemen who did not want to put on a speculative season of shows but were interested in the theatre for what he called 'other reasons'. Their money was as good as anyone's, indeed their credit was a great deal safer, and he accepted their offer. Cave put on his last show at the Old Vic on 13 June 1880, presenting *The Mountain Devil*, *The Iron Clasp*, and *Sweeney Todd*. As the *Era* described it, 'Pit and gallery were crammed with a demonstrative rather than an appreciative audience, the noise causing the performance to be one of dumb show. Mr Cave did not address the house, and Queen Victoria's Own Theayter closed without even God Save the Queen being sung. It is to be reopened as what a gentleman present called "Temperance Sing-song".'

Part Two

1880–1937

Cons, Baylis, and Shakespeare

6

Miss Cons and the Purified Hall

The committee of benevolent gentlemen were the principals of the Coffee Tavern Music Hall Company, devoted to temperance. They formed a trust and bought a lease, and in October 1880, through their hon. secretary, Miss Emma Cons, and with the support of the Archbishop of Canterbury and the Duke of Westminster, asked the magistrates for a music and dancing licence for the Royal Victoria Hall. The application was not in due form, and it was late, but the magistrates not only waived all objections but added their congratulations. God was on the side of Miss Cons. She had a splendid new theatre but all she wanted was a hall, so Delatorre's gilded auditorium became the Royal Victoria Hall. That as it happened was the distant beginnings of a national theatre, but Miss Cons had no interest in the theatre and in all her time there never even asked for a theatre licence. She called the hall her recreation and her playground, but not once in her thirty-two years there did she put on a play, and not for the next fifty years was an alcoholic drink served at the bar. She hated drunkenness and wanted the Victoria so that she could dispense wholesome food and 'innocent' entertainment – all for the moral benefit of the lower orders.

Emma Cons came from the German family of Konss which had emigrated to England in the eighteenth century.

She was born in 1838, the daughter of a piano-maker who had married a mill-owner's daughter. As a girl she trained at the Ladies' Art Guild in London. She made stained glass and engraved the back of watches. At art school she met Octavia Hill, who had friends in high places and many years later was one of the founders of the National Trust. Miss Hill built dwelling houses for the poor, Miss Cons assisted her, and by 1879 had for twenty years been concerned with model dwellings for the poor, herself building tenements, collecting their rents, and acting as adviser to her tenants. She was a Christian social reformer in the style of Elizabeth Garnett and her navvy mission society, only with better connections. She was a philanthropist with no means of her own but with friends in high places. Through Octavia Hill, she had met Ruskin. She was a close acquaintance of Lady Frederick Cavendish, who was maid of honour to the Queen.

A lease of the theatre was bought, sacks of shrimps' heads, nutshells and dried orange peel dug out of the pit, and the temperance music hall opened on Boxing Day, 1880. The *Era* was ironic, saying first that the name of temperance music hall seemed to suggest that all the others were intemperate, and then observing that a clergyman was stage manager and always at hand to regulate the length of the skirts of the lady performers. In its opinion two thirds of the audience had probably never been in a music hall before, and they would not have been there at all 'had not "respectability" set its seal upon the place and guaranteed its propriety'. That first night there were American songs and dances, a capital orchestra, a juggler, a troupe of Roman gladiators, and a lightning cartoonist who in one minute sketched the ocean with a ship under full sail and Captain Webb swimming the Channel. The whole front of the Victoria had been rebuilt into a coffee house, and tea, coffee,

A crowded Royal Victoria Hall (*above*) and coffee tavern (*below*), 1881

jam, ham, and steaks were to be had from twopence to sixpence. Smoking was permitted throughout the hall – strange,
since it was forbidden when the Victoria had been licensed as
a theatre.

The hall, when its programme settled down, offered on

Mondays and Saturdays purified variety acts without innuendo, spectacles such as 'The Burial of Sir John Moore', and acts by performing dogs, cats, and goats; on Tuesday penny lectures on the telephone, electricity, and the moon; and on Thursday ballad concerts, which soon became the Victoria's most popular attraction. There, operatic recitals were given, from *Faust*, *Trovatore*, and *Fidelio*. In the hall's first year Princess Frederica, the Queen's niece, came one evening and was presented with a bouquet by Miss Cons's niece, the young Lilian Baylis. And in February 1882 the Prince and Princess of Wales came to a special Irish ballad night. The hall owed these royal visits to Lady Frederick Cavendish, and it's important to know a little more about her, to understand the strength of Miss Cons's support.

Lucy Cavendish was born the daughter of Lord Lyttelton, one of Sir Robert Peel's ministers. Her mother's sister was the wife of W. E. Gladstone, making Lucy the niece of another prime minister. In her early twenties she became a maid of honour to the Queen and married Lord Frederick Cavendish, who happened to be second son of the Duke of Devonshire. Cavendish became Irish Secretary, and was murdered in Dublin the day he took the oath. Lady Frederick was not only in every way well connected, but famous.

And the attendance of the hall's annual general meeting of 1884 reads like *Who's Who*. The Duke of Westminster presided, Cardinal Manning was present, so was Lord Mount Temple (stepson of Melbourne, yet another prime minister), and so was Samuel Morley, a textile millionaire and newspaper publisher, and MP for Bristol. What they heard was that the Victoria Hall was flourishing but broke. In the previous year £3,260 was taken at the box office (and that in threepences and sixpences), and £2,739 in the coffee tavern, but

Poster for Miss Cons's coffee tavern and hall, 1884

the overall loss was still £1,000. The Hall always did lose but always attracted philanthropists. Morley was one such, and it happened that the technical college for working men later named after him was already establishing itself at the Victoria. Tuesday-evening lantern lectures had developed into regular classes. Classrooms had been built under, over, and behind the stage, and then bricked up to form a quite separate institution. The Victoria was the only music hall ever to give birth to a college. Its members put after their names the initials OVS, for Old Vic Student. The remains of the building, even after the quite separate coffee room was subtracted as well, were enough for Miss Cons. An auditorium and bare stage accommodated variety and concerts. With no plays, she needed no wings or backstage.

Only once, in 1886, did Miss Cons attempt to put on even a pantomime. At which Cave, formerly of the Victoria but by then running the Elephant and Castle theatre, summoned her before the magistrates, contending the pantomime was a play, unlicensed and illegal. Ada Clarisse, an actress, gave evidence in the Victoria's defence, saying that songs were sung but had nothing to do with what she spoke, and that there was no con- nected story whatever. Even this eloquence failed. Legal argu- ments were exchanged, with some laughter, on the difference between pantomimes 'à la Cave and à la Cons', but Cave had the law on his side. Not even the statement that the Victoria had the support of the royal family helped. The magistrate, evidently reluctant, said it was his duty to convict but that he would impose a nominal fine of half a crown.

A vivid account of Miss Cons's hall appeared in the *Pall Mall Gazette* in May 1888. This was a London evening news- paper, at that time with Liberal leanings, which considered itself a cut above the rest of the newspaper press. It praised the tableaux vivants and operatic arias of the concert evenings, and the classes offered at what it called 'almost an entire tech- nical school'. It praised the three temperance bars at the Vic, but did add that temperance was in a way optional since pass- out tickets were given between turns, so that members of the audience could slip out for a drink at the nearby pubs.

Outside, said the *Gazette*, there was hardly a face and fig- ure on which poverty and want had not left an unmistakable mark. Gaudiness there was, but hardly ever neatness; noise and laughter but no quiet mirth and contentment.

> The very road, wide and well-paved, forms a striking contrast to the small and narrow houses most of whose windows are brown and dull with a thick coat of dust. And high above all other houses, a very giant among pigmies, rises the 'Vic', its front windows lit up with many lights, its side walls gloomy and ugly as those of some strong old prison. But round no prison gates –

except perhaps when the Bastille was stormed – have ever yet been seen such eager crowds, clamouring for admission . . .

Inside, in the gallery, the reporter remarked that the gravity of the audience was truly remarkable. 'Nor is their taste uneducated . . . The most graceful steps in a graceful dance; the cleverest acrobatic feat though it may be the least showy; the best voice among the vocalists, are speedily detected and cheered.' But, he said, no one was more keenly alive to what was going on in the auditorium than the 'chucker-out', in a red shirt, arms folded across his chest, closely watching the young 'twopenny Gods' crowded closely against the railings. Then at eleven 'God Save the Queen' was struck and the audience dispersed 'with a bright vision of light and merriment in their mind which is marred by no shadow of what is vulgar or indecent'.

The *Birmingham Daily Post*, a little later, gave an even more glowing account of what it called 'the civilization of the roughs'. 'And the experiment', it wrote, 'has succeeded, to the glory of Emma Cons . . . Women with their children are there, boys and girls at the "dangerous ages", working men and slaving women; and over all hangs an atmosphere of purity and truth which must cause rejoicing in Heaven, for Emma Cons has found the way to console and pacify the troubled soul.'

In 1886 Samuel Morley died, and the hall lost its single greatest benefactor. But the trustees then launched an appeal to buy the freehold. A letter was written to *The Times* by Lady Frederick Cavendish, a meeting was again chaired by the Duke of Westminster, the owner reduced his price by £3,000, and the freehold was acquired in no ordinary way but transferred by Order in Council – that is to say of the Queen's Privy Council – to Emma Cons on behalf of a newly created trust.

Plainly the Vic was seen as Miss Cons's creation, but it was not her whole life. She remained acting director of the South London Dwellings Company. In 1889 she was appointed an alderman of the newly created London County Council but, because she was a woman, was not by law allowed to speak or vote, though she served on many committees. At the Vic she did make decisions. It was she who declined an offer from Henry Stanley to talk on Africa, an offer you would have thought she would welcome from the man who had found Livingstone. Her reason was that he was at the time Conservative candidate for North Lambeth, and that the Vic did not allow politics. It could have been objected that she was an evident Liberal. She is also said to have turned down an approach from the young Charlie Chaplin, who was born within a mile or so of the Vic, but this is probably legend. It was Chaplin himself who told the story, sixty years later. At any rate, Miss Cons did not run the Vic day to day. She employed a number of underpaid managers, and by 1898 the trustees were hoping, in their annual report, that Miss Baylis would, before long, be able to undertake the entire management.

But who was this Miss Baylis? The trustees did not even identify her as a niece of the hon. secretary of the Hall. Lilian Baylis was the daughter of Miss Cons's sister Liebe and her husband Newton, both musicians. Lilian later remembered being at the Hall at Miss Cons's very first night, on Boxing Day 1880, standing on a chair, held by her nurse, as the people rushed into the pit from the Webber Street entrance. The next year she appeared, as Miss Cons's niece, at a royal visit to the Vic, when she presented a bouquet to the Queen's cousin, Princess Frederica of Hanover. She was then seven, and was already learning the violin and banjo. She toured with her parents' concert party, performing ballads and scenes from operettas. In 1889 the Baylises formed a group called the Gypsy Revellers, and in 1891, when Lilian was seventeen, they set out on a nine-month tour of South Africa. They stayed for years, touring Johannesburg, Pretoria, Durban, and many other towns, travelling four thousand miles by ox-cart. Lilian played the banjo and sang in a clear soprano voice. She taught the violin, banjo, and mandolin. She taught dancing too, and Mark Twain, on a visit, was one of her pupils. She also became engaged to a gold prospector, and broke the engagement. Later she was reputed to tell stories of a manly man who waded across rivers with her flung across his shoulders. She may have been known later as a dumpy and always badly dressed woman, but she was a girl of spirit. And the cockney accent she was often accused of was not cockney at all but South African.

By the mid-1890s all-out war between the Boers and the British was becoming increasingly likely. A cart full of dynamite exploded close enough to shake the house, and Lilian ran into the street in her petticoat. In 1897 she had to have a kidney operation, and Emma Cons cabled from London offering to pay the fare so that her niece could recuperate in England. Lilian accepted. She left her family. Within a year, though she had certainly not taken over the entire management, she was helping her aunt to run the Vic at a salary of one pound a week. She was just twenty-four.

These were not prosperous days at the Vic. The trustees blamed this in part on the Boer war, but whether or not that was so the Lambeth audience was preferring the twopenny and threepenny seats to the sixpennies and shillings. The Thursday concerts still attracted full houses, but variety on Mondays and Saturdays did not, which Miss Cons attributed to competition from newer music halls like the Coliseum and the Lyceum.

And she made it clear where her heart lay, writing in 1902: 'The work of the Hall is primarily Temperance work . . . The workers at this Hall have been labouring for 23 years to provide such a "people's palace" – one that should furnish only innocent amusement . . .'

In that she had largely succeeded. Her coffee room right across the front of the hall, let out to John Pearce and called Pearce and Plenty, flourished as it served temperance tea and sandwiches. Music, after temperance, was her love, and that flourished too. She had in 1899 appointed Charles Corri as conductor of the Vic's tiny orchestra – a post he kept for thirty-five years. And she had a hand in appointing the young Gustav Holst as music director of Morley College in 1907, a post he held until 1924. But with only a music-hall licence no opera could be presented in its entirety, even if Corri could have scored it for an orchestra of eighteen at the most. So only arias and recitals could be given, and they were, from *Trovatore* and *Rigoletto*, from *Carmen* and *Faust*.

It was left to Lilian Baylis to introduce something new – moving pictures. In 1901 an Exhibition of Animated Pictures was offered after Donizetti's *Daughter of the Regiment*. By 1903 a change of pictures every week was advertised. By 1905 Monday night was film night, attracting audiences of two thousand, more even than the concert nights' sixteen hundred. This more than paid Miss Baylis's salary, which had by then been raised to three pounds a week, with an added bonus of twenty-five pounds a year. She helped in many ways. The London County Council had demanded alterations costing £3,000, including a safety curtain. These were made. Miss Cons was then adamant that everything was then as safe as could be. She said all the doors were tried before each performance, and they opened easily, so easily that wicked people pulled them open from the streets and got in for nothing. As for the safety curtain, that was let down every evening – 'and it is so easily worked that Miss Baylis lets it down herself, and I think it weighs 20 ton'.

What Lilian could not achieve was a theatre licence, which she suggested to the trust. The committee did not agree, in part perhaps because a music-hall licence permitted smoking and a theatre licence would not. So her aunt's firm conception of the temperance hall survived again. Not that the Hall was ever Miss Cons's only concern. In 1896 she visited Cyprus to help Armenian refugees who had been driven out of Turkey, and denounced the Sultan. She continued to manage her dwellings for the poor, and went to Canada to visit some of her former tenants who had emigrated. One of her pleasures was to spend her weekends with her friend Ethel Everest – daughter of the surveyor after whom Mount Everest was named – at Hever in Kent. She never came back without something, bunches of flowers or plants, for her tenants. And at Christmas she gave tea parties for them at the Vic, with a gift for everyone.

There was this simplicity, and also a certain grandness, and the two ran together. The 'People's Palace for South London', as Miss Cons liked to style it, maintained its association with the greatest in the land. In March 1910, thanks again to Lady Frederick Cavendish, the Prince and Princess of Wales – two months before the prince succeeded to the throne as George V – came to a Grand Concert of which the first half was Welsh songs and the second selections from popular light opera. Then the evening concluded with 'animated pictures'. At the time five dukes or duchesses and seven earls or countesses, along with three bishops, were on the hall's council, and the patroness was Princess Christian, daughter of Queen Victoria. There is a photograph of the evening, taken from the stage, which shows the prince and princess in the royal box, to the left on the first tier, Miss Cons in a ground-floor box beneath, and the audience, both in the stalls and the pit, more or less formally dressed. Red printed slips in the programmes asked for the gift of draperies, curtains, and evening dresses. The gallery was also packed, and soldiers, sailors, and postmen in uniform were admitted at half price.

Miss Cons was consistently generous to her niece. That same year, 1910, when Lilian was exhausted by her work at the Hall, Miss Cons sent her and a woman friend on a three-month world tour. Lilian and her friend crossed to Ireland, then to New York and Toronto, crossed the Rocky Mountains to British Columbia, and then crossed the Pacific by way of Hawaii and Fiji to Australia, to Sydney, Adelaide, and Perth. They sailed home by way of Colombo, the Suez Canal, Egypt, and the Mediterranean.

This extravagance shows another side of the frugal Miss Cons, though she was spending not the Vic's money but her own. It shows another side of Lilian Baylis too, who was happy to go round the world first class but later, famously and on principle, never paid an actor the going rate.

By this time, the animated picture shows were less profitable than they had been. The Vic had at first had a monopoly south of the river, but picture shows had sprung up everywhere. The operatic recitals continued, but they were expensive. Lilian pressed again for a theatre licence so that operas and plays could be given in full. Her aunt steadily opposed the idea. She still wanted a Hall. She had never wanted a theatre.

Miss Cons was coming toward the end. In May 1912 Princess Christian came to a concert performance of *Tannhäuser*. In the interval Miss Cons received a collection of £200. This was the last time she stood on the stage of the Victoria Hall. That July, at the age of seventy-four, she died on a weekend

Opera queue for the Old Vic gallery, *c.*1912, before Miss Baylis presented Shakespeare. The seats were not numbered, and people paid an extra threepence at the Early Door to get a better place

visit to Miss Everest at Hever. The King's secretary sent a message: 'The King and Queen have heard with great regret of the death of Miss Cons, whom they so well remember meeting at the Royal Victoria Hall, and for whose self-sacrificing life Their Majesties had a high regard.' Lilian scattered her aunt's ashes in a daffodil wood at Hever, in grounds which had been willed to the National Trust in Miss Cons's memory. It was sad that the Trust later declined the bequest.

And another thing. Lilian Baylis, in a memoir written twelve years later, recalled a last conversation with her aunt. '"What about the Vic, Emmie?" I said at last, and her answer was, "You are there, dear."'

Lilian wrote that she felt humbled by her aunt's faith in her. But just two months later, faith notwithstanding, Lilian Baylis had her way and the Royal Victoria Hall asked the Lord Chamberlain for a theatre licence. By November 1912 it was granted, with Miss Baylis named as lessee.

7

God, Shakespeare, and Miss Baylis

Once the Vic had a theatre licence, there was no more variety. A tradition that had lasted thirty-two years under Miss Cons was ended. This did mean that there were now two nights of opera, on Thursdays and Saturdays. It also meant plays had to be found, and within eighteen months the tradition of Shakespeare at the Vic was begun. It was not at all Miss Baylis's idea, and at first she was unhappy about it, and with some reason.

It happened this way. Late in 1913 Rosina Filippi appeared. She was a character actress and a teacher of acting, who had also adapted two novels of Jane Austen for the theatre. She claimed descent from the great Eleanora Duse. She was an instinctive self-publicist. She talked to several newspapers, making much of her ideas for a Fourpenny Theatre. When she spoke to the *Observer* it became her People's Theatre. To the *Manchester Guardian* she outlined her plans for what she then called a Theatre for the Poor, giving as an example such a theatre which had been established in Milan, in a drill-hall with 2,300 cushioned seats, where the best plays were presented to 'the intellectual poor, poor artists . . . and even the intelligent shop assistant'. She said that she would, furthermore, attach to her company a school of acting. After this publicity she proposed to the Victoria Hall trust that her own company should appear there four nights a week from the following

74

April, presenting Shakespeare. She would bring with her sets and costumes lent to her by Matheson Lang, a Shakespearean actor-manager of some reputation, who had just returned from a tour of India and Australia. She would, she repeated, sell some of the seats for fourpence. The *Guardian*, reporting this offer, described the Victoria as 'Miss Cons's brave venture for providing good and very cheap entertainment in days when picture palaces were undreamt of'. There was no mention of Miss Baylis, who had at the time, after all, produced little drama and no Shakespeare at all.

Miss Filippi with her talk of founding a People's Theatre was not likely to be congenial to Miss Baylis, who had much the same ambitions. The one had a company, of sorts; the other had a theatre, of sorts. They were rivals.

Miss Filippi and her company did come to the Old Vic in April 1914, though only for two nights a week, not four, playing *The Merchant of Venice* and *Romeo and Juliet*. And there was indeed no love lost between the two women. Miss Filippi accused Miss Baylis of scattering leaflets exhorting the audience to prefer the opera. According to the young Sybil Thorndike, who was there, 'They were both too violent to work together. They got on very well as long as they were apart. But when it came to doing anything together they would bawl at each other and have terrible rows. Rosina had such a temper, a terrible temper, and so did Lil.' There had been an agreement that, if the short spring season went well, Miss Filippi should stay for forty-two weeks from September 1914. But she lost money, and that was the end of her, and of her People's Theatre.

Miss Baylis retained hers. A man called Shakespeare Stuart offered his versions of Shakespeare, and did present *Twelfth Night, As You Like It*, and *Much Ado about Nothing*, but he too lost money. Miss Baylis then had a vision. Over the years she had several, generally of Jesus, but the dialogue of this one, as she reported it, seems to show that her interlocutor this time was Shakespeare. She had been crying, trying to sleep, when a strong manly voice out of the dark enquired: 'Why have you allowed my beautiful words to be so murdered?' She replied that it was not she but others who had done it. The voice then said: 'You must run the plays yourself as you do the operas.'

So she did. She turned to Matheson Lang, whose scenery was still on loan to the Vic, and he brought along his wife Hutin Britton and directed three Shakespeare plays, with his wife playing Portia and the Shrew. But then he had to go off on already arranged tour, leaving his scenery behind again. The Vic devoted itself to an appeal for £5,000 'to put the best forms of entertainment within the reach of those who are already seeking "higher things"'. The sponsors included Princess Christian, again, the Lord Mayor of London, and the conductors Thomas Beecham and Henry Wood. But the year was 1914, and by August the Great War overtook the appeal, which raised only £800, and things were so bad that the trustees wondered whether they would be able to continue to run the hall.

There was always God, and Miss Baylis was apt to consider any stroke of luck as an Act of God. One day, feeling ill and weary, she entered All Saints, near Oxford Circus, did not kneel, and, as she said, with no praise or thanks in her heart but only 'one hateful grumble', complained that the *Daily Telegraph* had taken no notice of her last Wagner performance. Now the great Nellie Melba happened to be in London and that evening came to see *Rigoletto* at the Vic, attracting several columns in the papers. This was good for the Vic, and Miss Baylis put it down to God.

But it was Ben Greet, who turned up at the theatre one

night and offered to do a season of Shakespeare, who saved her. Ben Greet, who is now pretty well forgotten, is one of the great men in the history of the Old Vic. He was the son of a navy captain, and was himself a naval cadet before he turned to the stage in 1879. He became an actor-manager, touring England and America, and when he came to the Old Vic that night had twelve times toured the United States, from where he had just returned. In the 1913–14 season there he and his Woodland Players had performed five Shakespeare plays and five by other authors – at Harvard, Princeton, Yale, West Point, Chicago, the White House, the University of California, and thirty other places. He too had the idea of a people's national theatre, but in America, which he saw as the co-inheritor of the glories of Shakespeare. So he was no threat to Miss Baylis. His Shakespeare theatre would be in New York. But he was English, his country was at war, he had returned to do his duty, and his duty as he saw it was to cheer the nation by presenting Shakespeare. When he first appeared that evening and presented himself to Lilian Baylis he was fifty-eight, and had a great shock of white hair. He stayed four years, the first for nothing and after that taking only his expenses. He more than anyone else created the Old Vic's Shakespeare tradition.

By then the Hall had been in constant use without renovation since 1871, forty-three years. The curtain was red cotton, the audience sat on hard benches covered in American cloth, and the floor of the auditorium was bare boards on which sawdust was scattered once a week. The actresses changed on stage in tiny corrugated iron boxes, and the only water was from a tap on the prompt side where there was also a gas ring on which Miss Baylis cooked her sausages. Lang's sets remained, and were adapted for the play of the moment. In these conditions Greet was the ideal director. In his fit-up tours he had never had grand sets, and was used to making do with what there was.

It was wartime. Yet strangely enough this helped the Vic. The West End managements were depressed, attempted fewer lavish productions and little Shakespeare, so there was room for a rival. Many young actors had been called into the army. Older actors were happy to find work even at the low wages the Vic offered. When there were not enough men to go round, women played men's parts. In one production of *Henry V* the Chorus, Orleans, Mountjoy, the Constable of France and eight smaller roles were played by women.

And the plays were adapted in other ways. Ideally, Greet would have presented the full texts, but he could not do this at the Vic with a weekly change of play. So he gave carefully arranged acting versions, saying that the intellectuals who studied the plays could supply the missing scenes from their own knowledge, while ordinary playgoers could understand the plot as it stood and use their imagination to fill the gaps. In this way, Greet presented in his first season, from January to April 1915, no fewer than nine plays of Shakespeare, including *Macbeth, Othello,* and *The Merchant of Venice.* The only exception to his notion of the 'acting version' was *Hamlet.* This he presented in its entirety, lasting five hours. This then became the Old Vic tradition.

There were occasional Zeppelin air raids in 1917, aimed perhaps at Waterloo Station, which reduced audiences and gave rise to legends which, if not exactly true, make good stories and perhaps capture the spirit of the time. One night, when there were said to be only five people in the pit and three boys in the gallery, Miss Baylis asked the company whether they wanted to go on, or should she tell the audience, such as it was, to go home. Ben Greet, and Sybil Thorndike (who told the story),

Shakespeare arrived in 1914 to supplement the opera. This is wartime, but in four months, January to May 1915, the Old Vic is offering on one of its famous green slips, which were the only advertising Miss Baylis allowed, no fewer than fifteen plays and seventeen operas

and the rest of the company voted to go on. Then there was the air raid during *King John*. Bombs were falling when Ben Greet, acting that night as well as directing, spoke the lines:

> Some airy devil hovers in the sky
> And pours down mischief.

Laughter from the audience. And at the end of the play two other and more familiar lines brought the house down:

> This England never did, nor never shall,
> Lie at the proud foot of a conqueror.

There is probably more substance to this second tale, since those words were put up over the proscenium for the rest of the war.

In four wartime seasons Ben Greet put on twenty-four Shakespeare plays. 'One of the things that astonishes American and colonial soldiers', said the *Manchester Guardian* in 1918, 'is that they have to go to an obscure and unfashionable theatre across the water to see Shakespeare in London. For the past five years the people at the Old Vic have been giving not occasional or selected Shakespeare but Shakespeare right through the rubric. They gave *Measure for Measure* the other day, a play that no commercialised theatre would look at these days . . . The performances are unambitious and sincere, without the disturbing influence of stars or expensive notions of scenery.'

Greet left after the 1918 season, but returned for a royal performance that October, just before the end of the war, that was given in the presence of Queen Mary. Hers was the first visit to the Vic by a reigning queen since poor distracted Queen Caroline's in 1821. The occasion celebrated the centenary of the theatre's opening, as the Coburg, in 1818, and those who had performed there over the years. Grimaldi and Paganini were impersonated, Matheson Lang appeared as a big bad buccaneer, Ellen Terry declaimed as Portia, and Ben Greet himself appeared in melodrama as a condemned felon, with Athene Seyler as his wife, in a gruesome scene from *The Murder of Five Fields Copse*.

The war and Ben Greet established Shakespeare at the Old Vic, but throughout this time opera continued and flourished, and that was Miss Baylis's first love. In 1920 she had established *The Old Vic Magazine*, published four times a year, at first typewritten and then printed with a circulation of 1,000, and always in effect edited and in part written by her. She did not hesitate to promote herself. In the issue for February 1920 she mentions donations to a reconstruction fund 'to celebrate the 21st anniversary of Miss Baylis's Management of this theatre'. That is to say, she was reckoning her management to have begun not on the death of her aunt in 1912 but from the time she returned from South Africa in 1898, as a twenty-four-year-old, on a pound a week. This was stretching it. But then she had done great things. As she wrote in the issue for January 1921: ' "Audace, toujours de l'audace" [Dare, always dare] is I am sure a fitting motto for the Old Vic. Last month it dared three things – *King Lear*, *The Magic Flute*, and *Tristan and Isolde* . . .'

Now this is astonishing, even though the orchestra numbered only twenty-eight and the choruses in all operas were amateur and unpaid. What single theatre could present such a programme today? Never, said Miss Baylis, had the management received more congratulatory letters from persons of high standing than after *Lear*. And the first performance of *Tristan* had been a red-letter night. At the end, she said, both the conductor, Charles Corri, and the manager (herself) had had to respond to call after call, until Corri finally cut short the demonstration by saying, 'Let us sing "The King" together.'

One of the Old Vic's great successes, though a financial disaster, was the matinée for schoolchildren. Greet started this in 1915. Tickets cost a penny. The London County Council then asserted that this counted as part of the children's education, and since education had by law to be free the children could not be asked to pay. The council itself then made a payment, until this was too was declared illegal by the auditors. The council then made an ex gratia grant, but this seems to have been paltry. As Miss Baylis wrote in 1920:

Our Manager [she almost always wrote of herself in the third person] is amused at several of the Vic audience congratulating her on receiving £1,100 grant from the LCC towards the Shakespeare movement for schools. Though half a million children have enjoyed the plays here . . . [only] £100 was presented to the Vic last autumn, the remaining trifle of £1,000 our patrons must seek elsewhere. One Vic friend remarked, believing the £1,100 had come to us: 'Something towards new wallpaper': but there is little likelihood of this £1,000 wandering into our coffers, leave alone gilding our walls.

Shakespeare production had been taken over in 1921 by Robert Atkins, who stayed five years. He had served in the army and before that acted as assistant to Greet. By 1921 even Lang's sets seem to have disappeared, and Atkins made do with draped curtains and artful lighting.

Neither Filippi nor Greet nor Atkins had set out with the

notion of performing all thirty-six plays of the Shakespeare First Folio, and it is not clear when this was first seen as possible, but by the early 1920s the Vic had performed most, and was putting on some of the least well known. On the first night in 1923 of the bloody *Titus Andronicus* – in which throats are cut and hands and heads severed – five members of the audience fainted. 'The actors', said the *Old Vic Magazine*, 'took this as a great tribute to their acting powers: word was passed every night to the stage-doorkeeper – "How many? Only two?" – and, quite dispirited, the artistes went back to redouble their efforts . . .'

The play which would give the Vic a full hand, *Troilus and Cressida*, was given in November 1923 at a gala performance before the Princess Royal. John Murray, the publisher, brought a copy of the First Folio which was displayed in a glass case in the orchestra pit. Many of the actors and actresses who had taken part in any of the plays assembled on stage after the final curtain, as many as still lived close enough to London to be rounded up. Miss Baylis again took rather a lot of the credit. A page of that night's programme was devoted to photographs of herself and of six Shakespeare directors, Ben Greet and Robert Atkins among them, and hers was in the centre and much the largest. And in her magazine she could not resist remarking – clean contrary to the recollections of Sybil Thorndike and others – that what she called the Shakespearean movement at the Vic owed its being to the enthusiasm of the opera audience, who she said had been urged to sample the play nights for themselves, and to encourage their friends to come. Without this, she said, the plays would have died for want of support. The Vic's early *Hamlet* had been played to a few hundred people and the takings had barely covered the cost of printing the programmes. 'The dear Old Vic has attained the honour of having produced every play generally accepted as Shakespeare's . . . I suppose that every great actor and manager during the centuries has desired to achieve this record, and, mainly thanks to the splendid fillip given by opera lovers at the start, the historic event has come to pass at the Vic . . . Deo gratias.'

At the time this record was achieved the Vic had just presented fifteen plays of Shakespeare in a season and a half, something unthinkable today and made possible only by the briefest of rehearsals. Just how brief was indirectly revealed by Miss Baylis when she was indignantly expressing her low opinion of critics. They came along, she said, and in half an hour dismissed the work which it had taken her people a whole week to perfect. No wonder John Gielgud, who made his first walk-on and spear-carrying appearances soon after, remembered the productions as rushed and unfinished. In March 1924, at a meeting of the Board, one member of the theatre Board suggested that the pre-season period of Shakespeare rehearsal should be increased from three to six weeks. This was not just for the rehearsal of one play, but for a review of the first several plays of the season. Miss Baylis opposed the proposal, saying it would be unfair to the opera artists who would be kept out of work by such extended drama rehearsals. Things were left as they were. This also shows that, even after the great achievement of presenting all the First Folio plays, Miss Baylis's first love was for the opera, and remained so.

That year Miss Baylis was given an honorary MA at Oxford. She described this in detail. Within three seconds of the announcement being made on the BBC, which she said had caught the habit of loving the Vic, her telephone bell rang and felicitations began to arrive. Only one other woman, she said, had received such an honorary degree, and that was the

Queen. She then described her journey to Oxford to receive the honour. Perhaps, she said, it was easier to recognise in the austere hush of the Sheldonian, even more so than among the enthusiastic scenes that had taken place in the precincts of the theatre, what a living force the Old Vic had become. She described the ceremony moment by moment – scarlet robes, silver maces, carved doors thrown open, and the Vice-Chancellor's Latin oration. What he said, in brief translation, was that she had known how to attract unlearned and common men to her theatre, and that if Shakespeare were to return to earth from the Elysian Fields he would regard her as his handmaid or priestess – *ministra aut sacerdos* – and heap her with praise and thanks.

Ever afterwards she wore her Master's cap, gown, and hood at first nights and last nights and galas and at any other opportunity, as if it were a uniform, and put MA (Oxon.) after her name in programmes, on her letterhead, and even in the Old Vic's small ads in newspapers. The board of trustees can be said to have encouraged her in this. When it conveyed its congratulations to her, it also resolved to present her with the cap and gown.

8

Melba and Heavenly Things

'God send me a good actor, and send him cheap.' This is the classic and undeniable Lilian Baylis story, and she probably did say something like it. It comes from Russell Thorndike, no great man of the theatre himself but the brother of Sybil Thorndike. It happened in 1915. He had been invalided out of the army and was with Miss Baylis in the theatre box she used as an office. She knelt down, put one hand on the telephone on her roll-top desk, and then, in what sounded like a business conversation, asked God if she should put on *Henry V*, which would mean taking on more actors and spending more money. 'The last sentence of the prayer', said Thorndike, 'was that God should send her some good actors – and as an afterthought she added the word "cheap".' He did not tell this story until after her death. Laurence Olivier then picked it up and used it in his autobiography, and it is now set in stone.

Miss Baylis's dealings with God were frequent. She was High Church, and took Mass every day. Among her closest companions, and her confessor, was Father Andrew, a monk of the Society of Divine Compassion, who floated round the theatre in a brown habit and was respected by some members of the company, thought sinister by a few, and mocked by others who had been obliged by the Manager to perform three years running the Nativity play he had written. He had founded a leper colony in Essex, which also became Miss Baylis's second favourite charity, after her theatre. She sometimes drummed up parties of actors to visit the colony with her.

As was perhaps suggested by the businesslike tone of her conversation about *Henry V*, Miss Baylis's beliefs could have their practical side. She firmly believed that money could not go to Heaven, but just as firmly that it could do heavenly things, and by 1924 she needed some such help. In the 1880s the Old Vic had been divided up to make room for Morley College, and the theatre had lost everything but the auditorium and the bare stage. The college was above, below, and behind the stage, and college and theatre were separated only by thin brick walls. By the 1920s the London County Council's safety regulations could not allow it to stay this way. It had to be restored to a proper theatre, and this would cost £30,000 the Vic did not have. Miss Baylis set about raising it, failed at first, and then was rescued by a most unlikely man who was hardly a champion of the deserving poor and certainly not of temperance.

George Dance was a showman who had started as a music-hall songwriter. He wrote 'Come Where the Booze is Cheaper' for Vesta Tilley. He then wrote the libretti for a dozen musicals, including *The Lady Slavey* and *The Gay Grisette*, then turned impresario and at one time had twenty-four companies on tour at once, in Britain and America. He gave the whole £30,000 to the Vic, and was knighted for services to the theatre.

By 1924 the college had moved out. A start was made on knocking the walls down, and then the builders went on a national strike, leaving the Vic roofless backstage, looking as though it had been heavily shelled, and letting the rain in. The builders' unions did however allow their members to continue work on hospitals and other such buildings for the public good, and it says much for the esteem in which the Vic was held

One of Miss Baylis's constant appeals for money. This is from 1922 and
appeared in the *Old Vic Magazine*. Hamlet holds a model of the Old Vic
with a 'Closed' notice on it

that such an exception was made in its favour. The builders returned, and then the Vic acquired the unheard-of riches of gallery seats from which their occupants could see the stage, a rehearsal room, dressing rooms with wash-basins, a lift, a stage door, and a wardrobe room so that the costumes could at last be brought in from the local pub that had been their previous home. The Old Vic also had a new constitution. When the college went, and theatre and college were legally separated, the old charter lapsed and the Charity Commissioners restated the purpose of the theatre as 'to provide in the theatre high-class drama, especially the plays of Shakespeare, and high-class opera . . . suited for the recreation and instruction of the poorer classes . . .' This seems innocuous but later caused the Old Vic some trouble.

Miss Baylis was by then a settled legend. At a dinner of the Elizabethan Literary Society in London, which happened to be in the week after Ramsay MacDonald took office as the first Labour prime minister in 1924, the principal speaker remarked that if that government should call a National Theatre into existence, Lilian Baylis would have taught them the way, and that neither Garrick nor Irving nor Herbert Tree had come within speaking distance of such an achievement. While the reconstruction of her theatre was going on she took a long holiday in southern Africa, returning to the country she had known as a girl Gypsy Reveller, and was there received as a heroine. She told the readers of the *Old Vic Magazine* in some detail about her drives with the archbishop in Cape Town and her adventures in Johannesburg and Victoria Falls. Just as later on, when she flew to Paris, she described the Farman Goliath plane, the circling, the clouds, the blue sea, and the forest of Chantilly seen from the air. She was the public face of the Old Vic. When in 1926 she acquired a little

Trojan car she reported that it had given her even more thrills than flying, and gave a list of the places in the West Country that she had driven to. And when she was invited to a garden party at Buckingham Palace she recounted this at length to her readers, adding that her Trojan had been parked next to the wonderful silver car of an Indian prince, with his chauffeur in scarlet and gold. Only after that anecdote did she turn to the next season of plays.

At the beginning of 1925 Robert Atkins, in his last season, was directing *Richard II* and *Othello*. As for opera, plans for the Vic's first *Aida* were announced. The Vic was flourishing and overcrowded, and Miss Baylis, with the renovations there by no means complete, promptly embarked on another scheme, this time to buy a second theatre – Sadler's Wells, across the river in Islington, a theatre which was derelict and being offered for sale as a site for a factory. By then she simply attracted money. The Carnegie Foundation gave £14,200 to buy it, but where was the money coming from to demolish the wreck and build a new theatre?

She launched yet another appeal and called in more favours, one from Nellie Melba, the great Australian soprano, who had as far back as 1914 promised to sing for nothing at the Vic one night. By 1926 she was sixty-five and had already given three farewell concerts that year, one at Bournemouth, one at the Royal Albert Hall, and another at Covent Garden before the King and Queen. But she would give another, on condition that it was for the People, in front of a true Old Vic audience. As *The Times* said, preference was given to those to whom a Melba gala night had always been a financial impossibility. Miss Baylis was an early mistress of public relations. The BBC, which paid the Vic ten pounds for an occasional excerpt from the plays and fifteen pounds for an opera, announced in *Wire-*

less Notes that Melba would be heard on virtually all stations from the Old Vic between 9.30 and 10 p.m., and would sing the Willow Song and 'Ave Maria' from Verdi's *Otello*. Then the *Manchester Guardian*'s reporter happened to be outside the theatre that day and the result was a paragraph headlined: 'Melba by Chance and for Nothing'.

The story said that the appearance of three magnificent shining motor cars outside the Vic had attracted a number of inquisitive children. One more enterprising than the rest pushed at the stage door and the sound of a piano and a woman's voice came through. 'Soon a small crowd of young and old had gathered at the half-open door, and Miss Lilian Baylis invited them in. She whispered to them that they should hear Melba sing, and all for nothing. They heard and saw Melba for over two hours as she rehearsed Mimi's part in acts iii and iv of *La Bohème*, and then Desdemona's part in act iv of *Otello*.'

Melba sang, but she made her demands. Covent Garden, where her word was law, lent scenery. She insisted on her own conductor, and that the best seats should be reserved for his friends and hers. She demanded that the orchestra pit should be enlarged to take thirty musicians. She specified the flowers in her bouquets – masses of violets. In short, for the day of the rehearsal and the evening of the performance, she took over the theatre from Lilian Baylis as no one had before, and Miss Baylis was even driven to sip brandy. Still, the evening – which Melba ended by singing ' Home, Sweet Home' – made a profit of £300 for the Sadler's Wells fund, and the larger orchestra pit remained as her legacy.

The new drama producer appointed in 1925 was Andrew Leigh, who, having acted at the Vic with Matheson Lang and been stage manager under Ben Greet, was hardly new at all. But what he did for the first time was to introduce two West

End actors to lead the company – Edith Evans and Balliol Holloway. Actors of the first rank had appeared there before – Sybil Thorndike in 1915, Maurice Evans in 1918, and Ernest Milton in 1921. Both men later became famous Hamlets – but they were at the beginning of their careers. No one already a star had ever before been sought out. And in 1926 the young Ninette de Valois approached Miss Baylis. She had had been born into the Anglo-Irish gentry as Edris Stannus, had danced in musical comedy, then at Covent Garden, and then with Diaghilev's Ballets Russes, and was running a ballet school in South Kensington. She was taken on at a pound a week to teach the actresses of the company 'how to move' – in particular Miss Baylis said they did not know what to do with their hands, and she preferred beautiful hands to beautiful faces. Miss de Valois would also be paid two pounds for arranging the choreography of any dance sequence needed for the Shakespeare repertory. So she came to the Old Vic, and stayed with Miss Baylis always dangling before her the uncertain prospect of a rebuilt Sadler's Wells where she could have her own ballet company.

The theatre's finances were always shaky, and not helped by Miss Baylis's insistence on presenting so many performances of *Everyman*. This is a fifteenth-century morality play showing what a Christian man must do to attain salvation, probably known today only to those reading English at one of the more demanding universities. It had been introduced by Ben Greet, and a performance now and then would have been splendid, but Miss Baylis insisted on performing it throughout Holy Week. Reginald Rowe, a governor who also acted as honorary treasurer, kept a notebook of the daily takings, which shows that in April 1927 *Everyman* was presented on six consecutive days, on one night taking as little as £16 14s. 6d. and never more than £48 14s. 6d. A donation of £17 6s. 6d. was made to Father Andrew's leper colony. The figures for the following week, that of Shakespeare's birthday (23 April), show that the traditional Old Vic Festival on the eve brought in £160 5s. 4d., and that *Hamlet* in its entirety, given at a matinée on the birthday itself, took £139 17s. 11d. But the one night of opera on offer did best of all. *Cavalleria Rusticana* and *Pagliacci*, 'Cav and *Pag*', took £144 17s. 1d. – and that on the evening of Shakespeare's birthday, after *Hamlet*.

But the real trouble, again, was the building. The backstage was done, but now the LCC was pressing for improvements to the auditorium. Miss Baylis had apologised to her patrons for 'rock-like stalls', but it was more than that. The auditorium was still lit by gas, and smelled: the only electricity in the place illuminated the footlights, an improvement that had been insisted on by Rosina Filippi as far back as 1914. There was only one lavatory for both stalls and boxes. There were too few exits. And Miss Cons's coffee house, run by John Pearce, still took up the entire ground-floor front of the theatre, where the foyer is today. Pearce's lease ran out in 1927, so all the work could be done together. But when it began the fabric was found to be crumbling and much of the façade had to be rebuilt. This left the company homeless for nine months, and it had to migrate to Hammersmith. It also left the theatre with two appeals going, one to build Sadler's Wells and another to patch up the Vic. Once again Carnegie and other charities found the money, and Miss Baylis, demonstrating the taste common to so many theatre managements, proceeded to butcher the splendid auditorium of 1871, hacking out six of the boxes. (Much later the National Theatre continued the desecration with gusto, and the auditorium was not restored until 1981.)

The Old Vic in 1928 or 1929 when part of the façade was found
to be crumbling. The artist, Arthur Moreland, was a newspaper
cartoonist with the London *Morning Leader*. One copy of the image
was inscribed 'To Harcourt Williams in memory of his work at the
Vic with loving greetings from Lilian Baylis 1929 to 1933'

At the Vic Miss Baylis was known as the Lady. In 1929 she was made a Companion of Honour, which outranks a damehood, the offer of which she had hinted she would decline because she feared that dames, like knights, tended to be overcharged wherever they went. She received the medallion at Buckingham Palace from the young Prince of Wales who seven years later became Edward VIII and abdicated for Wallis Simpson. The only other CH created in the same honours list was the composer Frederick Delius. Hers was the only stage honour that year. She was herself planning a memorial to her aunt Emma Cons, and £1,100 had been set aside for a bronze plaque in the new vestibule. That year Ben Greet was knighted too, though not particularly for his services to the Old Vic, which were by then ten years in the past.

The Old Vic, in February 1929, offered ten nights of opera and eighteen of plays. That season, *La Bohème* and *Otello* were in the repertory for the first time, and the next year *Tosca* and *The Force of Destiny*, which had not been seen in England for sixty years. And yet the theatre still seemed to be in some ways amateur. It still relied for some of its costumes on the generosity of its patrons. The *Old Vic Magazine* for that February thanks, among others, Mrs Bateman for real ostrich feathers; Miss Chippendale for three velvet dresses; Miss de la Force for a box of various goods; Dr Margaret Tyler for a tiger skin and an African king's burnous; and the Misses Tutton for a Victorian frock.

But a new ferro-concrete theatre was rising at Sadler's Wells, across the river, two miles to the north. It opened in January 1931 with *Twelfth Night*, telegrams from the Prince of Wales and Sir Ben Greet, and a speech from Lilian Baylis, in Oxford cap and gown and wearing the medallion of her CH. She carried a basket of fruit on her arm, and spoke with such animation and movement that first an apple and then a pear leapt from the basket on to the stage. John Gielgud remembered that, along with a fair number of the audience, he burst out laughing. But it was an evening of triumph.

What did not go quite so well was the first night of opera, on which *Carmen* was given. The *Manchester Guardian*, which could generally be relied on to be sympathetic, praised the wildcat performance of Carmen herself, said that the company was good all round and, mysteriously, that the orchestra continued to play the game. But, said the critic, the great interest of the evening was in watching the audience. 'It was clear that many people in the attractive and comfortable house tonight did not clearly distinguish opera from a smoking concert at which applause after every song is expected. There were far too many interruptions tonight . . .' He hoped that Miss Baylis would convey to her new admirers that applause at the end of each act was more thoroughly appreciated than constant expressions of gratitude. She did do this, through her *Old Vic Magazine*. No one retorted that spontaneous applause, if it was good enough for Italian opera houses, was good enough for London.

The opening of Sadler's Wells was the end of a triumphant decade for Miss Baylis, but she was not well. She had worn herself out. She weighed more than fourteen stone and had diabetes. And two weeks after the opening she was in a car accident. She was being driven back from a celebratory dinner in the Trojan, accompanied by her secretary, Kathleen Clark, when the car ran into the back of a coach. She was in the front passenger seat and seemed to be unconscious. When the ambulance men arrived Miss Clark told them to attend to Miss Baylis first, saying she was manager of the Old Vic. At which Miss Baylis, rousing herself, said, 'And Sadler's Wells.' More legend but, since both Miss Clark and the driver told the story, more likely to be true.

9

Two Theatres, and a Drift
to the West End

By the time Sadler's Wells opened Harcourt Williams had already been drama producer at the Old Vic for a season and a half. He was a strange choice.

He was forty-nine, a moderately successful character actor who, when Miss Baylis first approached him in 1929, had directed only one play in the West End. He had however directed his wife's Christmas matinées for children at the Vic, and his wife happened to be the daughter of Antoinette Sterling, who had for years been a favourite singer there. When the offer was made to him he hesitated, knowing he would have, as he put it, twopence-halfpenny to spend, and fearing that Miss Baylis would interfere with his work. As it turned out she did not, and it was he who introduced the Old Vic to modern times. It was he who brought there John Gielgud, Martita Hunt, Ralph Richardson, and Peggy Ashcroft. All are names familiar to modern audiences, though Miss Hunt is probably best remembered as Miss Havisham in David Lean's film of *Great Expectations*.

In accepting Gielgud, Miss Baylis was undoubtedly swayed by his being a great-nephew of Ellen Terry. And of course she quibbled over salaries, nearly losing Miss Hunt for the want of an extra ten shillings a week, but then supported Williams, in his first production, of *Romeo and Juliet*, when he was assailed

97

by the critics for making his players speak as rapidly as the Italians they were supposed to be. She and Williams quarrelled only once, when she criticised his production of *A Midsummer Night's Dream* in front of the company – and that incidentally was a cast that brought in Donald Wolfit as well. Williams's first season included *Hamlet, Macbeth, Richard II*, seven others by Shakespeare, and one by George Bernard Shaw, the first of three Shaws he produced. Having a Gielgud in the company had its small drawbacks. The *Old Vic Magazine* put it this way: 'As John Gielgud has an important and urgent film engagement the production of *The Merchant of Venice* in which he will be associated with Harcourt Williams must be postponed . . .' Still, a Gielgud was worth a postponement. On the last night of that first season the company, in an Old Vic tradition, assembled on the stage, receiving gifts from the pit and the gallery, and Miss Baylis, in her Oxford robes and wearing her CH medallion, introduced the company, made a speech, and kissed her producer.

For Williams's second season Gielgud and Hunt remained. Ralph Richardson was brought in from Birmingham and was a natural both as Prince Hal and Caliban. Shaw came to the dress rehearsal of his *Arms and the Man*, muttered and groaned his way through the first act, taking copious notes, and then, having lashed into the assembled actors, wished them luck and left. Still, the company was splendid. As for Miss Baylis, she, said Williams, 'with the genuine optimism that flames like a torch behind her customary façade of financial ruin, proclaimed that when the world was in trouble it came to the Old Vic for solace'. This was however in the middle of the Great Depression, and the cut in teachers' salaries had cut into the theatre's audiences. Fewer could seek solace there.

Miss Baylis was fulsome in her goodbyes to Gielgud. His

mother made a cushion for her, and in her letter of thanks she said:

> You knew how proud we were in the first instance to have a 'Terry' with us – we are prouder than ever now to feel that he is going out to conquer new fields with something added to his art, and himself, by the work he has done here . . . I know that he will miss the joy of playing a series of such parts, just as we shall miss seeing him in them, but I look forward with keen pleasure to the day when he will have his own theatre, and when we may hope to see him again in parts of huge size – nothing else will satisfy us for him ultimately.

In Williams's third season Anthony Quayle and Marius Goring appeared. Richardson was Henry V and Iago. And the young Peggy Ashcroft joined the company. She was already known as an actress of great delicacy, and of wholeheartedness. She had two years before played Desdemona to Paul Robeson's Othello in the West End. Some of the audience were scandalised that a white woman should be publicly embraced on stage by a black man. More than fifty years later she said that for her it had been more than a theatrical experience, and that she and Robeson briefly became lovers. At the Old Vic in 1932, she was expected to play ten leading roles in ten months. She began with Cleopatra in Shaw's *Caesar and Cleopatra*, and then in rapid succession played the great Shakespearean roles, only starting with Imogen, Rosalind, and Portia. Her Rosalind in *As You Like It* particularly caught the attention of Walter Sickert – a great artist, many would say – who adored her and came to see her performances to sketch her from the life, inscribing some of his sketches to 'The

Divine Peggy'. He also painted her often, working from news-paper pictures. Perhaps her greatest success of that long sea-son was as Portia, in a *Merchant of Venice* directed by Gielgud. Portia's famous speech about the quality of mercy showed the nature of Miss Ashcroft's originality: her biographer, Michael Billington, quotes her as saying she tried to do it not as an aria but as a way of advancing the argument.

At the end of a season in which she also played Perdita, Juliet, and Miranda she was exhausted, and so, at the end of his time with the Old Vic, was Harcourt Williams. When Lilian Baylis kissed him on stage at the end-of-season performance it was time to go. Though Williams held her in some affection he did think of his time there as three years' hard labour. In his mem-oirs he wrote that he imagined the Old Vic, in the beginning, was intended to educate 'the masses' but there were, he said, no longer any such masses of great unwashed and untaught. In the body of the theatre sat middle-class schoolteachers, the intellectual new-poor, young women who worked in the City, and students. They did not want a diet of buns and lemonade. As he put it, 'Pauperism, too, can be overdone. I know well enough upon what thin ice we habitually skate, but . . . we lose a certain dignity by perpetually uttering a cry of wolf.'

Miss Baylis would not tell him, her producer, how good business was, how full or how empty the week's houses had been. Such matters were for her alone. He remembered seeing her after one meeting during the world financial crisis. 'How did you get on?' he asked. 'Splendidly,' she replied. 'I had the Almighty in my pocket.' She may have done, but Williams still had an average of only twenty-eight pounds to spend on the costumes and sets of any new production.

He was not happy. It was, he said, difficult to get anything altered. He felt at times that he had strayed into the committee of some charitable organisation, which of course he had. 'Lilian Baylis, rightly or wrongly, holds the end of every string in her hand, and the only chance of change comes through her, and, as I have already said, she welcomes new ideas so far as they can be squared with her own wisdom.' To take small things, he could not stand matches struck by members of the audience in the middle of a scene, or tatty lantern slides shown in the intervals, or noisy crockery removed after tea served in those intervals, or cold draughts through doors carelessly left open. And tickets could still not be bought through the usual ticket agencies, only at the Old Vic box office.

And sometimes he thought she should praise her people a little more. 'One gets the impression that she belittles endeavour for fear one might ask for tuppence more. It is not necessary, dear Lilian, you would find no difficulty in saying No.' This is a little bitter. Perhaps Peggy Ashcroft put the matter more aptly when she remarked that Miss Baylis was both a power and a joke.

Lord Lytton, chairman of the Old Vic governors throughout the 1930s, had some small difficulty with Miss Baylis. He had been a Lord of the Admiralty, Governor of Bengal, and even briefly Viceroy of India, and a man who had ruled India should have been able to rule the most intransigent of women. Later he described how he did.

We all admired and trusted our manager, and consequently left her a free hand in all matters connected with the actual management of the theatres. But there were times when differences of opinion occurred and Miss Baylis would become engaged in heated argument with one or other of the governors. She would get very excited and explosive, giving expression to vehement opinions delivered at the top of her voice. At such times I had to intervene to keep the peace. But there was never any malice in Miss Baylis's outbursts – they were always in defence of some principle which she held sacred, and the storms would subside as quickly as they arose.

Williams and Miss Baylis had also disagreed on Sadler's Wells. It was her project. She was photographed first in the ruins of the old theatre, and then, often, by the walls of the new one as it rose. He refused even to look at it while it was building. When it was finished he loathed it, saying the acoustics of all that ferro-concrete were terrible. He was not alone in his opinion. Gielgud thought the new theatre resembled a denuded wedding cake. Sadler's Wells did have tip-up seats in both stalls and circle (which the Vic did not until 1950), and hot running water for the actors in their dressing rooms, and even, for the audience, two bars, which were not yet permitted at the Vic. But that was about the sum of its advantages. It was unknown. Even taxi drivers did not know how to find their way there.

The prime notion of the Vic-Wells, as the joint venture was named, was that opera and drama should be presented at both theatres. So *Hamlet* and *Othello* played ten days at the Vic and then ten days at the Wells, and the costumes and sets had to be ferried the two miles across the Thames either in Miss Baylis's Trojan or by costermonger's barrow, and if by barrow that had by law to be done before six in the morning because of the traffic. Shabby sets which had gone unremarked at the shabby old Vic looked their age in a new concrete theatre and, besides, those sets grew even tattier and more knocked-about with all the to-and-froing. One set for *La Traviata* tipped from its barrow into the river. There were other difficulties. Members of the audience confused the theatres and turned up at the wrong one. And it soon became clear that there was not much of an audience for drama at Sadler's Wells anyway. Only by 1935 was it decided that the drama should stay at the Vic and opera at the Wells. That was the year Charles Corri retired, after conducting a last double bill of *Cav* and *Pag*. He had served the Old Vic since 1898.

The great surprise was the sudden rise of the ballet. Ninette de Valois, as we have seen, had joined the Old Vic in 1926 to teach ' movement' to the actresses at a pound a week. She had stayed because Miss Baylis was forever dangling in front of her the promised opening, in some dim future, of Sadler's Wells and the formation of a ballet company there. But against all the odds the Wells did open, in its first year a ballet company was formed, and out of nothing de Valois assembled a company of names already famous or soon to be so.

Alicia Markova, born Alice Marks but dancing with the Ballets Russes at fourteen, became prima ballerina. Her first *Giselle*, danced on New Year's Day 1934, brought glory to her and to the company. There was Margot Fonteyn, born Peggy Hookham at Reigate, who studied with Russian émigré teachers in Shanghai, joined the Wells in 1933, and became in her turn prima ballerina. Not to forget Lydia Lopokova, late of the Imperial Russian Ballet School and then Ballets Russes, friend of Picasso, mistress of Stravinsky, later wife of the economist John Maynard Keynes, who danced Swanilda in the Wells's first *Coppelia*. All of these, along with Anton Dolin, the choreographer Fred Ashton, and the Australian Robert Helpmann.

So the ballet thrived, and was a social success too. In 1932 the Duchess of York, later George VI's queen, came to see de Valois' *Nursery Suite*, because Sir Edward Elgar had written the music for her daughters, later Elizabeth II and Princess

Margaret. Elgar was also in the audience. The Vic never did lack patrons. That same year the Vic-Wells's annual revel, under the patronage of Sir Thomas Beecham, Mrs Matheson Lang, Gwen Ffrangcon-Davies, and Sir Ben Greet, was held at the Royal Opera House, Covent Garden. Tickets were five shillings and the modest cabaret was supplied by the Vic-Wells ballet with Alicia Markova, arranged by de Valois.

By the early 1930s Lilian Baylis was losing some of her endless energy. She was not well, had to have a hysterectomy, and was beginning to realise she could not run everything. She also needed someone to drive her round London and help generally, and in 1932 took on the twenty-one-year-old Annette Prevost. Her letter offering the appointment speaks for itself:

> The post I have to offer of chauffeuse companion carries a living-in salary of one pound a week. I expect whoever is appointed to be accustomed to driving in heavy town traffic, and to keeping the car in good condition – very heavy cleaning is done by one of the stage hands. I also want my chauffeuse to help in the house, doing light work there, and while waiting at either theatre to do any odd work for which she is suited. Typing is an advantage but is not essential. I cannot promise regular hours off, because my own days are so full, but the work is not continuous, and is definitely interesting.

She probably made no greater demands even of her actors. The salary of a pound a week was the same as she had earned when she came as assistant to her aunt Miss Cons in 1898, but that was more than thirty years before. Prevost, as she was called in the theatre, lived with Miss Baylis at her house in Stockwell, two miles from the Old Vic. She was a pretty, well-educated young woman, with distant connections to a South African bishop, and gradually became not only driver and companion but also personal secretary. She stayed with the Vic-Wells into the 1960s.

From 1933 the new drama producer at the Old Vic was Tyrone Guthrie. He was thirty-three, by far the youngest to hold that position, and he was another step into modern times. He was the first producer at the Vic whose name became as important on the bill as that of the leading actor. After attending an English public school five of whose pupils had won the Victoria Cross in the First World War, he read history at Oxford, and then failed to establish himself as an actor. He spent two years at the very new BBC in Belfast, which he found too like the civil service, then directed at the Festival Theatre in Cambridge, returned to radio in Canada, and then directed at the new Westminster Theatre. It was there that Harcourt Williams saw his production of *Love's Labour's Lost* and recommended him to Lilian Baylis. It was only the second Shakespeare Guthrie had directed, and he was lucky that it was not fashionably done in modern dress. Miss Baylis went to see the play with Prevost, taking a box and keeping up an incessant conversation with her new young companion. Guthrie thought Miss Baylis looked like a parish worker, and he was perhaps a good judge since there were clergymen in his family and a great-grandfather had been Moderator of the Church of Scotland. He nevertheless accepted her invitation to come for tea, with his young wife, at her cottage in Kent, and spent a sodden afternoon there in constant rain. He was then asked for another interview at the Vic, in the box she still sometimes used as an office, in the presence of her snarling dogs Scamp and Sue and underneath a print of Dürer's praying hands. She still did not offer him the job for another three months and then, on paper headed 'The People's Theatre' and 'The Home of Shakespeare and Opera', proposed to engage him for the 1933–4 season, starting in September, at £700 a year, which in a way was a generous salary since it was the same as her own. She did, however, require him to do what she called the preliminary work of getting to know the company, from June to September, for nothing.

He accepted, introduced Flora Robson as his leading lady, and then Charles Laughton, the star of eleven films who had just become famous in his film of *The Private Life of Henry VIII*, as his leading man. Miss Baylis overcame her objections to Laughton's never going to church, to his never having played Shakespeare, and – only just – to his requiring a salary of £20 a week, a twentieth of what he could earn in films. He was to play in *The Cherry Orchard*, in Shakespeare's *Henry VIII*, and in *Measure for Measure*, *The Tempest*, and *Macbeth*. He was dismayed by the Vic's own shabby stock of costumes and instinctively used his personal fame as a film star to secure from the new Pilgrim Trust, backed by American money, a grant to buy new costumes for the play in which he appeared. Miss Baylis regarded this as a flagrant trespass into her territory. Who did he think he was? She was the Manager, she did the begging, and she grudgingly countenanced the gift only when it was explained that the Vic would inherit the costumes. She thought Laughton an upstart using her theatre as a stepping stone. He thought her a shrew.

The season started with *The Cherry Orchard*, the first time the Old Vic had done Chekhov, and ran for six weeks, an unprecedentedly long run for the theatre. Guthrie thought it essential that if a play did well it should be able to run. He thus attempted only seven productions, compared with twelve in Williams's last season, and the twenty-six Greet had done in

1917–18. Laughton's Angelo in *Measure for Measure* was a triumph, his *Henry VIII* an inevitable commercial success, and his Prospero in *The Tempest* terrible. But he certainly drew a West End theatre audience across the river. This was an audience Miss Baylis did not want. The season ended in magnificent ill will with *Macbeth*. It was not Laughton's most convincing performance, and he knew it. After the first performance Miss Baylis, in MA gown and hood, swanned into his dressing room, smacked him on the shoulders, and said: 'Never mind, dear. I'm sure you did your best. And I'm sure that one day you may be quite a good Macbeth.' He never forgave her, continued to fill the house, but turned his back on her. On the last night, when by tradition all the company received little gifts on stage, there was nothing for Laughton. He thought she was taking revenge for the Pilgrim Trust affair. Guthrie did not agree. He knew she was not petty. If she had wanted revenge she would not have been catty in a dressing room but rather, he thought, would have called down the Lord of Hosts upon Laughton and had her dogs lick his blood.

Guthrie himself had not been welcomed by all. His season made a profit of £6,000, which more than covered the losses on opera and ballet. But another Pilgrim, a Miss Pilgrim from the gallery, had got up a letter of bitter protest against his new ways. Many of the old guard agreed. It was not their kind of Shakespeare. Miss Baylis showed Guthrie the letter. His response was that the old guard failed to understand that tradition was not a stagnant pond but a river. He cited the American critic Robert Benchley as saying that at this time the Old Vic was interesting at its worst, and at its best was the most important experimental theatre in the world. But he doubted if the *New Yorker* was much read in The Cut. For himself, he admitted he might have been youthful and immature, but thought Miss Baylis tired and a little discouraged. He thought it best to part on friendly terms at the end of the season.

His successor was Henry Cass of the Croydon Repertory Theatre, who is best remembered for reintroducing Maurice Evans. Evans had made a name by playing a part the young Laurence Olivier did not want in R. C. Sherriff's *Journey's End*, perhaps the greatest play about the First World War. He stayed for only a year. His *Richard II* and *Hamlet* made such an impression that Katharine Cornell, the first lady of the American theatre, invited him to play Romeo to her Juliet on Broadway. He also played in *Macbeth* opposite Judith Anderson, gave 283 performances of *Hamlet* on Broadway, and for many years played the great Shakespearean parts in the American theatre and, after the war, on television. So he was lost to America, and seldom returned to England until his old age, but Cass and the Vic had him first, though only for a year. If he had stayed in England he would have become a theatrical knight.

Cass stayed for two seasons, and the most notable event of his second, in February 1936, was *St Helena*, a new Sherriff play about Napoleon's imprisonment on that island after Waterloo. The critics did not like it and the audiences at first were sparse. Then Winston Churchill, out of office for six years and in the political wilderness, wrote a surprising but most Churchillian letter to *The Times*. He had first been put off by the critics but had then seen the play, and in his opinion 'as a voracious reader of Napoleonic literature' it was a work of art of a very high order and an entertainment which riveted the attention of the audience. 'Nor need the sense of inexorable decline and gloom sadden unduly those who have marvelled at Napoleon's prodigious career. There is a grandeur and human kindliness about the great Emperor in the toils which make a conquering appeal . . . Here is the end of the most astonishing journey ever made by mortal man.'

And there was the beginning of a run on the box office that Miss Baylis called sensational. Tired she might have been, but the theatre, in one way and another, on stage and off, was flourishing. At the Vic's costume dance at Covent Garden Pearl Argyle, Robert Helpmann, and Margot Fonteyn had given a cabaret, Edith Evans made an appeal, and the prizes were presented by Gertrude Lawrence and Noël Coward. All of which raised £2,167 16s. What other theatre could have raised such a cast?

Early in 1936 Miss Baylis's doctor and the theatre governors told her to take a rest. She took a cottage by the sea in the wilds of Wales, ideal, she said, for peaceful recreation. But she was tempted to speak at an Eisteddfod where she said the Vic had done something for music too, having presented fifty-two operas, but badly wanted dramatic tenors. Nor could she resist an invitation to a conference of international businesswomen in Paris. She flew there. The British ambassador gave a lunch for her. At the People's Theatre she saw a performance of *Le 14 Juillet*. At the end a minute's silence was observed in memory of comrades who had fallen, fighting Franco, in the Spanish civil war that week. 'Then [she wrote in the *Old Vic Magazine*] the Marseillaise was sung, and the great multitude stood with raised arms and clenched fists to sing their own anthem – The Red Flag – twice through . . . It was most moving and I was thrilled from my toes to my hair.' It is probable that she innocently had no idea of the political implications of what she was saying. She had to explain in the next issue that she was not a communist, and that there was no room in her life for Right, Left, Centre, or for anything but the Old Vic, Sadler's Wells, and full houses.

That year Ben Greet died, to whom she owed so much. He had last been at the Vic for the previous year's Shakespeare's birthday gala, on 23 April. She had asked him to say a few words, but he could not. She remembered he had put his hands to his face, saying 'I can't bear it,' knowing he would never address an audience again.

After two years Cass left. There had been too many empty seats, he lost money, and at one point was told he could spend no more than ten pounds on the next production. He said this broke him professionally, and he did little in the theatre afterwards, but he did go on to direct no fewer than twenty-seven films, into the 1960s.

Guthrie returned. He had done well in his two years away, having directed four West End plays and two on Broadway. Miss Baylis seems to have reconciled herself to him, even to his West End tendencies. In the magazine she wrote that he was 'full of life and ideas well worth trying out'. For his part he admitted that his motives in returning were a mixture of artistic ambition and worldly calculation. He wanted to be part of an institution more permanent than the commercial theatre. He also admitted that awful crises would probably occur, like receiving telegrams from actors saying: DEEPLY REGRET CANNOT PLAY OTHELLO FOR YOU TONIGHT STOP SAILED HOLLYWOOD YESTERDAY.

He then outlined his first season. Edith Evans would be returning. She would play in Wycherley's *Country Wife* – a bawdy play that would hardly have been seen at the Vic in Lilian Baylis's earlier days – with the American actress Ruth Gordon. Alec Clunes would be coming, and so too would Michael Redgrave, 'a potential star'. And this:

'For the later part of the season we shall have Mr Laurence Olivier.'

10

Olivier, and the Last Baylis Season

It seems strange to think so now, but in 1936 Laurence Olivier was known not as a Shakespearean actor but as a promising film star and a West End matinée idol of the swashbuckling kind. He had, very early, spent two years in Hollywood, and by the mid-1930s had made ten films. On the stage his longest run had been in Noël Coward's *Private Lives*, and his most typical West End role that of John Barrymore in a rapier-rattling performance of *Theatre Royal*, a send-up of the celebrated American acting family. But at the age of twenty-eight he had played only one Shakespearean lead, alternating Romeo and Mercutio with John Gielgud. In 1936 he had just finished shooting *Fire Over England*, a Korda epic with Flora Robson and Vivien Leigh, which he knew would make his name – in films. It was then that he decided to become a Shakespearean actor. It was a cool decision. As he said, he was determined to be a great actor and he knew that unless he could make a reputation in the classics he could not achieve that. 'My ambition required it. I required it of myself. I knew it wouldn't happen unless I crashed that market. So I had to go on with the critics giving me bad notices, saying I couldn't speak the verse to save my life and all that, and I just went on and on, and after about a year the Press referred to me as "that Shakespearean actor". Then I knew it had been done.'

The only place, in those days, where a man could do a whole season of Shakespeare was at the Old Vic, and Olivier gave two accounts of how he came to do his first Shakespeare season there. The first was this: 'In those days if one was a leading West End actor one phoned up Lilian and said, "I'd like to come." Sure, and they were thirsty for you. You only cost £25 a week and you were welcome. I mean, you know, the smell of a leading man to Lilian was like oats to a racehorse.'

The second and more likely version was that in September 1936 he and his first wife Jill Esmond invited Tyrone Guthrie down to the country to discuss the coming Old Vic season and, again according to Olivier, the conversation went like this:

OLIVIER: You think we should start with *Hamlet*?
GUTHRIE: Yes, agreed.
OLIVIER: Well then, let's see. I'll stay the season and we'll pick up parts as we go along, shall we?

As Olivier later said, he would have been dumb not to know that he was 'quite a snip, for Lilian and for Tony'. To reassure himself, he phoned Ralph Richardson in New York and said, 'Ralphie, shall I go to the Old Vic?'

'Think it's a very good idea,' said Richardson.

'Thanks, goodbye.'

That settled the matter.

In this second version, after the agreement was made with Guthrie, Olivier was summoned to meet Lilian Baylis, in her curtained-off box, after he had already been rehearsing *Hamlet* for two weeks. He was giving up five hundred pounds a week in films for twenty-five at the Old Vic, and she knew it. He entered a room with faded photographs on the walls and her pet dogs snarling at his ankles on the floor. He could not remember what she said, except that she ended by remarking, 'Of course you really oughtn't to come here at all when you can get so much money elsewhere but still it's your business. Goodbye.' Olivier warmed to her. 'She was very friendly,' he said. 'She loved me. Well, she was thrilled because I was naturally the biggest name up to then. And she knew I'd pull them in so she loved me. I brought this great socking movie public into her theatre.'

It was a fair bargain. Olivier would get his season of Shakespeare. The Old Vic would get its leading man. As he put it:

> They had to have a so-called star to whom they need pay only £25 a week. They'd had Maurice Evans, they'd had Gielgud, they'd had Ralph . . . but I'd done these films, you see, and I had a fantastic name for them. I'd said we should start quite boldly with *Hamlet*, and Guthrie swallowed that . . . I had something John Gielgud never had, which was extreme athleticism, and I really founded my Hamlet on [the American] John Barrymore. Nobody recognised that, but I was a very physical Hamlet, which they had never seen. We had to be real people. We don't necessarily do that at the expense of the verse . . . Find reality through the verse, and if the verse is a sort of veil in front of reality you go through that veil and take a little bit of the veil with you.

These two accounts are from Olivier's recollections in his seventies, when he could speak more candidly than he had before. But it may also be that he was not, in 1936, quite as brash as he remembered himself to have been. He was a catch for the Old Vic, but he would not have been, at the time, the biggest star to have appeared there. As he said, Gielgud had famously played there, and in 1934 Charles Laughton had played seven leading roles in a season.

Olivier and Guthrie's productions of *Hamlet* were to be played uncut, four hours of them. Olivier called them 'Eternity Hamlets'. Guthrie adopted the Freudian thesis of a recently published book by Dr Ernest Jones that Hamlet had an Oedipus complex and was almost incestuously in love with his mother. They both went to see Dr Jones and hear him expound his theory. As Olivier remembered: 'He said Hamlet offered an impressive array of symptoms: spectacular mood swings, cruel treatment of his love, and above all a hopeless inability to pursue the course required of him.' From that meeting Olivier believed in that particular reading of *Hamlet*.

> Audience after audience for nearly 400 years have watched it with infinite patience trying to make it out because it's so interesting. A man in black is always interesting, and I think you've got to realise, as an actor, that the only thing is to try and make the audience follow the journey from mood to mood, and you can work out quite easily that when he was fucking Ophelia, which unquestionably he was, that that simply represented his nymph and shepherd period: the mood took hold of him. Everything he does is a mood taking hold of him: the man of action is a mood, and he can ginger himself up to giving a great performance of that.

This Oedipal treatment of the play, though faithfully followed, went almost unnoticed by the audience and critics. Even Hamlet's lascivious kissing of his mother Gertrude was little remarked. The play opened on 5 January 1937. The reviews conceded the virility of the performance but lamented its lack of Gielgudian pathos. Dr Jones himself was sniffy, writing to Guthrie: 'You will not, of course, expect me, who have known Hamlet himself, to be content with any human substitute. Mr Olivier played well and understandingly the scenes with the queen. But temperamentally he is not cast for Hamlet. He is personally what we call "manic" and so finds it hard to play a melancholic part.'

In March Olivier continued his Shakespeare season as Sir Toby Belch in *Twelfth Night*. But for him the great event of that time was the opening on 24 February of *Fire Over England* at the Leicester Square cinema. This was attended by a vast crowd, nine admirals, the First Sea Lord, the Duke and Duchess of Norfolk, the French and Portuguese ambassadors, H. G. Wells, author of *The War of the Worlds*, A. A. Milne, creator of Winnie-the-Pooh, and Lady Diana Cooper, wife of the Secretary for War. Olivier and Vivien Leigh commanded full pages of pictures in no fewer than three society magazines – *Harper's Bazaar*, *The Sketch*, and *The Bystander*. The film strangely became one of Hitler's favourites. He liked it better than James Agate in *The Tatler* who wrote that it had cost £75,000 to make and found it 'melancholy to think how far this sum could have gone towards a National Theatre'.

It was Coronation year. In 1936 Edward VIII had preferred Mrs Simpson to the throne, abdicated, and become the Duke of Windsor; his brother the Duke of York was to be crowned George VI on 12 May 1937. The Old Vic needed a Coronation play and the choice fell on *Henry V*. Ralph Richardson again helped Olivier. 'I know he's a boring old scout-master on the face of it, but being Shakespeare he's the exaltation of all scout-masters. He's the cold bath king and you'll have to glory in it.' At first Olivier could not bring himself to glory in it enough. His Crispin speech, which he later ended in the film with a rising howl of 'Cry God for Harry, England, and St George,' fell flat in rehearsals at the Vic. He insisted on taking it gravely and quietly until Guthrie told him he was taking all the thrill out of the play, which, for goodness sake, he said, was all it had.

Olivier went from strength to strength. He played Iago to Richardson's Othello. He played Coriolanus, with a spectacular death scene, much admired, throwing himself down a staircase in a complete somersault which shook the stage, rolling over three times on his side, and crashing dead at the footlights. *John O'London's Weekly* declared that he was 'the only sign of a great actor in the making in England today'. He played six of the great Shakespeare roles in sixteen months. His gamble of making a name as a Shakespearean leading man – and it had been a gamble – had come off triumphantly.

Lilian Baylis had been invited to take the company to Denmark to perform *Hamlet* at Elsinore. Olivier flew to Elsinore, saw the mayor and corporation, arranged everything, and flew back. By then, three weeks before the whole company was due to leave for Denmark, he had determined to leave his wife, Jill Esmond, for Vivien Leigh. He had somehow got her cast as Ophelia for the Danish trip, replacing the actress who had played that part in London. When the Old Vic company sailed for Denmark on 27 May, Olivier was accompanied by both his wife and Vivien. Jill was a spectator. Oliver and Leigh were a carnal Hamlet and Ophelia. 'We could not keep from touching each other,' he later wrote in his *Confessions of An Actor*, 'almost making love within Jill's vision.'

The company rehearsed until three in the morning at Kronborg, Hamlet's castle, watched by Miss Baylis with knitting needles, in a sealskin sou'wester, and huddled in a pile of rugs. It was courageous of her to be there at all, let alone to stay up until the early hours in filthy weather. She was in no fit state. In a letter to the Swedish organisers asking to hire a car for Prevost to drive her about in Denmark, she had added in her own hand: 'I suppose the hotel has a lift otherwise I must ask to be allotted a bedroom on the 1st floor, as I must not do many steps.' She added that she would like Miss Prevost to have a small room near hers.

The company gave six performances. All should have been in the open air but the weather was so bad that Miss Baylis, so strong against drink, procured a keg of rum for her company. Rain fell constantly, but it was impossible to cancel what was to be a gala performance for the Crown Prince of Denmark. So the company and the audience moved to the Martienlyst Hotel, where eight hundred chairs were hastily arranged in the ballroom. The other performances were in the open air, though one had to be called off after two acts. This was seen by the young John Steinbeck, who years later reminded Olivier of the event. 'It was on a scaffold in the courtyard,' he said. 'I and three thousand [others] sat on wooden trestles. The rain poured down and your black tights grew blacker with the moisture. Finally, to save your lives, you, a wet and melancholy Dane and your prematurely damp Ophelia, called the non-existent curtain down.'

Olivier, Jill, and Vivien flew back together. Within a week Olivier had left his wife for Vivien Leigh. Olivier had had to use some persuasion to get Miss Leigh to Elsinore at all, and Prevost attempted to reassure Miss Baylis: 'Someone mentioned to me that you were worrying yourself about a certain trio at Elsinore sorting itself out into the wrong 2 plus 1. But it's common knowledge that things were wrong ages before then and I'm convinced the same end would have been arrived at whether they'd gone with us or not.'

Back at the Old Vic, Olivier gave what many thought his best performance of the season as Macbeth. His Lady Macbeth was Judith Anderson, an Australian actress who had made her name on Broadway but who came for a season at the Vic. It played to the best houses the Old Vic had ever known. James Agate, one of the most powerful critics, said that the last act was the best of any *Macbeth* he had seen. 'Mr Olivier, who has made enough noise, and some people think too much, now gives the part the finest edge of his brain. "Liar and slave" is uttered with a cold Irving-esque malignity. If the voice . . . still cannot accomplish a cello, it achieves a noble viola.' But the opinion of even the most esteemed critic is worth less than that of Elizabeth Bowen, a novelist of high distinction, who wrote:

> Played as it is at the Old Vic, *Macbeth* might be called, first of all, a play about a marriage; the instinctive complicity of these two people, their powerful natural tie, the hypnosis they exercise over each other, is palpable the whole time . . . As for Mr Olivier, he has that gift, above price for a Shakespearean actor, of speaking every majestic, well-known line as though it sprang, only now, direct from his own heart.

All this is high praise, so it is surprising that a dissenting voice should have been that of John Gielgud. He thought it the best *Macbeth* he had seen, and Miss Anderson's performance finely conceived, but considered Olivier's to be 'a modernism awfully unequal', continually slipping from the classical style to ranting. It was a violent evening, exhausting to watch, but Olivier's scenes with Judith Anderson had real harmony and moving tragic intention. In that at least he agreed with Miss Bowen.

15 Emma Cons's passion was temperance, not theatre. Not once in thirty-two years did she put on a play, only 'purified' variety acts and concerts

16 The Victoria Coffee Hall's penny matinées packed the gallery of Delatorre's lavishly gilded auditorium with the very young, as shown in this engraving from *The Graphic*, 1882

17 Royal visit to the Vic, 1910. The Prince and Princess of Wales are alone in the second box in the dress circle. Miss Cons is in the box below. The evening was devoted to a ballad concert. Two months later the prince acceded to the throne as George V

18 Opera was Miss Baylis's first love, the Old Vic was as much opera house as theatre, and Charles Corri was conductor from 1898 to the mid-1930s. The Vic was too poor to employ a full orchestra, and he played Wagner with eighteen musicians

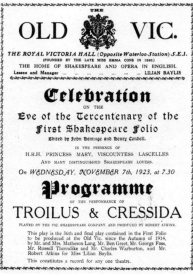

THE

OLD ⚜ VIC.

THE ROYAL VICTORIA HALL (Opposite Waterloo Station) S.E.1.
(FOUNDED BY THE LATE MISS EMMA CONS IN 1880.)
THE HOME OF SHAKESPEARE AND OPERA IN ENGLISH.
Lessee and Manager ... ... LILIAN BAYLIS

Celebration
ON THE
Eve of the Tercentenary of the
First Shakespeare Folio
Edited by John Heminge and Henry Condell.

IN THE PRESENCE OF
H.R.H. PRINCESS MARY, VISCOUNTESS LASCELLES
AND MANY DISTINGUISHED SHAKESPEARE LOVERS.

On WEDNESDAY, NOVEMBER 7th, 1923, at 7.30

Programme
OF THE PERFORMANCE OF

TROILUS & CRESSIDA

PLAYED BY THE VIC. SHAKESPEARE COMPANY AND PRODUCED BY ROBERT ATKINS.

This play is the 36th and final play contained in the First Folio to be produced at the Old Vic. since the Autumn of 1914, by Mr. and Mrs. Matheson Lang, Mr. Ben Greet, Mr. George Foss, Mr. Russell Thorndike and Mr. Charles Warburton, and Mr. Robert Atkins for Miss Lilian Baylis.

This constitutes a record for any one theatre.

19 Programme from 1923 when the Old Vic became the first theatre to have performed all thirty-six plays in the Shakespeare First Folio

20 Ben Greet, an actor-manager who worked at the Old Vic for nothing, in 1915–19 produced up to twenty-six plays in a season, and did more than anyone to establish the Shakespeare tradition there

21 This page from an Old Vic programme of 1933 shows Miss Baylis, in MA cap
and gown, surrounded by eight producers who from 1915 on worked at the Old Vic.
She still finds no place for Rosina Filippi, who in 1914 first produced Shakespeare
there when Miss Baylis, whose first love was opera, did not want it at all

22 (*Right*) Tyrone Guthrie, dominant producer of the 1930s at the Old Vic, who introduced the likes of Charles Laughton

23 (*Below*) Laughton, whom Baylis thought a mere film star. He in return thought her a shrew.

24 Lilian Baylis's new office, after the 1928 modernisation. Note the souvenir knick-knacks and, on the left, the ancient telephone. She also continued to use her old box, from which she could hear rehearsals

25 Diana Wynyard as Eliza Doolittle in Shaw's *Pygmalion* at the Old Vic, 1937. She was then best known as a film actress, but returned to the stage after the war, and played Gertrude to O'Toole's Hamlet in the first production of the new National Theatre at the Vic in 1963

26 Walter Sickert, a great painter, was attracted to Peggy Ashcroft, a great actress, and often painted and drew her. In this drawing, inscribed 'To the immortal Peggie', he shows her as Rosalind in the Old Vic's 1932–3 production of *As You Like It*

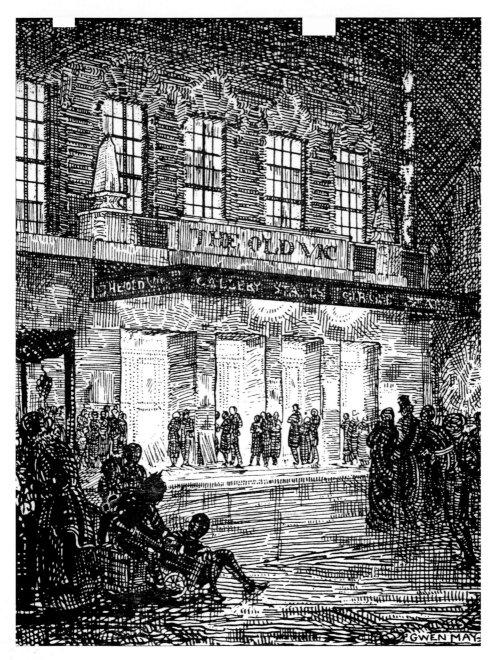

27 This woodcut of the 1930s, showing the Old Vic's audience arriving in The Cut
for the evening performance, was probably intended to be used as a Christmas card.
The artist, Gwen May, exhibited at the Royal Academy, and made ends meet by painting sets for the theatre. The obelisks on the theatre's façade, either side of the name,
have long since vanished. The stall on the left is part of the market then on The Cut

28 (*Above*) Laurence Olivier and Vivien Leigh as Hamlet and Ophelia at Elsinore in May 1937. It rained throughout the open-air performances

29 Lilian Baylis, seen here wearing the insignia of a Companion of Honour in 1937. She died later in the same year having been manager since 1912

But it was not a fortunate production. First it was not ready, so the opening had to be postponed from a Tuesday to the Friday, on the pretext that Olivier had lost his voice. Then Lilian Baylis fell ill, and on the day before the new first night suffered a heart attack and died. She was sixty-three, and she was exhausted.

To many she *was* the Old Vic. Should the show go on, or be postponed again? Annette Prevost, who had been at her bedside, reported that among her last questions had been: 'Is everything all right at the Old Vic?' So the play opened on Friday with Miss Baylis's chair in her box left empty. The audience stood in her honour before the play began. Olivier knew how ill Miss Baylis had been. Years later he said he had spoken that season from the stage in support of the Old Vic becoming the home of an eventual national theatre, and that he had done it chiefly, he thought, 'in order to bring a smile of approval to [her] sad, half-paralysed old lips'.

On the day of the funeral it rained persistently. The requiem mass at Kennington was crowded with the Old Vic's actors, stagehands, carpenters, painters, with a scattering of the faithful galleryites, and with the theatre and opera-house notables – Olivier, Helpmann, Thorndike, Fonteyn, de Valois. Patricia Don Young, one of the Vic's drama students, felt that with the banks of flowers and the opera choir it all felt like a scene from Verdi, and that at any moment Miss Baylis might come bustling down the aisle with a dog under each arm, exclaiming, 'Stop this, stop it at once. The idea of such a thing. It's costing far too much money.'

Her obituary notices were what an actor would call mixed. Some were sincerely devoted. Dame Sybil Thorndike recalled her as having said the Vic could not fail because it was God's work, a home for Shakespeare and for the People. 'She was a mystic – and the fire of a saintlike St Joan "going violently down her path like a thunderbolt" – a life ruled by prayer. Those who did not recognise the religious in her did not know Lilian Baylis. God bless her – the saints never die.'

Others were dutiful expressions of devotion with a certain hesitation about them, hardly a wholeheartedness. Tyrone Guthrie devoted most of his remarks, as published in the *Old Vic and Sadler's Wells Magazine*, to a description of her box, remarking that the first time they met at the theatre she kept him waiting so that he had time to take stock of the rickety black leather sofa, her roll-top desk with its knick-knacks, presents from Margate, rusty paper clips and perished elastic bands, three telephones, and, pinned to the top of the desk, a postcard reproduction of Dürer's Praying Hands. That, he said, was the room in which she interviewed her people, scolded them, and won their deep love. Harcourt Williams also remembered her famous box. It was, he said, screened from the auditorium by a heavy curtain through which a streak of light would sometimes escape so that those onstage were aware of her presence. 'That streak of light,' he wrote, 'if it may stand for a symbol of her presence, must never go out.' John Gielgud could only say that he saw little of her when he worked at the theatre and left it knowing her hardly at all, yet came to think of her over the years no longer as a distant and slightly eccentric employer but as a personal and devoted friend.

Only one obituary was downright hostile, but that was in the *Observer*, and at great length. The writer was St John Ervine, former manager of the Abbey Theatre, Dublin, not only a critic but a dramatist and at the time president of the League of British Dramatists. No one, he wrote, would have guessed Lillian Baylis ran a theatre and an opera house. He would have taken her for the superintendent of an orphanage. The Old Vic was the beginning and ending of her life. The British Empire might have perished without causing her a qualm but if a brick had fallen off the Old Vic roof somebody would have heard a lot about it. She had a single-track mind – 'the awful concentration of the saint'. He supposed she sometimes saw plays other than those produced at the Vic, but it was not apparent from anything she said. When her actors went to the West End and became renowned she regarded them as renegades. She was as hard as nails and utterly tactless, not a grateful woman, and could be unimaginably cruel in her criticism. 'She would have scrubbed floors for the Vic. She would have sold lavender from door to door for the Vic. She would have gone hungry for the Vic. She would have made you go hungry for the Vic . . . So long as you were working yourself to the bone for it you were alive, but the moment you stopped working for it you were dead and damned.' He supposed she read books, but there was no sign she read at all. She was not in any real sense a cultured woman. It would not astonish him to hear that she had little or no knowledge of music.

Moreover, he said, the Old Vic was not the marvellous institution that some people imagined. A great deal of flapdoodle was written about it. She had been called a producer but she was not. She was the manager of a theatre, adroit at cutting costs. Many of the productions would have been booed off the stage of any other theatre.

Yet such is the glamour this woman managed to cast over her theatre, the critics seldom if ever complained of them, though they would have flayed alive other managers who had offered such botched productions to the public. The theatre depended on her only to this extent, that she had a miraculous ability for making people give money to the theatre; but the production of plays will not be affected for the worse by her death; it may be affected for the better.

Six months later Ervine was at it again, after Miss Baylis's will had been published showing that she, the mistress of pinching and scraping, had left £10,037, about £1 million in today's money. He wrote in another *Observer* article that the passage of time would turn her into a myth. 'There will be an apocrypha about her . . . A time will come when a man who denies the Baylis hagiology will run the risk of incineration.' One legend was that she had sacrificed herself to help her aunt run the Old Vic. What, he asked, had she sacrificed? In London she was the unconquerable controller of two world-renowned theatres, an honorary MA of Oxford, and a Companion of Honour. Could she, as an indifferent music teacher in Johannesburg, have done better than that? Her passion for economy had become a mania. St Peter, when he opened the door for her, had probably been told he was much better paid than old Bob at the Vic, and less efficient. So, said Mr Ervine, when emotional men and women invited him to remember how she had slaved for the Old Vic for little money he begged them to remember that others had slaved no less and for as little money, and that Miss Baylis's estate amounted to £10,000. How much had Ben Greet left, or Rosina Filippi? (As it happens we can answer the first part of this question. When Ben Greet had died in 1936 he left £193.) Miss Baylis's notions of herself, Mr Ervine continued, were entirely romantic. She was her own heroine. She might have married and had troops of children in South Africa, but had sacrificed herself for the good of humanity in the Waterloo Road. 'It kept her going,' he concluded, 'though we may doubt if there was a word of truth in it.'

There may have been some truth in what Ervine wrote, even much truth, but it was harsh and in writing it he had shown himself no more graceful than he had painted her. At the very least, she had served the Old Vic for thirty-nine years, at first with her aunt and since 1912, as Manager, on her own. Above all she had preserved the theatre against all odds, and sustained it when others more rational but less determined, and above all of less faith, might have been overcome by difficulties and let the place founder in poverty. Under her stewardship it had become one of the most famous theatres in the world, attracting many of the great actors and actresses of her time, and making the names of others. Her detractors had a point, but Ninette de Valois, a woman of undoubted substance and genius, and equal strength of will, probably got closer to Miss Baylis when, some years later, she wrote that Lilian Baylis had a fearless simplicity, and was mentally not unlike a sincere, shrewd, devout peasant.

De Valois also remembered something else, that showed Miss Baylis knew she was getting near the end. At the beginning of each season she had traditionally given each member of the company a sprig of heather. Elsinore was in June. That autumn, at the start of the new season, and for the first time, she gave everyone rosemary, for remembrance.

Part Three

1938–1976
Old Vic to National Theatre

11

The War, and Homeless Wandering

By 1938 the fear of war was everywhere. Hitler had made himself war minister as well as Führer, the Czechoslovak crisis threatened, Germany mobilised and so did the British fleet. Gas masks were distributed in English cities. The Old Vic's 1937–8 season had gone ahead, notably with Olivier's Coriolanus, and even more notably with *A Midsummer Night's Dream*, which was sumptuous by Old Vic standards. The sets were not old hand-me-downs but by Oliver Messel; the Vic's own orchestra played the full Mendelssohn score; and Ninette de Valois, from her Sadler's Wells ballet, provided the fairies, who not only danced but flew on wires. Ralph Richardson was Bottom, Robert Helpmann Oberon, and Vivien Leigh played Titania. On 12 January 1938 the Queen, carrying out an old promise to Lilian Baylis, brought the Princesses Elizabeth and Margaret Rose, aged eleven and seven, to see their first performance in any theatre. Guthrie said Princess Elizabeth was so excited she nearly fell out of the royal party's box trying to discover how the fairies flew. And when in the interval Helpmann and Vivien Leigh went round to be presented, as he bowed and she curtsied their elaborate wire head-dresses as fairy king and queen became so entangled that they had to back away with lowered heads and locked horns until the Queen and the delighted princesses helped to separate them. That, at any rate, was Guthrie's story.

In the 1930s the shabby Old Vic had become an amazing theatre in many ways, but no more so than in the actors it attracted, for a pittance. Everyone remembers Gielgud, Laughton, Richardson, Olivier, Guinness, Flora Robson, Peggy Ashcroft, Judith Anderson, and Vivien Leigh. But those were the stars. The names of others on cast lists are often extraordinary. The smaller parts in a 1933–4 production of *Henry VIII* were played by James Mason, Richard Goolden, Ursula Jeans, Marius Goring, and Elsa Lanchester. And in September 1939 a Who's Who of the company included Constance Cummings, Max Adrian, Andrew Cruickshank, Stewart Granger, and no less a man than Robert Donat. All these achieved distinction, most on the West End stage, many in classic post-war British films and in Hollywood. Alec Guinness once said James Mason was the best Caliban he ever saw. That was at the Old Vic in the 1930s, and Mason, in *The Wicked Lady*, *The Desert Fox*, *Lolita*, and more than a hundred other films, became one of the best known post-war film actors in England and America.

The theatre remembered its faithful servants. The *Old Vic Magazine* for December 1938 carried an obituary of Orlando Whitehead, wardrobe master, who had started work when the costumes were kept in a disused pub nearby. In the days when both theatre and opera played at the Vic he would tear the costumes off the back of Shakespearean actors after a matinée to have them ready for that evening's opera, and could fit up an operatic cast of fifty extras, some of whom he had never seen before, with cloaks, hats, tights, and swords. He knew the history of everything, whether a costume had been bought, given, vaguely acquired, or had evolved from something quite different. In the frightful days when performances were interchangeable between the Vic and Sadler's Wells he saw to the transfer of twenty or thirty baskets across London. He lovingly catalogued his stock, from 'Sword, jewelled, very fine, would do Lohengrin' – his highest words of praise – down to 'Cloak, furred, chiefly inhabited by moth'. He worked to the end and died suddenly. His obituary appeared above a paragraph recording the death of the Duke of Westminster, a vice-president of the Vic-Wells.

For the 1938–9 season Guthrie offered another *Hamlet*, a brave thing to attempt so soon after Olivier's. This was a full-length production, over four hours, and in modern dress – though not aggressively so; there were no cigarettes – and the actor was Alec Guinness. 'Alec', said Guthrie, 'is much better in the part than Larry, but Larry with his beautiful head and athletic sexy movements and bursts of fireworks is what the public wants.' But the public did not turn up. War scares continued. At times the Underground lines beneath the Thames were closed for fear that air raids might flood them. The Old Vic's takings fell to fifteen pounds one night. And yet in January 1939, when after the meeting of Hitler and Chamberlain at Munich the fear of war had for the moment receded, the company set off on a three-month Mediterranean tour of Portugal, Italy, Malta, Greece, and Egypt funded by the British Council, presenting not only Guinness in *Hamlet* but also *Henry V*, and three other plays. Guinness had recently married, took his wife Merula with him, and regarded the tour as a second honeymoon. When they were in Milan they made an excursion to Lake Como. Merula had given him as a wedding present an expensive Leica camera of which he was hugely proud. 'Somehow,' he said, 'it fell into the lake, glug-glug to the bottom.' At Athens there were scarcely any tourists, and they could stroll almost alone round the Parthenon. King George of the

Hellenes came to the theatre almost every evening, attracted by the company's leading lady, Cathleen Nesbitt. When she was in her twenties, he had once chased her round and round the rotunda of the Midland Hotel, Manchester, in the early hours of the morning, or so she said. It was a surreal tour. There was no war yet, but there were alarms. Halfway through the performance of *Henry V* at the Valletta opera house a naval officer came on stage and ordered all naval personnel to report to their ships immediately, and all the women to remain. The play continued to a half-empty house of women, whose minds must have been with their men, elsewhere. On tour the company all thought war was inevitable but somehow deluded themselves that by some miracle it would pass them by. As Guinness wrote in his memoirs, it would have astonished him profoundly if, looking into his make-up mirror, he had caught a shadowy image of himself returning to Malta in four years' time as a sub-lieutenant RNVR on the eve of the invasion of Sicily, by which time the opera house had been bombed into rubble.

There had been much opposition from the Old Vic audience to the tour – which was seen as 'shaking the bloodstained hand of Mussolini'. Scotland Yard feared that there would be demonstrations in the theatre. One man threatened to jump from the gallery unless the tour were abandoned. Guthrie said he was all ears for the thud of a body landing in seat L76, but the man did not jump. The tour went on, Cairo was a triumph, so was Rome, and the Italian crown prince invited the company to return soon.

By then Guthrie had been appointed Director of both the Old Vic and Sadler's Wells at £1,000 a year, with directors of ballet and opera working under him. He was in overall charge of what he called the Troika. He told the *Observer* that the change in title from manager to director had been deliberate. 'There is no idea of my being . . . the inheritor of the mantle of Miss Lilian Baylis and so forth. Miss Baylis had her own qualities and cachet. History never repeats itself.' He was anxious to make his point about the Old Vic's audience, saying that it came from all quarters of London. 'Watch the rush to the Underground as soon as the curtain comes down. The West come in their cars, the East come by the Underground.' It was true; but so much for Lilian Baylis's beloved Lambeth playgoers.

War broke out in September 1939. London theatres closed, but in what became known as the phoney war the expected air raids did not come. The theatres reopened in February 1940. Guthrie addressed an eloquent appeal to the Old Vic audience. He wrote that a long-term artistic policy could be no more than a daydream. It was possible, in daydreams, to see the Old Vic, with its extraordinary hold on public goodwill, its mixture of classical tradition and informal atmosphere, established as it should be in close collaboration with Stratford-on-Avon and a National Theatre, and to see Sadler's Wells as the house of opera and ballet, endowed by public funds. 'Alas, the awakening from these dreams is a cold douche – we are at war; at any moment it may be necessary, without warning, to suspend all theatrical plans; our young men are being called up; there is a black-out; income tax is at 7/6 [thirty-seven pence in the pound]; we have no money. At this point, however, let me make it clear that *the greatest need of the theatre is not for money but attendance.*' In normal times, he said, the Old Vic could manage at half capacity; now with an ambitious season to come, and higher costs, they needed three quarters. 'So far the Old Vic and Sadler's Wells have swum; but we are swimming for our lives . . . We need you in the gallery, in the circle, in the pit and the stalls; we need 3,000 of you, every night. The serious theatre cannot be kept alive like Tinkerbell if its well-wishers are content just to clap their hands and believe like mad in fairies.'

He was never going to achieve such audiences, and he knew it. But Guthrie's ambitious season opened that April with *King Lear* and *The Tempest*, both with John Gielgud. The opening night was ecstatically received by *The Times*. 'To be at the Old Vic last night, waiting in the somewhat dingy but much-liked auditorium for the curtain to rise, was to enjoy a sense of the first genuine theatrical occasion of the war. Occasions of the kind declare themselves not in the sheen of fresh paint, diamonds, and gardenias, but in the unmistakeable stir of a common intellectual expectancy.' Gielgud achieved a 'nervous force' and a 'stillness of beauty' rarely seen on the stage. He concerned himself little with the corporal infirmities of the old king. 'He trusts the verse and his power to speak it, as a solitary silver figure in the dark loneliness, he speaks the storm, and his trust is never at any vital point betrayed.'

In retrospect it seems incredible but there were plans, in spite of the war, to take these two plays to Paris. As it happened Paris fell to the Germans first. But in May 1940 the Sadler's Wells ballet really did set out on a tour of Holland, which now seems crazily risky. At first, after the austerity of wartime England, the company was amazed by the plentiful food. After a performance at the Hague the dancers were showered with tulip petals. A Dutch baroness, one of the welcoming party, presented to Miss de Valois her eight-year-old daughter, who grew up to be Audrey Hepburn. But then the company encountered refugees on the roads. The ballet had intended to dance in the garrison towns of the British Expeditionary force in the Netherlands, but this adventure was cut short because the invading Germans chose the same dates to march through those same towns. The ballet company was at Arnhem the day that town was attacked. The company escaped, just, after five days, by way of Amsterdam and a fifteen-hour crossing of the North Sea to Harwich, and arrived back in London with a trainful of refugees at 2.30 one morning. All its sets and costumes had been abandoned. At the Old Vic, *The Tempest* continued until 22 June, the day France surrendered.

In September 1940 the London blitz began. Sadler's Wells was requisitioned for those made homeless by air raids. Both theatres were closed for the duration of the war, and then in May 1941 the Old Vic was badly damaged by a bomb. The roof needed to be shored up and the backstage walls were partly down. In the rehearsal room, at the top of the theatre, the outside wall was blown out, though Cabanel's bare roof trusses, dating from 1818, still survived above. A man standing in that room, looking west through the hole in the wall, had a clear view of Big Ben on the skyline. Repairs would have cost £6,000 but were pointless since there might be more air-raid damage, which there was. London was impossible. The only option was to tour. The theatre company set up its head-quarters in the Lancashire cotton town of Burnley, and toured thirty-eight northern cities and Wales. The opera and ballet companies toured widely with two pianos for an orchestra. This was an ironic success story. As *The Times* reported in March 1943, while the pre-war financial history of the Old Vic and Sadler's Wells had been a perpetual struggle, from 1940 on it had been a record of continuous success, particularly with the ballet and opera, and in unexpected parts of the country. As to the Old Vic theatre itself, the same report went on to say that by then, with air raids having fallen off, it was being re-roofed but no other repairs would be made until after the war.

Another of the Old Vic's provincial outposts was at the

Liverpool Repertory Theatre under the young Peter Glenville. He had been the youngest president of the Oxford University Dramatic Society, had acted in films, and played Dubedat in Shaw's *Doctor's Dilemma* in the West End. Then he went to the Liverpool Rep for Guthrie, who later said it had been at the time the liveliest theatre in the country. There Glenville not only directed six plays – most notably Ibsen's *John Gabriel Borkman* – but also played the lead in *Hamlet*. After the war he was lost to the Old Vic, and directed on Broadway and in Hollywood, with Olivier, Richard Burton, and his friend Alec Guinness among his actors.

In England the war changed everything. Just as the First World War helped the Old Vic by bringing about its first Shakespeare seasons, so the Second changed everything by introducing public subsidy for the first time. The Council for the Encouragement of Music and the Arts (CEMA) was meant to raise war morale through the arts. It became the Arts Council. So there was public money to fund a new Old Vic season in London, plainly not at the bombed Old Vic but at the New, in St Martin's Lane. Guthrie remained in overall charge of drama, opera, and ballet but in 1944 Lieutenant Olivier and Lieutenant Commander Richardson were seconded from the Fleet Air Arm to form two thirds of a triumvirate running an Old Vic company. The third man, John Burrell, was from radio. It was at the New that Olivier gave for the first time his celebrated *Richard III*. In 1945, just after the war, this company toured the newly liberated Europe – Paris, Antwerp, Hamburg, and Belsen.

It is important to say here that this book is primarily a history of the Old Vic theatre, of that building, of the companies that played there, and of the plays they presented. For ten years from 1940 to 1950 the theatre was closed. Old Vic companies did, as we have seen, tour in England and abroad, but that is another, separate history which we shall only sketch here, eminent though the dramatis personae may have been.

In 1945 Guthrie, fearing that the Troika of drama, opera, and ballet was falling apart, resigned. And it was coming apart, triumphantly. At the end of the war, with all things new, the Vic-Wells ballet moved to Covent Garden, which had been a dance hall in the war, later became the Royal Ballet, and went on to the great days of Fonteyn, Shearer, Somes, Ashton, and MacMillan. The first season there opened with *The Sleeping Beauty* in 1946. Ninette de Valois went on to be made Companion of Honour, like Miss Baylis, but then trumped her by being created a member of the Order of Merit. As the *Sunday Times* ballet critic remarked: 'Let us remember with gratitude Miss Baylis, who believed in Miss de Valois, and Miss de Valois, who believed in herself.' The opera company moved back to Sadler's Wells and opened with the world premiere of Benjamin Britten's *Peter Grimes*. In 1968 it would move to the Coliseum and become the English National Opera where operas were sung, as always at the Vic in Miss Baylis's day, in English. And another theatre company had been established in 1946, as an offshoot, at the Georgian Theatre Royal in Bristol – the Bristol Old Vic.

After her death, Miss Baylis's ambitions were being realised, and more successfully than she could have dreamed, except at her beloved Old Vic in the Waterloo Road. That was still bombed and unusable as a theatre. But enough of the fabric had been patched up to enable it to house a drama school, which opened in 1947. It was a school with three extraordinary teachers in George Devine, Michel Saint-Denis, and Glen Byam Shaw – men who had directed in Paris, London, and New York. They were not only teachers but practising professionals. Joan Plowright, later Lady Olivier, was one of their pupils and described them as godlike. They all worked in a theatre where the auditorium was still full of rubble and left-over scenic debris from past productions. Classes were held in the foyers, the bars, and the old rehearsal room at the back of the stage. The place was so full of atmosphere and tradition that no one cared about the discomfort.

There was constant talk, but little more, of a National Theatre, of which the Old Vic might or might not be part. The *Manchester Guardian* said England was centuries behind France and other European countries in providing a national repertory theatre and it was up to the Old Vic to recover lost ground. Guthrie repeated his opposition to Baylis's ideals by restating his views of the 1930s, that the aim of any restored theatre should be 'high artistic standards and not cheap seats as a form of social service'.

As to the company in the West End, at the New, Burrell looked after the administration but the other two directors were also film stars and earned most of their living that way. In 1947, after *Lear* at the New, Olivier filmed his famous *Hamlet*. Richardson made *Anna Karenina* with Vivien Leigh. Proposals for a National Theatre persisted. One day, when Olivier and Richardson were coming away from a meeting about such prospects with the chairman of the still-notional National and the chairman of the Old Vic, Richardson suddenly said, 'Of course, you know, don't you, that all very splendid as it is, it'll be the end of us.'

'Why?' asked Olivier.

'Well, I mean, it won't be our dear friendly, semi-amateurish Old Vic any more. It'll be of government interest now with some appointed intendant swell at the top, not our sweet old friendly governors eating out of our hand and doing what we tell them. They're not going to stand for a couple of actors bossing the place around any more. We shall be out, old cockie.'

They were out before either expected. Richardson went off to make another film in Hollywood. The Old Vic company from the New, with Olivier and Vivien Leigh, set out on a tour of Australia and New Zealand, taking *Richard III*, Sheridan's *School for Scandal*, and Thornton Wilder's *Skin of our Teeth*. Olivier and Leigh were treated like royalty. Olivier was asked to respond to loyal toasts to the King. In the middle of a year-long and highly profitable tour, he received a telegram in Sydney telling him that his contract and Richardson's would not be renewed. The discarded Olivier, after an exhausting tour that lasted ten months, returned with a profit of £20,000. While he was away the Old Vic company at the New – even with Trevor Howard, Celia Johnson, and Alec Guinness – had already lost half the profit made in Australia.

But the governors of the Old Vic required the full attention of its directors, also wanted to avoid the continuing and costly rent of a West End theatre for its company, and so set about acquiring public money to repair and reopen its own theatre in the Waterloo Road. The drama school of course did not want to go, and prevaricated, but in the end was obliged to move to a former girls' school in Dulwich, four miles out. The pupils of the Old Vic School helped to load the removal vans.

12

Last Years of the Old Old Vic

In January 1950 the governors of the Victoria Hall, having
borrowed the better part of £50,000, began to patch up
and in parts rebuild their old theatre. The auditorium was a
wreck, the seats were gone, and holes in the roof were covered
by tarpaulin. After the war the theatre's continued existence
had been precarious. It had been bombed. It had been in the
way of grand post-war plans to widen the Waterloo Road
and was due to be pulled down, until those grand plans were
abandoned for lack of money. And everyone had been talk-
ing for years about a *new* national theatre; a new theatre was
demanded and expected, and few were eager to patch up an
old one. It was only when those plans were put off too, again
for lack of money, that the Old Vic was repaired. It was seen as
a second-best. But, still, the time was propitious. The following
year, 1951, would be the centenary of the Great Exhibition of
1851, which was to be celebrated by the Festival of Britain, to
be held on a site south of the Thames near Waterloo Bridge,
not half a mile from the Old Vic. The Festival, in those drab
days of austerity, was seen as a necessary Tonic to the Nation,
and it was confidently hoped that some of the visitors to the
South Bank would want to stay south of the river to see a play
at the Old Vic.

When work started on the theatre there was no attempt to

restore the gilded grandeur of the 1880s auditorium within its Regency walls. Those post-war days were before the time of loving and costly restoration. What was wanted was a plain, dull, auditorium that did not leak, and with no decoration that could distract attention from the stage. So, in the tradition of Lilian Baylis who in the 1920s had pulled down four of the original six boxes, the builders of 1950 pulled down the remaining two. In the fashion of the day, the proscenium arch was also demolished, and a forestage projected into the stalls. On stage the cyclorama was painted a neutral colour. The auditorium was painted grey and dark red. The stalls and circle seats were new and upholstered, and, for the first time at the Vic, all of the tip-up kind. The theatre seated 1,100, of whom 400 were in the gallery. The seats there were also upholstered but backless benches, not separated by armrests but for the first time numbered. The best stalls cost 10s. 6d. [53p], and the gallery 1s. 6d. [7p] and 2s. There were bars – again for the first time at the Vic – and the traditional draughts coming in from the Waterloo Road were at last blocked off.

The remorselessly increasing cost of all this is classical. Theatres always cost more than any reasonable estimate. In 1950 the budget was for £30,636, within a year £38,885 had been spent, and then another £1,450 was needed for the bars. By 1956 the total sum needed had risen to £75,000, and when the works were finished, in 1957, they had cost in all £85,000.

None of this was foreseen in 1950. The reopening was eagerly looked forward to. The *Manchester Guardian*, which consistently covered the Vic more thoroughly than the London papers, expressed its pleasure, in an editorial, that 'much of the hysteria had fallen away' since the company dropped its flirtation with what it called the West End planetary system – a crack against the Oliviers and Richardsons of only two years before. 'The management now has to keep its theatre full and find a middle course between the pioneer methods of Lilian Baylis and the occasionally meretricious policies of later years.' The *Guardian* also published a reminiscence from a reader, who remembered the gallery of before the war, and, all around her, 'the familiar, warm, sharp odour of oranges'.

The opening night, 14 November 1950, was, whether the theatrical puritans liked it or not, a great social occasion. *The Times* reported general rejoicing. At least 3,500 people had applied for tickets in the first two weeks they had been on sale, so the audience was largely selected by ballot. 'Everyone knew, of course, that the seat he was occupying had been sought in vain by others left fretting in the outer darkness' – and that was true, except that by tradition a few gallery tickets had been held back, and people queued all night for them. Among many telegrams of good wishes to the company was one from the 'traders and barrow boys' of The Cut, whose territory was invaded that evening by mink stoles, evening dress, and expensive cars.

The occasion was one thing, the performance another. The play was *Twelfth Night*. Most critics tried to be kind. The consensus was that the director feared his treatment might be seen as unadventurous, and consequently avoided the conventional as a cat avoids water. Ivor Brown in the *Observer* wrote that part of Illyria was set in what appeared to be a sailors' dive on a grey river front, and that there was much whinnying and clowning from the cast, in part relieved by the charm and tenderness of Peggy Ashcroft as Viola. The general critical opinion was that the production was intended to be a rollicking romp. That was the first night. Three weeks later the King, Queen, and Princess Margaret came to see the play. Since there was now no box in which to put them, let alone a royal box, they sat in the stalls.

The director of *Twelfth Night* was Hugh Hunt, brother of John Hunt who led the British ascent of Everest in 1953. He had been brought in after his success with the Bristol Old Vic. But by then the Vic had no fewer than five directors, one of whom was also the administrator. It was not clear who was in charge, and there were soon press headlines like 'More Trouble at the Old Vic'. By May 1951 the three at the Dulwich drama school – Saint-Denis, Devine, and Byam Shaw – offered resignations in a huff, which were promptly accepted. The administrator was also invited to resign, and then Tyrone Guthrie was brought back – for the fourth time since 1933. He said in an interview with the *Observer* that artistic experiment needed the Common Touch. And what was that? 'I can only say that Shakespeare had it; Molière had it; Gracie Fields has it . . .'

So Guthrie was in charge, with Hunt. For the next season Guthrie brought in Donald Wolfit to play *Tamburlaine*, a play by Marlowe not done for three hundred years. The play was a triumphant success, and Wolfit was a grand actor. But he was also an actor-manager of the old school, a courageous man who had tatted his company round the provinces, earning his own living, expecting no grants. He certainly had the Common Touch, but his whole history made him a bit of a tyrant, he fell out with the company who were used to gentler treatment, and then himself resigned. At the end of that season Guthrie went too. The other directors had scattered – Saint-Denis to France, Devine eventually to the Royal Court, Byam Shaw eventually to Stratford-upon-Avon, and Guthrie eventually to Stratford, Ontario. That left Hunt who demanded and got a vote of confidence from the governors.

He was in charge for the 1952–3 season, which brought

Claire Bloom to play Juliet. Now the Old Vic had always attracted film stars, but Miss Bloom was only twenty and the film she starred in was with no less a man than Charlie Chaplin. When she was sixteen Olivier had auditioned her for Ophelia in his film of *Hamlet*. She lost that part to Jean Simmons, but at seventeen did play Ophelia to Paul Scofield's Hamlet at Stratford, and was then in a long West End run of Christopher Fry's *The Lady's Not for Burning*. Then Chaplin summoned her to America to play opposite him. It was in *Limelight*, a film that tells the story of a young girl sacrificing herself for a man who could be her grandfather, and it made her name. After the filming she joined the Old Vic company and happened to be playing in *Romeo and Juliet* at the Vic at the time when Chaplin came to London for the English premiere of *Limelight*. He, who had been born in south London only a mile or two away, came to the Old Vic to see her perform, and went backstage to meet the cast. Then she, on the night of the Leicester Square premiere, was whisked away from the theatre after her performance to be presented, with Chaplin, to Princess Margaret. Her face appeared on the cover of *Time* magazine. Few actresses can ever have been so famous so young.

In her memoirs many years later she was not kind to the Old Vic of that day, saying all was decorous and unremarkable, that there was little investigation into the motivation of the character, and that the only interesting conversations were in the dressing rooms later, among the actors themselves. This is strange since Hunt's briefings to his actors were later published and are full of sense. The stage, he told them, was an ephemeral affair, and the taste of an audience changeable. In his notes for Juliet he clearly set out the inevitable, death-marked progress she must make from girl to woman and wife. His *Romeo and Juliet* was a great success but still, as Hunt also wrote after the production, bad luck, bad judgement, and internal dissension had lowered the prestige of the Old Vic.

So he left too, but not before he had directed a *Merchant of Venice* with Paul Rogers that sold out for the whole of a seven-week run, and a production of T. S. Eliot's *Murder in the Cathedral* with Robert Donat. He was succeeded by Michael Benthall, who had directed Shakespeare at Stratford and who in July 1953 announced that he would repeat the Old Vic's earlier feat, from 1914 to 1923, of performing all the plays of Shakespeare's First Folio, with the histories in chronological order. For the next five years, until 1958, only Shakespeare would be presented at the Vic.

The first play of the thirty-six performed was *Hamlet*, with the young Burton, already a Hollywood star, and Claire Bloom again, with the glamour of *Limelight* still all around her. As she says in her memoirs, their courtship was brief. They were lovers in a fortnight. They lay on the grass in Regent's Park, daydreaming. And, at the Old Vic, she said, 'our dressing room had a communicating door, and we had a private life in the theatre we were unable to have outside . . . Sometimes even our lovemaking took place in the darkened room, between the matinée and the evening performance.' The notices were excellent. It was, besides, all in the Old Vic tradition, very like Olivier and Vivien Leigh at Elsinore in 1937.

This was a time of which the best-remembered nights at the Old Vic were indeed those of Burton and Bloom and, a little later, those of 1955–6 when Burton and John Neville alternated the roles of Othello and Iago. Burton then returned to Hollywood but Neville was very much a man who made his name at the Old Vic and remained there for four seasons, playing among other parts Romeo, Richard II, Troilus, Hamlet, and Angelo, before he too left, and went on to become artistic director at the new Nottingham Playhouse.

Not all of the Old Vic's imports succeeded. Ann Todd had made a name in British films like *The Seventh Veil*, with James Mason. This was a celebration of Chopin, kitsch, and Freud, in which she played a tormented concert pianist, the pounding out of piano concertos being very much a fashion of the times. As *The Times* gently put it: 'Miss Todd is perhaps more widely known on the screen than on the stage, but it would be a mistake to suppose that the Old Vic is pursuing some policy of attracting larger audiences by bringing in film stars. Though it cannot be disagreeable to the Old Vic to know that Miss Todd has a large following among cinemagoers, the reason she is coming to the Old Vic is, of course, because Mr Benthall sees her as a good Lady Macbeth.' That production of *Macbeth* was thought to be vivid but noisy. And reviewing the second offering of the season, *Love's Labour's Lost*, Kenneth Tynan remarked in the *Observer* that the girls in the cast giggled so incessantly 'that one applauded Miss Ann Todd when, quite early on, she adopted a frozen simper and stuck to it'.

The Old Vic, even with its Arts Council grant and film actors, had to make a living, and one way to do this was to tour. Such a tour, and most profitable, was that of *A Midsummer Night's Dream*, after the Edinburgh Festival of 1954. The company of sixty actors and dancers in all, led by Moira Shearer, Robert Helpmann, and Stanley Holloway as Titania, Oberon, and Bottom, opened with three weeks at the Metropolitan Opera, New York, then crossed to Los Angeles and San Francisco, and then came back to Toronto. Everywhere the whole of the Mendelssohn score was played by a full orchestra. In America the company travelled by train, but it flew the Atlantic, with a second plane needed for the sets. It was said to be the largest theatrical flight ever to cross the Atlantic.

The Shakespeare canon was completed in 1957–8. That season began with *Hamlet*, with Neville in the name part and Coral Browne as Gertrude, and continued with *Measure for Measure*, the three parts of *Henry VI*, and another *Dream*. Paul Rogers came back from Australia to play Lear. The thirty-sixth and last play to be presented, in May 1958, was *Henry VIII*. This provoked headlines like 'An Old Vic Occasion', which was to be expected, and 'Misfortunes of a First Night', which was not. The casting was splendid – Edith Evans as Queen Katharine and John Gielgud as Cardinal Wolsey, both returning to the Vic after years away. The performance was uneven. The costumes were grandiosely absurd, and it soon became a question whether the players would trip more badly over their trailing drapery or over their words. In the first scene Edith Evans and Harry Andrews as Henry VIII competed with each other in first fluffing and then helplessly drying, so much so that all eyes were on Gielgud to see whether he would join them. He did not, and went on to rescue the evening with a display of a Wolsey changing from ostentation, to malevolence, and then to pathos.

At the end of that season *Henry VIII* and *Hamlet* were both taken to Paris, at the Théâtre Sarah-Bernhardt. Four nights of Henry were not received that enthusiastically, and some of its lines were lost in the vastness of a theatre half as big again as the Vic. But *Hamlet*, given for the first time in France for something like half a century, was another matter. The occasion was splendid and memorable. True, the eccentrically nineteenth-century costumes, like something out of a Victorian levee or a glimpse into the Austrian court under Franz Joseph, puzzled the audience and the critics. *France Soir* likened the setting to that of an operetta. But the critic of *Le Monde*, though remarking that Polonius looked like Charles Dickens, considered this the definitive *Hamlet*, writing that John Neville had established for ever the prince's madness and his courage, and that the production was one of lucid revelation. Judi Dench, in one of her first principal parts, was praised for her Ophelia, quite mad but played 'without trying to look like something out of Botticelli'.

That same year, mainly with the profits from overseas tours, the Old Vic spent another £90,000 building an annexe next to the theatre, to store costumes, properties, and scenery. It was an extravagance. Only the Shakespeare Memorial Theatre at Stratford had anything like it, and certainly no other London theatre. The theatre's remarkable royal connection continued. The annexe was opened by the Queen and the Duke of Edinburgh, who were then entertained by a performance of scenes from Shakespeare. They saw Paul Rogers as Falstaff in the recruiting scene from *Henry IV Part II*, John Neville in the central scenes from *Hamlet*, Barbara Jefford and Keith Michell in the wooing scene from *The Taming of the Shrew*, and the play scene from *A Midsummer Night's Dream*, with Moira Shearer as Titania and Frankie Howerd as Bottom. The actors and actresses were the theatre's finest, with Frankie Howerd, not a straight actor but a great stand-up comedian, brought in, as he had been before, to add variety. And everything was Shakespeare, as it had been for the previous five years. That was the Old Vic's strength and weakness. Having presented the thirty-six plays the Old Vic was seen as a Shakespeare theatre. In the next two years it did notably less well with a wider repertory of Schiller, Ibsen, Chekhov, Shaw, and Wilde.

One production that did stand out was another *Romeo and Juliet*, in 1960, by Franco Zeffirelli, seven years before he made his famous film of the play. No one has better described it than Michael Blakemore, later a director at the National. It was, he said, such a relief and a revelation when the Chorus walked on stage and in the most normal tones simply explained: 'In fair Verona where we set our scene . . .' Or when Judi Dench said to her Romeo, John Stride, 'Parting is such *sweet* sorrow,' and the wearisome familiarity of the line fell away.

That was all freshness and light. But the sad fact was that just at the time when the Old Vic appeared strangely prosperous – prosperous enough to spend £90,000 on an annexe – the old assumption that the Vic, or at least its company, would eventually become the National was coming under question. The Memorial Theatre at Stratford had throughout the 1950s attracted international stars like Olivier, Richardson, Gielgud, Vivien Leigh, and Peggy Ashcroft, and now it had the young Peter Hall as its new director, had become the Royal Shakespeare Company (RSC), and had a London branch at the Aldwych Theatre. The story of the National Theatre and its tortuous beginnings has been often told. First the state would provide the money, and then it wouldn't. A new building would rapidly rise, and then it wouldn't. A foundation stone was laid, and then moved. In 1961 the government did at last agree to come up with a million pounds, provided the London County Council found rather more than that. A National Theatre Committee, which had met and done nothing much for years, quietly approached Olivier to be director. The RSC, declining to surrender its autonomy, ruled itself out, and by the summer of 1962 Olivier was appointed. A splendid new theatre would be built but not yet, so the governors of the Victoria Hall agreed that the Old Vic should be the National's temporary home, 'for some years'. So much for the bricks and mortar. As for the new National company, it would be substantially the same as Olivier was running in the new theatre in the round at Chichester. The Old Vic governors did not say so in as many words, but this left their own company with just one last season to go before it was disbanded.

For that season there was a new director, Michael Elliott, who, as if there were still money to spend on alterations that would last only a year, built a new apron stage and yet again refashioned what was left of the proscenium. Guthrie briefly returned to direct Ben Jonson's *Alchemist*, and Elliott himself did *The Merchant of Venice* and *Measure for Measure*. That second play was the last given by the Old Vic company.

Philip Hope-Wallace, the gentlest and most learned of critics, was there for the *Guardian* on the Old Vic's last night in April 1963. 'It's all over,' he thought, looking round the dingy auditorium. 'Bar the shouting,' he added, listening to the howls of the Old Vic players whooping it up. Then he wrote his notice:

True, the stones of the theatre as such, its lighting equipment and its coffee urns, will still be there in the autumn when it will pro tem house Sir Laurence's new National Theatre. But will it be, phoenix-like, Miss Baylis's Old Vic reborn? It would be pleasant to think so. And yet . . . immediately I began to feel the difference . . . I heard her say: 'What's all this talk about the national theatre? We know that we are the national theatre,' and that *we* was royal.

But was she? Had she that in her? Save souls, do good, my dears, but don't go wasting money on extravagances or what the public doesn't want. She was cautious in her role of manager: the least hint that the public were staying away and off it came, with Gounod's *Faust* instead. An essential part of old-vick-edness was a sort of wholesome cheeseparing, as in a well-run vicarage nursery. Very different must any national theatre be: there, white elephants must be put on for prestige, and costed regardless . . . Let us hope for rebirth in Miss Baylis's old theatre; but it won't be quite the same; it has not been quite the same since Miss Pilgrim is no longer there. O, well-named Miss P. You were the real Vic thing, who solo sang the National Anthem from our seat in the sixpenny gods.

Meanwhile let us not fail to savour the end of the brave effort which Michael Elliott has made. Hearing that strident shouting I could at least reflect that they are going out lion-like.

13

The National Comes to the Vic

By the end of 1960 Olivier had no doubt that the central duty of his career was the creation of a National Theatre. He had not always thought anything of the sort. He had wondered whether institutional theatres were a good thing anyway. Weren't they – as he later asked himself when he came to write his autobiography – weren't they supposed to develop an unimaginative, uncreative, sepulchral sort of atmosphere? He must have overcome these doubts, because he found himself by late 1960 director-designate of the National Theatre, though that was still no more than being the director-designate of a notion. In 1962 the government found the money and the notion became reality. Olivier's contract as director was for £5,000 a year for five years, during which time he could take off not more than fifty weeks to work on films, television, or plays outside the National. The directorship, in other words, would pay him in a year one twentieth of the £100,000 he had earned for a supporting role in the film of *Spartacus*. He accepted because he regarded it as his destiny.

It was part of the deal that there would be a new National Theatre building on the South Bank, but not yet. The company's first home, as we have seen, was to be the Old Vic. In spite of Olivier's long connection with the theatre, since 1937, he felt little affection for it, and once went so far as to say he

30 The Old Vic auditorium, 1938. Oil painting by Oliver Messel

31 Judith Anderson as Lady Macbeth opposite Olivier's Macbeth in Michel Saint-Denis's 1937 production. She was an Australian who made her name in America and played Mrs Danvers, also opposite Olivier, in the 1938 film of *Rebecca*

32 John Gielgud as Lear, 1940. This production was due to go on tour to Paris, even in wartime, but the invading German army got there first. Costume design and sketch by Roger Furse

33 Alec Guinness as a modern-dress Hamlet, at the Vic in 1938, a role he also played in early 1939 on a Mediterranean tour to Lisbon, Rome, Egypt, Greece and Malta

34 The Old Vic was bombed in an air raid of 10 May 1941. This picture of the auditorium with a hole in the roof was painted by Roger Furse, stage designer, in 1942. The theatre was even more badly damaged backstage, and did not reopen until 1950

35 Richard Burton
and Claire Bloom as
Hamlet and Ophe-
lia, 1953. She had
just become famous
by playing opposite
Charlie Chaplin in
the film *Limelight*

36 The young
Eileen Atkins
as Miranda and
Alastair Sim as
Prospero in *The
Tempest*, 1954.
He was then best
known as the
headmaster in
Ronald Searle's
St Trinian's films

37 The Queen at a gala performance of *Henry VIII* at the Old Vic in Coronation year, 1953, with Paul Rogers as the king and Leo Genn as the Duke of Buckingham

38 John Stride and Judi Dench in Zeffirelli's *Romeo and Juliet*, 1960

39 Laurence Olivier as Othello and Maggie Smith as Desdemona, 1964

40 Geraldine McEwan in
Somerset Maugham's *Home
and Beauty*, 1968. This poster,
with its bold diagonal letter-
ing, is typical of the distinctive work of Ken Briggs at
the National Theatre

41 A sketch by Feliks Topolski of Tony Harrison's version of Molière's *Le Misanthrope* at the Old Vic, 1975. Left to right are Alec McCowen as Alceste, Robert Eddison as Philinte, Diana Rigg as Célimène, and Gawn Grainger as Oronte

42 John Stride and Edward Petherbridge in Tom Stoppard's *Rosencrantz and Guildenstern Are Dead*, Old Vic, 1967

43 John Gielgud and Ralph Richardson in Pinter's *No Man's Land*, 1975

44 Sing-song in the Old Vic rehearsal room on 21 March 1974 after Laurence Olivier's last performance there or on any stage. With him are his wife Joan Plowright, and Denis Quilley at the piano

hated the place. Others did not love it. Kenneth Rae, secretary to the joint council for the proposed National, complained to Olivier that taxpayers' money would be spent 'shoring up that moribund building in the Waterloo Road', and forecast that the National would be kept in the 'crumbling Old Vic until such time as it falls down'. The place was indeed shored up, redec-orated, and re-upholstered at the then great cost of £93,000. Sean Kenny, a theatre designer with a hatred of prosceniums, said that if he had his way he would put a bomb under the place. He could not do that, but he did destroy what proscen-ium was left and put in a complicated revolve which often failed to revolve. Olivier then set about bodging the rest of the theatre. He took out the first two rows of the stalls and built yet another forestage which jutted out in front of the proscenium, making the Old Vic neither one thing nor the other. He also was disaffected with the idea of a proscenium theatre. 'As each and every family in Britain has a baby proscenium arch [he meant a television set] in their "through lounge" it would seem wise to offer them another sort of experience when they come to the theatre.' He was very jolly about what he was doing to the Old Vic: 'We are rebuilding the stage again, bringing it yet more forward. We shall be playing in the foyer eventually, with the public outside in the New Cut.' His improvements had the unlooked-for effect of ruining the acoustics. People couldn't hear. 'I don't know what it is we did to the theatre when we did the rebuilding,' he told one friend, 'but we did something that changed a theatre remarkable for acoustics for 150 years into a constant cause of complaint.' He then had everything painted sludge-green. He had, as he later cheerfully admitted, ruined the place.

As his second-in-command Olivier had wanted his old friend George Devine, but he saw no reason to leave the Royal

Court, so as associate directors Olivier recruited two younger men from the Court, John Dexter and William Gaskill. And Kenneth Tynan became literary manager, occasional inspirer, and publicist for the National Theatre and for himself. He was a critic whose stock-in-trade was vivid hyperbole, and had just slated an Olivier season at the Chichester Festival Theatre. He then wrote offering his services as dramaturge at the National. The word 'dramaturge' was a German affectation. Olivier contemptuously showed Tynan's letter to his wife Joan Plowright and she said: 'Wait a minute. I mean, look what he's got to offer you . . . He will rid you of the accusation of being an old-fashioned actor-manager. He will bring to you – he's the most modern influence in the English theatre today, and he will bring that to you.'

So Olivier put Tynan up to the board for the post of dramaturge. The board changed the title to literary manager, and defined his duties as being to help plan the repertoire, look for new plays, and to act as the theatre's spokesman on policy matters. Olivier thought he had neutralised a potentially damaging critic. Tynan put it more bluntly: Olivier would rather have him inside the tent pissing out than outside pissing in.

Then Olivier held auditions for his company. His old friends from the Old Vic and from his films were not chosen. He wanted to move on. Esmond Knight, who had appeared in all three of Olivier's Shakespeare films, offered himself and was offended to be turned away. One of the newcomers was the young Michael Gambon, later Sir Michael, who was at the time working as a fitter on the floor of an engineering shop in Islington, and had the splendid nerve to offer as his audition piece a speech of Richard III's. 'God, you've got a bloody cheek,' said Olivier, but heard him out and then, when the young actor cut his hand on a pillar he grasped for added effect, patched it up for him. Gambon remembers Olivier as a god – a god who wore his suits cut wide at the shoulders and fitting at the waist, and wore his watch loose on his wrist so that it hung on his hand, like a piece of jewellery, a god who liked to be seen at times in the props room or in the canteen as one of the boys, telling jokes: but when Gambon got carried away one day and ventured a joke of his own, he got his head bitten off.

A young Gambon was just right for Olivier, who noted him as 'to be renowned'. Among the younger actors who made their reputations at the National were Anthony Hopkins, Derek Jacobi, Maggie Smith, and Geraldine McEwan. For the new National, Olivier wanted all things new. He declined as 'fearsome clobber' an offer to the theatre of the bells from Henry Irving's famous play, *The Bells*, one of his earliest great successes. They were offered by Irving's grandson. 'Do we want reminders and mementos or a clean sheet and no ghosts?' asked Olivier, adding that theatrical memory was so short that the name of Henry Irving would soon mean precious little.

For its first season the National's plays included *Uncle Vanya* and Shaw's *Saint Joan*, both transferred from his previous year's Chichester season. *Vanya*, with its extraordinary cast of Olivier, Michael Redgrave, Joan Plowright, Sybil Thorndike, and Lewis Casson, was a natural. So was the Shaw, in which Joan Plowright, directed by Dexter, had perhaps the greatest success of her young career. Also among the National's first plays were *The Master Builder* with Redgrave, and, later on, Olivier in *Othello*. The theatre opened on 22 October 1963 with a production of *Hamlet* with Peter O'Toole, then newly famous for David Lean's vast film of *Lawrence of Arabia*. Olivier explained this choice to Tyrone Guthrie, who was then running a theatre in Minneapolis, and had asked what the National would be doing. 'This is a special engagement,' Olivier wrote, 'and rather outside our general policy [which] concerns itself with a longed-for permanent ensemble (the old, old yearning), such an ensemble not to have its nose put out of joint by the invitation of outside stars except on very rare occasions, the sales talk being that, in the beautiful future, to be a National Theatre player is to be a star.' But, never mind the sales talk, he brought in the biggest star he could lay his hands on.

As it happened, O'Toole was not a success. Olivier's two associate directors wanted nothing to do with him. Dexter did not like him. Gaskill was opposed on principle to any star. Olivier tried to win them round by explaining that people would always be asking, 'But who's in it?' and that a National without stars was next to impossible. Then, as he would have done anyway, he directed the play himself.

O'Toole's hair was dyed blond, as Olivier's had been for his 1947 film, but there the director's absolute power ended. On the opening night, O'Toole wilfully departed from Olivier's carefully plotted moves. 'It was tragic actually,' said Olivier. 'If O'Toole had given on the first night the performance he gave on the last dress rehearsal it would have been an absolute sensation.' As it was he pleased himself, but neither Olivier nor the critics.

Still, the National Theatre of Great Britain was open at last, and at the Old Vic. Olivier lived in Brighton and commuted on the Brighton Belle to London, working fifteen or sixteen hours a day. The director's office was not at the theatre but in a row of workmen's wooden huts, of a style known in the trade as Terrapin 19, bought second-hand and erected at a cost of £6,200 on an old bomb site a quarter of a mile away, ten minutes' squalid walk past a grim park infested by meths drinkers and through streets of crumbling terraces. Olivier did not only do the work of artistic director. He had an administrator but

wanted to run everything himself. He insisted on being provided with a list of the names and nicknames of the stagehands and electricians: the master carpenter was George and
the head flyman Ted. He compiled lists of Christmas presents
– handmade shirts for John Dexter, a bottle of Rumeur Lanvin
for a press officer, a bowl of flowers for Maureen in reception.
He signed a chit to authorise the purchase of an electric stove
for Annette in the huts, to give the actors one meal a day, and
agreed in principle that a girl should be taken on to do the
washing up. It sounded as frugal as in Lilian Baylis's time. Only
after all this could he turn his attention to *Othello*.

This was far and away the most memorable production in
the early years of the National. It was put on to celebrate the
four-hundredth anniversary of Shakespeare's birth in 1664,
and Olivier's performance in it was one of those that last in theatrical memory. The play stayed in the repertory for nearly three
years. Olivier murdered Maggie Smith as his Desdemona at the
Old Vic, in Moscow and Berlin, and in the English provinces.

Olivier always insisted that he had to be persuaded into
Othello, and that he was reluctant for many reasons, particularly
because his voice was a natural light baritone and Othello's
was a dark, velvet bass. In early 1964 he began to prepare
himself. For *Lear*, he had once bellowed at a herd of cows. For
Othello he came in early to the huts and yelled away there. He
took voice lessons, roaring lower by the semitone as each week
went by, and then he had the voice of the Moor. Except that
he had decided not to be a Moor at all, but a full-blooded black
man. It took him two and half hours to make up.

It was grease on the face first of all, black grease on the
face and round the neck and then the rest was pancake,
absolutely all over my body black pancake. I remember

155

the number, Max Factor 2880. And then I applied a slightly lighter one called Negro No. 2, which was browner, and so the application of a brown coat on top of a black gave it a very rich ebony, sort of gold somehow. Then the great trick was that glorious half yard of chiffon with which I polished myself all over until it all shone.

Then, working from the outside in, he visualised the character of the man. Othello was dignified.

But of course he has to be at first so goddam innocent, and then so goddam cold blooded. You know the old sort of definition of Shakespeare's tragic theme, a perfect statue with a fissure in it; shows how the fissure crumbles the statue . . . There's an infinite world of self-deception in Othello. He makes himself out to be so cold to the senate, and it's only got to be strawberries on Desdemona's handkerchief and a day and a half later he strangles her. He actually says, 'Then you must speak of one who loved not wisely but too well, of one not easily jealous.' Not easily jealous? When in twenty-four hours after he's seen her handkerchief he kills her?

The critics varied in their opinions. Some did not like the idea of Othello as black. All, one way or another, were astounded. The notice most worth quoting is again that of Philip Hope-Wallace of the *Guardian*. He wrote:

In great tragic acting there is always a strong element of surprise. Othello, on the rack last night, was agonising in the sheer vehemence of his anguish, but it was the inventiveness of it above all, the sheer variety and range of the actor's art, which made it an experience in the theatre altogether unforgettable by anyone who saw it . . . the General self-broken, self-cashiered. 'Othello's occupation's gone.' We saw it go.

Tynan believed he had inspired Olivier to do this *Othello*. But since he first arrived as literary manager, his advice had been treated with no great respect. He suggested the National should look for a resident playwright and should advertise for one in the posh papers. Olivier replied that he could not think of any such announcement that would not be slightly comic. 'Like a sort of poet laureate?' he asked. 'Well, we'd soon get sick of him, whoever it was.' Then, for the benefit of an international drama conference at the Edinburgh Festival, Tynan submitted to Olivier a list of earnest questions. He received derisive answers.

What elements in the theatre did he think most likely to damage its chances of survival? – Olivier: 'The theatre would seem to have been trying to kill itself for years and years, but does not seem to have found anything lethal enough yet.'

Which trends (a long question, this) in contemporary playwriting would most influence the future course of the theatre? – Olivier: ' Sorry, love, have not the faintest idea.'

By the autumn of 1964, after only a year at the National, the burden on Olivier kept on increasing. He had taken Coward's *Hay Fever* into the repertory, with Coward himself directing. It was trying out in Manchester when an urgent summons came from Coward: would Olivier come up and fire Edith Evans? She did not know her lines and was fluffing around quite lost. He did go, and was dismayed. Dame Edith recovered herself, but only just. It was a nightmare time. Olivier, who had taken over from Michael Redgrave as Solness in Ibsen's *The Master Builder*, was for the first time struck down by stage fright. He, with his talent for guilt, thought this some punishment for the sin of pride; however that might be, he was too tired to remember his lines. On the first night he went on stage in the grim certainty that he would not be able to remain there for more than five minutes. He began to watch for the instant at which his knowledge of the next line would vanish. His voice faded, the audience began to go giddily round anti-clockwise, he feared he would be written off – and then he got on with the play. That should have been that, but for the next five years, in *The Master Builder* and particularly in *Othello*, but also in any other role, the fear remained.

At the Old Vic, Olivier was directing Arthur Miller's *Crucible*. He wrote to Arthur Miller saying he was delighted, and was determined to get the seventeenth-century New England accent right. Should it be a countrified lilt? To which Miller replied: 'You delighted? Not half as much as I am to think that at last the play will be done by a man who actually is concerned with its language . . .' He said it should be almost a brogue. He had found a few old men whose speech reflected if not the word usage then at least the temperament behind the older speech. It was gnarled, terse, with a stiff-lipped humour delivered with hardly the flicker of a smile, and with an imminent cruelty. The *Crucible* people would always have sounded honest, and would have found it difficult to distinguish between religion and fanaticism. No one could have taken more trouble than Olivier; Miller's plays had always been better received in England than in America, and his faithful production did well.

Tynan continued his barrage of memos to Olivier. One at that time takes the cake. 'I asked the director of the Prague National Theatre why his theatre worked so smoothly. He said,

"It's simple. I decide on the repertoire with the dramaturge, and then we tell the other directors what they are going to do. Is there any other way?" Perhaps there's a lesson for us all here.' Tynan had already inquired whether three directors at the National were not too many, and had fallen out with Dexter. He soon attracted the hostility of Gaskill as well. Olivier and his two associates were at Brighton discussing the new season's plans. Tynan said more stars were needed, to which Gaskill objected, saying that he could understand why Olivier might wish to rely on Tynan's advice about the choice of plays, but that it was not the business of a literary manager to dictate the choice of actors. It developed into a row, Gaskill became angry, Olivier left the room and went upstairs, and reappeared half an hour later to say he must have Tynan involved in all decisions. At that point Gaskill decided there was no point in going on.

In 1965 the National Theatre company went to Moscow with *Othello*. A tour to Moscow, in those cold-war days, was infinitely more important than it would be now. There was no way into Russia, except for a theatre or ballet company, and the trials of socialist hotels and oppressive hospitality only added a perverse glamour. Olivier, since his reading of Stanislavski's *My Life in Art* in the late 1920s, had thought of Moscow as some sort of Mecca of the theatre arts. He was himself known in Russia for his patriotic wartime films, particularly for *Lady Hamilton*, which had been Stalin's favourite, and *Othello* was to Russians what *Hamlet* is to the rest of the world, the best known of Shakespeare's plays. Olivier, getting into the Russian spirit, wore a cloth cap throughout the visit. The performances were given at a theatre inside the Kremlin itself. The Russian audience knew its Shakespeare so well that it was able to follow *Othello* in English. The ovation after the first night of *Othello* lasted a full ten minutes, and so delighted Olivier that by the time he came to write his memoirs his memory had lengthened it to thirty-five. At any rate, the audience surged forward in its enthusiasm. Hundreds from the circle came down to the stalls to add to the crush. When he was finally able to begin his curtain speech the first word he uttered, 'Tovarichi' (Comrades), brought a new storm of applause, and then he delivered, in Russian, an address he had learned phonetically, word for word. Parties followed. Vodka and champagne flowed so plentifully that by the small hours, staggering back down the corridor of his hotel, guided by his wife Joan, he broke free from her and victoriously entered a linen cupboard. After Moscow, Olivier and the company travelled home by way of West Berlin, and then returned to the treadmill of the National's London repertory.

When Olivier acted or directed at the National all was happy. But the Board, and particularly its drama panel, was uneasy about some of the other plays proposed. Tynan had wanted to do Wedekind's *Spring Awakening*, an 1890s German play of erotic fantasies, but was headed off by the panel whose members included Kenneth Clark, art historian and former director of the National Gallery, and Binkie Beaumont, a West End impresario. In June 1966 a production of *The Architect and the King of Assyria* by the Spanish playwright Fernando Arrabal was proposed. Clark thought it 'pretentious nonsense and inexpressibly tedious . . . a mixture of Beckett, Ionesco, and Anouilh; gimmicks from all three.' By August 1966 Clark was more alarmed, and wrote a strong letter to Lord Chandos, chairman of the governors, saying three quarters of the plays the executive presented to him seemed to be fashionable nonsense.

I often try to analyse why the National Theatre has taken a direction so very different from what most of us had anticipated. Apart from our director's obsessive fear of being thought old-fashioned, there are two factors I had not reckoned on: first that producers would feel themselves incapable of putting on straightforward productions, and secondly that famous actors would refuse to repeat their great performances of the past. This last seems a peculiarity of the English stage, and would be perfectly incomprehensible to all the great actors of France, Italy and Germany, who repeated their parts exactly as the great singers do. I confess that I had never realised that contemporary English actors would take this point of view, and had looked forward to seeing Richardson as Falstaff etc.

The difficulty was not going to lie with Olivier's ideas for the new season. He wanted to do a Molière, and there was talk with Gielgud of their doing *Tartuffe* together. Olivier also intended to direct *Three Sisters*, and this was more than another play to him. Next to Shakespeare he revered Chekhov as an acute observer of human nature and its depths. He had played the name part in *Uncle Vanya* with the Birmingham Rep in 1927, and the doctor Astrov in the same play at Chichester and at the National in 1962–3. The ending of *Three Sisters*, with the sisters left bereft in their garrison town, with the lover of one of them just killed in a duel and the regiment commanded by the lover of another setting off for Siberia, was as exact an illustration as there could have been of Olivier's own sense that sometimes one must do without hope. 'Oh,' he said of Chekhov, 'he sees the end of the world. There's no question. All the soldiers are going to Siberia. They'll never meet again. Chekhov was always writing plays about the end of the world. That's what makes them so bloody marvellous.'

A difficulty of the kind Clark had foreseen – of Olivier's being out of touch with his Board – would certainly come with Tynan's grand new proposal. The play was by Rolf Hochhuth, a German dramatist who had had a success with a piece that accused Pope Pius XIII of collaborating with the Nazis, and now had a play which accused Churchill of cremating German cities and of a convenient political assassination. Tynan wanted to present this play, and he wanted Olivier as Churchill. He wrote to him: 'We can try [Patrick] Wymark. We can tempt Burton. We can look for a Lunt. But the P.M. is you . . . It is the kind of history you ought to be making.' Olivier demurred. But Tynan persisted, and his stubborn infatuation with Hochhuth would cause no end of trouble.

14

Watch it Come Down

The first months of 1967 were as taxing as any in Olivier's life. He was still appearing in the last performances of *Othello*. He was rehearsing the part of Edgar, the passed-over Captain in Strindberg's *Dance of Death*, a story of love and hate in a marriage, which was, as he said, nine-tenths hate. It became one of his greatest and most memorable parts, and he played it with a demanding athleticism which only he could have brought to it. He was planning the production of *Three Sisters*. He had a tour of Canada arranged for the autumn. And he lost John Dexter, his only remaining associate director, in a quarrel over an all-male *As You Like It*.

The old stage fright remained. Peter Hall one night saw Olivier in the wings waiting to make his entrance, with the stage manager holding him.

> Just before his cue Larry said, 'Right, push, push, push,' and the stage manager pushed Larry on stage, and one saw Larry walk on stage and become Olivier. I remember saying to him, 'Can anyone help you?' He said, 'It's the curse of being me. Some nights I walk on stage and I think the audience is saying, "And *that's* Olivier?" '

Laurence Olivier as the captain in Strindberg's *Dance of Death*.
The original pen-and-ink drawing, by Claude Marks,
was signed by Olivier, as shown here

Throughout all this time Tynan was set on a wrecking
course, pursuing notoriety, picking a public quarrel with the
National Theatre Board, and embroiling Olivier in what he
was beguiled into seeing as a matter of principle and artistic

164

freedom. Tynan should have been Olivier's support and ally. If he had set out to damage him he could hardly have done worse.

The occasion for all this was Hochhuth's play *The Soldiers*, which damned Churchill's saturation bombing of German cities, and accused him of complicity in the assassination of the Polish leader Sikorski. Tynan wanted a political play. It was the fashion. The RSC had presented *US*, which vilified the Americans in Vietnam, and Jean-Louis Barrault had presented a play in Paris which reviled the French army for its Algerian atrocities. Tynan asserted that the theatre was 'a sleeping tiger that can and should be roused whenever the national (or international) conscience needs nudging'. He no doubt felt he was speaking up for freedom, but given his record he may just as well have been influenced by his taste for the sensational and the outrageous. In November 1965 he had been the first man to say 'fuck' on English television. At the same time as the Hochhuth affair dragged on, he was inviting writers to contribute sketches to *Oh! Calcutta!*, the sex revue he later put on in the West End and New York. He wanted *Soldiers* at all costs.

The choice of plays was normally the director's, sometimes with the advice of the drama panel, but in the last resort the Board had the legal responsibility. In a matter of such controversy the Board was bound to decide. The chairman of the Board, Lord Chandos, had after all as Oliver Lyttelton been a member of Churchill's War Cabinet. Tynan was picking a fight, on his and Olivier's behalf, which he must have known they could not win. The Board unanimously decided not to do the play. When Lord Chandos told the *Sunday Times* in an interview that he thought it odd that Tynan should conduct a campaign against his chairman and Board while retaining his salary, Tynan wrote grandly to that newspaper, 'My first loyalty is to the National Theatre, not to its Board.' He then summoned reporters to the huts and held forth about resignations while Olivier sat silently and unhappily at his side. The Board wanted to sack Tynan but Olivier defended him. Chandos gave way, but warned Olivier: 'He is a man completely lacking in probity and loyalty, and is unscrupulous and untruthful . . . This is the man we are to keep, temporarily, at your request, and for your sake, dear Larry, I am willing to do it, out of friendship and out of gratitude to you . . .'

By the end of May 1967 Olivier was ill. In his diary for 25 May, three days after his sixtieth birthday, he wrote: 'Prostate pain.' He carried on playing *The Dance of Death*, sometimes twice daily, but then did at last consult a surgeon and entered St Thomas's Hospital, London. He had prostate cancer and underwent radiation treatment as an out-patient. While this went on he continued, although much weakened, to rehearse *Three Sisters*, and to commute between London and Brighton. On the night of 18 June, the week before the play opened, he found he could breathe only with great difficulty. He had pneumonia. His Brighton doctor was called, but against his advice Olivier insisted on being driven to London, to St Thomas's. They started in the early morning. He told the driver to take detours to pass through villages he had known, and Joan realised he was seeing it as perhaps his last journey. When they got to London, and within a mile or so of the hospital, he told the driver to go to the Old Vic instead. By then it was early morning, 9.30. There were few people at the theatre, but he wanted to see whoever was there. Harry the caretaker rounded up carpenters, electricians, and someone from the props department, and Olivier shook hands with them all. They were frightened to see the state he was in. Harry kept whispering to Joan, 'You must get him out of here,' and at last they got him back into the car and to the hospital.

This time he was kept in. *Three Sisters* opened triumphantly on 4 July and afterwards the cast went to his hospital room with champagne.

Blow then followed blow. Vivien Leigh, Olivier's second and divorced wife, whom he had probably never ceased to love, died suddenly. A close friend was killed driving back from the funeral. Olivier contracted appendicitis. Then came a blow at the Old Vic. He had brought in Peter Brook to direct *Oedipus*, with Gielgud. Brook wanted to end the tragedy on a note of jollification, and to have his actors dash up and down the aisles to what Olivier called 'a hideously jazzed up version of God Save the Queen'. To bargain him out of this, the patriotic Olivier agreed that if Brook would cut these antics, he would in return undertake that the national anthem should not be played again at any performance at the National. It had been a theatrical custom for years to play it at each performance, but this offended a new generation of directors who were happy to take the state's money but unhappy to play the national anthem. Brook made this bargain and then sold Olivier down the river. At a dress rehearsal a monolith six feet high and draped in a cloth appeared on stage. After the blinded Oedipus was led off the cloth was torn from this object, which was seen to be a huge golden phallus. Olivier was adamant that it should not remain. Brook was adamant that it should. Tynan supported Brook. Olivier was exhausted and gave in. When *Oedipus* opened the actors invited the audience to join them in a fertility dance round the phallus. Gielgud refused to take part. The whole charade was derided by the critics and disappeared after a few performances.

Olivier still defended Tynan. He wrote to Chandos going over the National's repertory since its beginnings, almost play by play, saying there had been twenty-two hits out of thirty-eight, and that a great many things which had given the National an aura of success had come from Tynan. He particularly mentioned *Othello* and Tom Stoppard's *Rosencrantz and Guildenstern Are Dead*, which could be their 'greatest money-spinner'. He told Chandos that if Tynan were got rid of he would be stricken, and Tynan once more survived. In two years, from 1967 to 1969, Olivier had been harried by recurrent serious illnesses, by the death of Vivien Leigh, and by the fear of his own death. He had been humiliated by Peter Brook, and mesmerised and betrayed by a self-interested Tynan. He was at a low ebb.

At about this time Noël Coward wrote to Olivier from Switzerland with a sensible and impossible suggestion. 'Darling Larry-boy, Don't administer the National Theatre. You have already made it and given in it several of the greatest performances of this century. Administration is more frustrating and tiring than prancing about and shouting "Ho there," or "In fair Verona's lofty cunt." What you need is a full year off duty. Please listen . . .'

Olivier took no notice. By the spring of 1970 he was playing Shylock to Joan Plowright's Portia in *The Merchant of Venice*, which turned out to be one of his last two great roles. Joan had agreed to play Portia when the Shylock was to be either Paul Scofield or Alec Guinness. It was only when both these actors pulled out that Olivier stepped in, not altogether reluctantly. The new director, Jonathan Miller, was setting the play in the nineteenth century and Olivier had been surreptitiously looking at portraits of Disraeli and the Rothschilds.

Olivier had bounced back again, and was taking control of everything. He decreed that the colour of stage wine should be improved: the magenta pink of the Ribena they used would not do at all. And he sent a sharp memo to Frank Dunlop, his new associate director, to Tynan, and to six others saying that acrimony, edginess, tantrums, and bitchiness were to be avoided at all costs. 'And I beg and request, in fact I bloody well command, that this advice be most carefully taken from now on and for ever. Any infringement of this in the future will cause trouble, big, big, trouble, I do most faithfully promise.' He had a little trouble with a persistent fan called Zena who inveigled her way into his dressing room, shouted from the gallery, and made much of her grand connections. It was eventually discovered that she was claiming to be the fiancée not of David Merrick, the New York impresario, but of the Messiah.

Later in the spring of 1970 he gave a long and jolly interview to a *Guardian* reporter. It started at the huts in the afternoon, and continued in his car to Victoria and then in the train home to Brighton. Olivier, who had just come from a rehearsal of Shylock, was in a high old mood. 'It's all right,' he said, looking round at the wooden walls of his makeshift office, 'but seven years in a hut?' He volunteered that he was playing Shylock as a last resort, and said: 'I'm reaching an age when I have to be cajoled, caressed, persuaded, stroked, before doing anything on the stage.' He named the trees he had planted – limes, oaks, willows, walnuts, poplars, apple trees, umbrella pines. He agreed he had just subjected himself to two of the busiest years of his life, with films as well as plays, but said: 'I haven't got much money; I worry about my children and the future, dying and leaving nothing, and my wife with three hulking kids.' Having caught his train by two minutes he talked about his petition to restore kippers to the breakfast menu of the Brighton Belle. The day kippers reappeared the waiter asked: 'Kippers, sir?' 'No thank you,' he said. 'Scrambled eggs this morning.' That evening on the train with the reporter he was unrecognised, and looked the most unactorly of men, but his sense of the sound of words was there. About the National he said: 'It is the chief labour of my life.' And: 'What is life about? Strife, torment, disappointment, love, sacrifice, golden sunsets, and black storms.' Had he been near resigning over the Hochhuth affair? 'I was bitter. But resigning? No, that would have been an hysterical thing to do. Actors are not the most theatrical people.'

That summer, confident that the new National on the South Bank would after all be completed and that he would be able to leave the Old Vic at last, he accepted the life peerage he had been offered three years before. Terence Rattigan sent a telegram saying: I SHALL LIFT UP MINE EYES UNTO THE LORD. Peggy Ashcroft called him 'the lordly one'. Richard Burton cabled: BY THE LORD HARRY, LARRY. The white swan Olivier wanted on his crest was the same as Henry V's.

He had decided to do the musical *Guys and Dolls* at the National, himself playing the gambler Nathan Detroit and with the American Garson Kanin as director. On stage he was a greatly praised Shylock, and during its run he had lost the stage fright which had plagued him for five years. Then, on 1 August, he was taken to hospital with a right leg ten pounds heavier than his left. It was a thrombosis extending from mid-thigh up to the vena cava. *Guys and Dolls* had to be abandoned and it was announced that he would not perform for a year. He remained director, but there immediately followed a period of great confusion about his eventual successor.

Olivier wanted an actor to succeed him. He wanted Albert Finney, but Finney did not want it. He went so far, after a good dinner, as to offer it to Richard Burton, but had to admit the next day that it was not his to offer. Chandos retired, and made a robust farewell speech. He said educated people should be allowed to recognise fustian, and pretentious fustian, for what

it was, and that public interest and public taste were not neces-
sarily ridiculous. He asked for more Shakespeare, saying that in
his time no *Julius Caesar*, *King Lear*, *Macbeth*, *Antony and Cleopatra*,
Twelfth Night, or *Midsummer Night's Dream* had been done. He
warned the National against hubris, and against pronounce-
ments on statecraft. And then, as loyal as he always had been
to Olivier, he said that the directors generally – and he made
the point that he was *not* speaking of Laurence Olivier – should
repeat to themselves, '*Nemo sapis omnibus horis*,' which he said he
might translate as 'Nobody need be clever all the time.' It was
the dignified farewell of a civilised man.

For persuading Olivier was exhausted, but he was preparing for his last
great part with the National, and indeed his last great part on
any stage. This was James Tyrone, the decayed great actor in
Eugene O'Neill's darkly autobiographical play, *Long Day's Journey Into Night*. It was Tynan's idea that Olivier should play the
part, but Olivier himself chose Michael Blakemore as director.
It was a fortunate conjunction. Blakemore considered Olivier
the most remarkable actor of his generation – the successor to
Garrick, Kean and Irving – and Olivier later put Blakemore
forward to be his successor as artistic director of the National.
The O'Neill is a long night's play, and Olivier wondered to
Peggy Ashcroft whether he would *ever* learn the bloody part.
But when it opened it was splendid, and he played it, through
more illness and through a bitter controversy over his successor, for one hundred performances. Olivier, a great actor at the
end of his stage-acting life, was playing Tyrone, a celebrated
actor at the end of his. 'For once,' he said, 'when people say,
"You were born to play that part," it isn't all that cheering.'

For persuading Olivier to play that role Tynan deserves
credit. But Tynan's real view of Olivier was next to contemp-
tuous. He concealed this at the time, but later called him a man

of no imagination or sense of contemporary theatre, sluggish of mind and insensitive to current definitions of talent, interested only in hanging on to power.

Olivier's contract would end in 1973, his health would not allow him to continue, and he had himself put forward no one acceptable to the Board. The Board then made the natural choice of Peter Hall. This was a secret to few in the theatre, but came as a distressing surprise to Olivier. It came at a time when the National was about to go through a splendid period. Michael Blakemore directed Hecht and MacArthur's *Front Page*, and then there were Jonathan Miller's *School For Scandal*, and Dexter's production of Molière's *Misanthrope*, in Tony Harrison's verse translation, all of which filled the theatre. When he heard of the new appointment Tynan wrote in his diary: 'Larry has behaved appallingly. He has sold us all down the river without a single pang – by refusing to nominate a possible successor from his own colleagues he has passed a vote of no confidence in us all.' He called him an Uncle Tom and a traitor. He also called Hall a burned-out conservative. Hall for his part thought him a Flash Harry, and one of his conditions for accepting the directorship was that Tynan should go.

The last play Olivier directed at the National, or anywhere else, was Priestley's *Eden End*, with his wife Joan. And for his last part at the Old Vic he played not Prospero or Lear but the part of John Tagg, a Glaswegian Trotskyite in a new play by Trevor Griffiths called *The Party*. It was not the lead, but it was a virtuoso performance in which he could demonstrate yet again his mastery of an accent, and it demanded from him one speech twenty minutes long in which Tagg lamented the failure of his beloved communism. Olivier had not long recovered from his stage fright and his fear of drying. That speech took him four months to learn in the summer of 1973, stretched out on a garden seat from six to eight every morning, adding another twelve or fifteen lines a day.

All this time Hall was constantly pressing Olivier to say what he might like to do in the future. In a taxi one evening Hall suggested Prospero in *The Tempest*, saying he ought not to be played as a remote old man but a man of power, as shrewd, cunning, and egocentric as Churchill: Olivier listened. For a whole weekend he appeared to have agreed to do Prospero, but then withdrew. Joan Plowright remembers that Olivier just wanted to stay away from the theatre, and did everything he could to obstruct Peter Hall. Hall accepts this, saying, 'The man was God in the theatre. He had been asked to leave his Heaven. Although without him there would not have been a National Theatre, he knew he would not actually enjoy it. I just tried to be as forgiving as possible. But he didn't make it easy. No he didn't.'

In July 1974 Lord Rayne, the new chairman, wrote repeating his suggestion that Olivier should become life president of the National, and offering to commission a portrait of him by David Hockney. He declined both offers. Both Hall and Rayne were dealing with a sick man, and it was more than the cancer and thrombosis and other ills he had suffered. Blood tests showed he was suffering from a rare wasting disease called dermatopolymyositis, and that he should prepare himself to stay in hospital for six or nine months.

The new National Theatre had risen slowly. It was to open in 1974, then 1975, then 1976. From all this, Olivier withdrew himself. He was still a consultant director. His name appeared before that of the chairman in the theatre programmes. He could have attended Board meetings, but when a copy of the minutes was sent to him he scrawled across the top, 'Keep Out.' He had withdrawn himself so effectively that, although he did write to tell Peter Hall when he went into hospital, saying he would not be able to play Father Christmas for his children that year, it was four months before Hall realised how seriously ill he was.

Peter Hall did direct *The Tempest*, but with Gielgud. He also directed Albert Finney in *Tamburlaine* and in *Hamlet*, but his most distinctive achievement of the National's last season at the Old Vic was probably Harold Pinter's *No Man's Land* with Richardson and Gielgud, the two old lions as he called them.

The last play presented by the National at the Old Vic, in January 1976 – greeted with boos, cheers, and indifferent notices – was John Osborne's *Watch It Come Down*. Some thought that, with the National going, the old place might do just that. The very last evening of the National's tenancy, on 28 February 1976, was devoted to a gala performance of *A Tribute to the Lady*, a memorial to Lilian Baylis. Olivier was still too ill and said he could not face an audience. Albert Finney, deputising for him, narrated a show that related the career of the lady. John Gielgud spoke Hamlet's 'rogue and peasant slave' soliloquy. Ralph Richardson ambled round the stage before ambushing two fellow actors into the barge scene from *Antony and Cleopatra*. The ninety-six-year-old Sybil Thorndike was present in a wheelchair as Susan Fleetwood, on stage, impersonated her as she had been back in the Shakespearean days of the First World War. Peggy Ashcroft, as Miss Baylis in her box, picked up a trampled sausage from the floor, wiped it on her skirt, devoured it, and then damned theatre critics for hastily belittling work it had taken her producers and boys and girls 'a whole week to prepare'. And finally Miss Baylis, acknowledging and half-lamenting that her boys and girls were about to leave for a posh new theatre costing *thousands*

Peter Hall rehearsing John Gielgud in Pinter's *No Man's Land* at the
Old Vic, 1975. Drawing by Feliks Topolski

and thousands and thousands, threatened to come back and haunt them all should her work at the Old Vic, or the Old Vic theatre itself, ever be put at risk.

Peter Hall thought the evening went well, not too much sentiment, not too much nostalgia, though to him Peggy Ashcroft's portrayal of Lilian Baylis had been like a reincarnation. But when reporters asked him if this was not a rather sad occasion he kept on saying he had no regrets at all. He was delighted to be leaving the Old Vic. This was the moment he had been waiting for. He had not, he said, joined the National to run the Old Vic. It was a fine old theatre but not what he came for.

Others were more sentimental. Jimmy Hannah, stage-door keeper and actor *manqué*, son of a Glasgow miner, left the farewell party at six the next morning, in tears. Molly Panter-Downes in the *New Yorker* described the evening as brilliant and emotional, the last night of the Old Vic as itself, a unique and greatly loved bit of London's theatrical history. Robert Cushman of the *Observer* wrote: 'I grieve and hope for the place as much as anyone: the fact that it has now had a perfect requiem is the more reason for not laying it to rest.'

When it came to the much-delayed royal opening of the grand new building in late 1976 the Old Vic was remembered, by Olivier at least. After the last-night gala Lord Rayne had been generous, writing to Olivier that he had been sorely missed but that his spirit had dominated the occasion. But then he and Olivier fell out over an opening date that would suit the Queen. Rayne considered the particular date to be of no special significance. Olivier was outraged. He wanted the opening in October, and he wanted it on the twenty-second. That, he said, was the date on which the National had opened at the Old Vic in 1963. He wanted this 'in recognition of the first eleven years

of the National Theatre, and of what those years achieved'.
If, he said, that date was too unsociable for Her Majesty, he
proposed the day before, the twenty-first, which was Trafalgar
Day and Agincourt Day. Eventually the twenty-fifth was settled upon. Then the Board hoped that Lord Olivier might be
prepared to speak a prologue. He said he might, or might not.
He first suggested that there should instead be a ball, with the
Queen dancing on stage. Hall wrote in his diary, 'Larry was
at his most Richard III: smiling, charming . . . but obstinately
refusing to agree to anything that we wanted him to do.'

Olivier did in the end make a speech, giving in a few minutes one of the great performances of his career, dominating
the evening. What he said was of less consequence than the
manner of his saying it. It was, he said, a nationally character-
istic understatement to say that he was happy to welcome them
all, the Queen, and lords, ladies, and gentlemen, in that place,
at that moment. And for that moment they must be grateful to
many. He did not ask to be forgiven if he did not mention by
name all the contributors to that achievement since 1818, as it
might be harder to forgive him were he able to achieve such a
feat of memory. But he did not forget the Old Vic. There was,
he said, an unkind dictum which declared that a true artist
must not expect satisfaction from his work. But let him, he said,
wish the theatre such a blessed sense of dedication as had been
inspired, many years before, by Lilian Baylis.

15

Prospect and the Fragile Soul

The Royal Victoria Hall Foundation, left with the bricks and mortar of the Old Vic but no company, first extracted £96,000 from the National Theatre to repair its depredations to the Old Vic. This sum included £32,000 to restore the stage flooring and £47,000 for decoration and furnishings. Then the Foundation looked for an impresario to put on plays in its theatre. Since 1912, when Lilian Baylis took over, the theatre's purpose had always been clear. The Old Vic had had a company, generally a distinguished company, and, though there were constant cries of poverty the money was somehow raised. Then the National Theatre had turned up. Those sixty-four years, from 1912 to 1976, were the Old Vic's golden days. The five years after the National left were one long desperate adventure, as colourful as at any period in the melodramatic nineteenth century.

The first company to make any approach to the Old Vic in 1976 was Bullfinch Productions, which reopened the theatre in July with Glenda Jackson in Webster's *White Devil*. It was a modern-dress version in a Fellini-esque *La Dolce Vita* setting and not even Miss Jackson could save it. The critics condemned its mumbling and gabbling, and said it looked like a showbiz party that had got slightly out of hand. Bullfinch was unable to complete the play's run. The only good thing to come out of it was that Joe Papp, founder of the Public Theater in New York, who happened to be in London, saw Miss Jackson's performance and offered her the part of a female Hamlet in New York – and she quietly declined.

Other ventures did even worse. A visiting African dance company lost £4,000 in a week. Nottingham Playhouse came with experimental plays for a season of six weeks but left after a fortnight. Then along came Jimmy Verner, a former child actor who had had an interest in the erotic musical *Hair*, who offered two farces and a revival of a 1923 thriller called *The Ghost Train*. He called himself administrator of the Old Vic, which he was not, and gave disarmingly candid press interviews saying the theatre in London was a Bad Scene, less jolly than betting on horses, and that if you looked at his record you might not want to invest in him. He was right. In a few months he went bankrupt, having also contracted debts in the name of the Old Vic, and departed to go into banking in places like São Paulo.

Then Prospect appeared, and was most welcome to the governors of the Victoria Hall. Prospect was a distinguished touring company that had flourished since 1961. It was perhaps most memorable for its *Cherry Orchard* with the Russian-born Lila Kedrova as Madame Ranyevskaya, and for Ian McKellen in *Richard II* and Marlowe's *Edward II*. Prospect came to the Old Vic in May 1977 with *Hamlet, Antony and Cleopatra*, and *St Joan*, and returned in November, but in the meantime it had to tour, which was after all its principal purpose. This left the Old Vic dark for months. That year the theatre lost £72,000. The usual appeals were launched. London councils contributed £63,000, and in July 1978 a panoply of great names – Margot Fonteyn, Olivier, Peggy Ashcroft, John Betjeman, Gielgud, Katharine Hepburn, Ninette de Valois among many others – wrote a letter to *The Times* asking for £1.3 million. No such amount was forthcoming. The theatre made a profit only when Prospect returned, bringing the likes of Anthony Quayle, Derek Jacobi, Eileen Atkins, and Dorothy Tutin. By that October, when Prospect was presenting Quayle in *Lear* as part of a four-month London season, its director, Toby Robertson, was saying that the glamour of the Old Vic, with its historic and emotive name, had given the touring company a whole new dimension; touring was flourishing as never before, and in towns where they previously played for two or three weeks they were now asked to stay for six. Already, he said, they were known as Prospect from the Vic and might have to start calling themselves the Old Vic company.

This was exactly what Prospect wanted, pressed for, and got. That December the Vic's governors entered into a five-year contract, agreeing that from 23 April 1979 Prospect should be known as 'Prospect Productions Ltd, trading as the Old Vic company'. On that day, Shakespeare's birthday, six trumpeters played a fanfare from the balcony on the Old Vic's façade. It was all very grand, but it celebrated an agreement that was disastrous for both the Old Vic and Prospect. Prospect would continue to tour the English regions for eighteen weeks a year, as it was obliged to, and then it would tour abroad, so what time could be left for London? Prospect had over-extended itself. Its touring was indeed flourishing, but that very success kept it away from the Vic for six months of that first year, leaving the trust again in debt, this time to the tune of £170,000. And at Prospect, the artistic director and his own board were in deep disagreement. Robertson, artistic director for seventeen years, even wanted to bring opera and ballet to the Old Vic. His board on the other hand was very conscious that the Arts Council's grant, without which Prospect could not exist, essentially required it to be a touring company. The Arts Council had no intention of subsidising a third national company, after the National Theatre and the Royal Shakespeare, and in November 1979 the Council insisted that Robertson should stand down as artistic director. He was in China at the time with a tour of *Hamlet*. The Arts Council was rather exceeding its powers, but if Prospect wished to retain its touring grant its board had no real option but to comply. Robertson resigned, and was succeeded as artistic director by Timothy West, an actor with the company for many years, but no actor-manager, and with no experience of running a company. West as an actor owed a great deal to Robertson, apart from which they had been friends for years and were godfathers to each others' sons, but, as West put it in his memoirs, Prospect's continued existence was more important than 'what might be conceived as personal loyalty'. Having been deposed when he was in China, Robertson's advice to his successor was never to go beyond Godalming.

West was sanguine about the future, reckoning that the Old Vic was a brand name as famous as Rolls-Royce. And for the 1980–1 season he was going to put on a Rolls-Royce of an actor in a dead-cert play. The actor was Peter O'Toole, the film star of *Lawrence of Arabia* fame, who in 1963 had also played Hamlet in the National Theatre's opening production. For Prospect, trading under the name of the Old Vic company, O'Toole would act Macbeth. He would have complete artistic control. The play would be co-directed by O'Toole himself and by Bryan Forbes, the director of *King Rat* and of many other films in Britain and America. O'Toole, aiming high, at first wanted Meryl Streep for his Lady Macbeth and Gielgud as Duncan. And according to West, O'Toole was convinced everyone was intent on sabotaging the show.

It was a memorable first night. First, effectively dissociating himself from the production, West slipped a printed statement into the programmes saying that this one play was under the direct artistic control of O'Toole, which it was. Then O'Toole gave a full-blooded performance in the tradition of Edmund Kean. The audience giggled. When he appeared drenched in gore from head to foot, paused, and then declared, 'I have done the deed,' there was helpless laughter. The critics were unanimously scathing. Michael Billington in the *Guardian* thought it shaming: 'With one flying, scarcely credible leap, the Old Vic *Macbeth* takes us back about a hundred years to the days of the barnstorming, actor-manager Shakespeare.' In the same paper James Cameron, a celebrated war correspondent, wrote in his column that he could not remember such shovelfuls of critical ordure ever being heaped on a production in a famous and beloved theatre. 'If I did not know a bit about the rush and hurry of the theatre critics' demanding job [half an hour to write and phone over a piece] I could have suspected a conspiracy; a concerted plan to demolish the Old Vic for employing a movie star and a film director to present the holy writ.' The *Daily Mail* did in fact accuse Forbes of taking a 'British B-movie approach'. *The Times* mercifully had nothing to say because the printers were on strike. Asked about the laughter, O'Toole replied that *Macbeth* was a very funny play and that the audience didn't laugh enough. It emerged that the gore splashed round the stage had been the idea of Princess Margaret, who had been to a rehearsal and suggested the use of Kensington Gore, the dummy blood used by the St John Ambulance brigade in that part of London, where she happened to have a palace. She said it looked more real than the usual stage blood. Forbes explained that she had very kindly come to the rehearsal in the first place to take the curse off the play, because she had been born at Glamis.

The morning after the first night Timothy West disowned the production, the actor, and the director, and was in his turn denounced as a Judas. Everyone wanted to see what was so outrageous about O'Toole's performance, and one way and another *Macbeth* became the hottest ticket in town. The Old Vic was booked up for six weeks. Kenneth Griffith, an actor and film-maker living in Italy, wrote a letter to the *Guardian* saying he admired the audacity or bloody cheek of O'Toole, who had achieved something of a scandal which 'brought to the British theatre the first bit of honest excitement in at least twenty years'. Edmund Kean, he added, had done it regularly.

Macbeth then went off on a provincial tour. The *Observer* carried a story, under the headline 'Is This Success I See Before Me?', which reported that at the Liverpool Empire the play had been a sell-out, that the Bristol Hippodrome had seldom had such an attraction in its sixty-eight-year history, and that at Coventry the play did as much business on its last night as the previous play had done in a week. On that tour *Macbeth* had played to ninety-eight per cent capacity and, alternating with *The Merchant of Venice*, had taken £160,000. It then returned to The Old Vic, again to full houses, and altogether, in seventy-two performances, took £200,000 at the box office. That at any rate was the figure given by O'Toole in a resignation statement he made two days before Christmas 1980. He had spoken earlier in the year of going on to play Lear, but the company claimed to know nothing about that, and anyway he had had enough. He was reported to have described Mr West as Miss Piggy.

By this time Prospect, trading as the Old Vic, was in desperate trouble. In the year 1978–9 it had a deficit of £398,000,

more than the Royal Shakespeare's £300,000, and astonishingly more than three times as much as the Covent Garden opera and ballet companies' £102,000. In November
1980 the Arts Council had reached the end of its patience
and announced that it would not continue its annual grant of
£300,000 to Prospect. The company did have other income
– ticket sales, business sponsorship, and grants from London
councils – but in spite of this, and in spite of O'Toole's scan-
dalous success, it could hardly go on for long.

It did try. In January 1981 a company left for Hong Kong
and Australia on a pre-arranged tour, with *The Merchant of Venice*
and Pinero's *Trelawny of the Wells*. The last new Prospect production mounted at the Old Vic was Vanbrugh's *The Relapse*,
an ominous name, and it had no luck at all. The first night had
to be cancelled after the actor playing Loveless sent a telegram
from Heathrow saying: CAN'T GO ON CAN'T COPE HAVE GONE.
He had not even told his wife. The *Merchant of Venice*'s company returned from the Far East and gave a few more performances at the Vic before appearing for the last time, in Rome,
on 14 June. Prospect continued to protest bitterly against the
withdrawal of the Arts Council grant, claiming that it had in
1980–1 made a profit of £20,000. To this the Council chairman replied that this had to be set against an accumulated debt
of £400,000, and that to pay this off the *succès de scandale* of
O'Toole's *Macbeth* would have to be repeated year in, year out,
for twenty years. The company then dispersed and that was the
end of Prospect, trading to the last as the Old Vic. A liquidator
was appointed.

A creditors' meeting was told that the company had debts
not of £400,000 but £523,295. Of this, £100,000 was a
generous but unwise loan from the Victoria Hall, almost all of
which it lost. In the best traditions of the nineteenth-century

Old Vic, Prospect's props and costumes were auctioned on stage – Yorick's skull from the 1981 *Hamlet,* Eileen Atkins's scarlet coat as St Joan, Dorothy Tutin's gold robe as Cleopatra, and O'Toole's own bloodied tunic from *Macbeth.*

The Old Vic was dark. From Paris, Jean-Louis Barrault – actor, director, and honoured artist of the Comédie-Française – wrote to *The Times* as only a Frenchman could:

> Every evening, at sunset, the spirit of English theatre awakes and, just over the Old Vic, hover the spirits of Shakespeare, the Elizabethans and the Restoration play-wrights, whose links with today's dramatic poets have never been severed . . . Today we emphasise our frater-nal solidarity with English actors in their pleas that the Old Vic should not be closed. The soul is fragile without the body, and the Old Vic company forms as it were, part of the body of English theatre. Such an act would not only be cruel, it would darken the glow of British theatre in the world at large, which we love, admire and need. We would like our English friends to know that we are with them in their request, the aim of which is only to serve the artistic genius of England.

Companies come and go. Prospect, calling itself whatever it might, had disappeared, but what of the Old Vic theatre itself? The governors of the Royal Victoria Hall Foundation, owners of the freehold and the heirs to Emma Cons and her phil-anthropic friends, struggled to preserve the Trust that dated back to 1880. They had to take whatever they could get. For six months the auditorium was used by Channel 4 and Mobil to shoot an eight-hour television version of the Royal Shake-speare's production of *Nicholas Nickleby.* Then the theatre's seats

were covered by dust sheets. The governors, becoming desperate, entertained a proposal from a television company based
in Kuwait to bring over Egyptian actors to use the stage of
the Old Vic to film seven Shakespeare plays, translated into
Arabic.

Nothing came of this exotic scheme, but it was hardly less
fantastic than that put forward by Equity, the actors' trade
union. Marius Goring, vice-president of Equity and a man
who had acted at the Old Vic in the 1930s, proposed that
the governors should themselves form a production company
and, as in Lilian Baylis's time, become a People's Palace. To
get this modest plan started the union offered the grand sum
of £2,000. The Foundation at the time had no substantial
means, and was indeed stuck with a debt of £380,000, so
nothing came of that scheme either. Then, in what must have
been a last resort, the National Theatre of Great Britain, once
a tenant in the Waterloo Road but now thriving in its concrete
bunker on the South Bank, was approached and asked for help.
The governors learned at their meeting of 3 November 1981
that the National had unsurprisingly 'declined to take over the
Old Vic'. The Foundation had already tried to sell the annexe,
opened in 1958 by the Queen, but planning regulations laid
down that it could be sold only as the annexe or store of a
theatre, and for no other purpose. No buyer wanted it on those
terms. By the beginning of 1982 it was clear that if the Royal
Victoria Hall Foundation was to survive in any form, it could
do so only by selling its principal asset – the theatre itself.

Part Four

1976–2014
Honest Ed to Kevin Spacey

16

Honest Ed and the New Old Vic

The governors of the Old Vic had done their utmost but had got nowhere, and were on the point of closing down when in mid-March 1982 an offer came in from Andrew Lloyd Webber, the composer and impresario, who already had to his credit *Jesus Christ Superstar*, *Evita*, and *Cats*, three famously successful musicals. He wanted the theatre to stage four new musicals a season, the most successful of which would then transfer to the West End. He would also use the annexe as a training school for singers and dancers. He had already tried to buy the Aldwych but had been outbid by an American buyer. Lloyd Webber had made no secret of his wish to buy the Old Vic, which had been well reported in the national newspapers. He was a keen buyer, and on 6 April the governors agreed unanimously to accept his offer.

But the Old Vic, formally the Royal Victoria Hall, was not a commercial company that could be sold at will. It was a charity that went back to the days of Emma Cons, and was bound by two schemes of 1892 and 1925. Any sale of the theatre required the consent of the Charity Commissioners. The governors confidently submitted Lloyd Webber's offer to the commissioners, who however insisted that formal, sealed bids should be invited. The governors protested at the delay, and here Colin Benham, their chairman, played a gallant part.

Mr Benham was typical of many professional men and women who then as now give their time and experience to the arts for the love of it. He had been at Oundle and then Cambridge, where he read mechanical sciences. By 1982 he was running his family firm of heating and ventilation engineers, was on the board of this and that public institution, and had been awarded the OBE. He took on the Charity Commissioners and put to them the bald facts of the matter. 'Let there be no doubt', he wrote, 'that this is a loss-making theatre.' He said the National Theatre, when it was there, had needed an annual Arts Council subsidy of nearly £1 million. Without this, three of its successors at the theatre had gone into liquidation since 1976. He believed that the governors would be taking an unjustifiable risk if they did not sell very soon, if they did not, in effect, take what was on offer. Not to find a buyer would be disastrous. He doubted whether there would be any other bids. A number of West End theatres, commercially better situated than the Old Vic, were known to be available, and he hoped the Commissioners would take into account the fact that the Old Vic was dealing, or hoped to deal, with business people who refused to be kept waiting indefinitely.

That was in May. The Commissioners still insisted on sealed bids, but did at least fix an early date, for 11 June. The bids were to be in by noon.

The day came and at first there were no bids at all. Then at 11.15 the first came in, from Ash Beacon, a company of which nothing was known. At 11.45, with fifteen minutes to spare, a second bid arrived, the expected one from Andrew Lloyd Webber. At three that afternoon the bids were opened in the presence of eleven governors and a charity commissioner. The bid of Ash Beacon, which turned out to be a company owned by Ed Mirvish of Toronto, Canada, was for £550,000, and accompanied by a required deposit of £55,000. Lloyd Webber's bid was for £500,000, with a deposit of £50,000, and enclosed with it was a letter of support from Trevor Nunn. There was a third attempted bid which was invalid because it made conditions about planning permission for the annexe and failed to include a deposit.

The governors unanimously voted to accept Lloyd Webber's lower bid. Mr Benham wrote to the Charity Commissioners reminding them that the terms of the tender document included a clause stating that the vendor did not undertake to sell to the highest bidder and explaining why the governors preferred the lower bid.

> We consider it a very important part of our responsibility to pass on the running of this famous theatre (possibly the most famous in the world) to a new owner who will provide entertainment of high standard for the people of London. By letters received from Mr Lloyd Webber with his tender and before it we believe there is no doubt he will do this. The proposed participation of Mr Trevor Nunn (at present the greatly admired chief director of the Royal Shakespeare Company) means that the Old Vic will be in the hands of two of the most eminent men in contemporary theatre . . . As I think you know, Mr Lloyd Webber is intending to do something unique in British Theatre – to develop a centre for song and dance theatre of a higher standard than exists at present in Britain and to couple it with a training school for its participants. This is, as far as I know, unique in the world . . . In contrast, the Ash Beacon proposal carries no indication of what programme they will provide, and we doubt whether these people have any real knowledge

of the London theatre scene . . . In our view the Old Vic
and British theatre as a whole will be much the poorer if
Mr Lloyd Webber's offer is not accepted. Therefore we
strongly urge you to accede to our advice.

But again the governors were rebuffed by the Charity
Commissioners who pointed out that the charity's purpose, as
stated in its founding charter, was to further 'the recreation and
instruction of the poorer classes' in London. All that mattered
was how much could be realised from the sale to be devoted
to that purpose, no other considerations could be entertained,
and the governors were consequently obliged to sell to the highest bidder, whoever he was. As Benham put it: 'The matters of
artistic policy and historical association, which the governors
have always regarded as of great importance, apparently mean
nothing to the Charity Commission. That, they tell us, is the
law, and we have no choice.'

On 23 June it was formally announced that Mirvish had
bought the Old Vic. Newspapers, scraping around for any
facts about this unknown buyer, reported that he was a substantial businessman and impresario in Toronto. He was the
son of Lithuanian Jewish immigrants. He had left school at
fifteen and liked to say that he had a few things in common
with Abraham Lincoln: both had grown up poor, and he had
taught himself business the way Lincoln had taught himself
law. He had started from nothing, opened a sort of Canadian
Woolworths, a bargain store where he sold red flannel bloom-
ers for nine cents. In a nearby warehouse he had opened a
restaurant for 1,300, decorated in a style he himself called
bordello baroque, serving bargain roast-beef dinners. He was
brash, a natural showman, and liked to be known as Honest
Ed. He made a fortune, and in 1963 bought the Royal Alex-

andra Theatre in Toronto. It dated from 1907, was the oldest continually working theatre in North America, and he restored it to its Edwardian grandeur. He had never seen the Old Vic when he made his bid for it, and it turned out that it was only by chance that he even heard it was for sale. Moreover, he did not know until the sale was completed that he had also bought the annexe, which was thrown in.

The deal was done, but there still was a great fuss. Lloyd Webber was reported to have said he was prepared to top Mirvish's bid by another £50,000 and that he would like the Charity Commissioners or the High Court to rule that the sale by sealed tenders had been out of order. He had some support. The author of the standard textbook on the law of charities questioned whether the duty to secure the highest price had been achieved by sealed bids and suggested that a public auction, with open bids, might have been the only proper way to do this. It was also made known that the secretary general of the Arts Council, and the Minister for the Arts, had both favoured Lloyd Webber.

A few came to Mirvish's defence. B. A. 'Freddie' Young, novelist and critic for the *Financial Times* and *Punch*, had been to Toronto, did know Mirvish, and wrote: 'We shall be lucky indeed if the Old Vic becomes as charming and comfortable as Mr Edwin Mirvish's Royal Alexandra in Toronto. Luckier still if it is even half as prosperous . . . He may not be as good a composer as Mr Lloyd Webber, but there is no doubt about his talents as an impresario.' Anyway, it was too late to complain. The theatre was Mirvish's. He came to London in August 1982, gave his cheque to the governors, and the next day held a press conference on the Old Vic stage. The reporters were hostile at first, but came round. He said he had looked over the place. It had had a hard life and was a bit threadbare, so he would spend £1 million restoring it and would reopen it in September 1983. He said everyone was calling him a foreigner, but he was really just a lad from the colonies. That got a laugh, and by then the hostility was evaporating. Even the chairman of the Old Vic governors, who could not have stated his opposition more strongly, wrote in a letter to *The Times* that since the bids he had visited Mirvish in Toronto. 'I found him to have the means, the will, the experience and the business ability to make a really serious effort to create a new life for our well-loved theatre . . . So, we have found a new future for the Old Vic. I welcome Mr Mirvish most sincerely.'

There was still much muttering about the strange closeness of those two blind bids. The *Guardian* went so far as to say, in a leading article, that Mirvish 'just happened to bid £50,000 more'. Some clandestine foreknowledge was hinted at. All this was not cleared up until Mirvish published a ghosted autobiography in Canada ten years later. In this he said that when he bid for the Old Vic he had never seen it, and had never even been to London. One day in 1982 he was phoned by Bert Stitt, a lawyer who years before had helped him buy the Royal Alexandra in Toronto, who told him the London Old Vic was for sale. Mirvish asked how much, was told about the sale by sealed bids, and then asked how he could possibly bid when he had no idea what the place was worth. Stitt said he would try to find out, and later called back to say he'd heard Lloyd Webber had bid £500,000. Mirvish couldn't imagine why anyone, let alone someone as canny as Lloyd Webber, would announce any price before a secret bid, unless he was bluffing, but he decided to go for it. There were only three days left before tenders had to be in so he flew a lawyer over with his bid of £550,000. He still thought Lloyd Webber was bluffing but wasn't sure. Two weeks later – that is, after the governors had failed to win round the Charity Commissioners – he got a cable telling him he had won. Then, he said, there wasn't just the shock and pride of proprietorship; he also discovered that Lloyd Webber *had* bid £500,000 and that he, Mirvish, a guy who considered himself pretty shrewd with a deal, had unnecessarily overbid him by about a hundred thousand Canadian bucks.

Even Mirvish's legally binding purchase, and his handing over of the cheque, was not the end of the affair. First, as Mirvish later said, Lloyd Webber immediately offered to buy the theatre from him for £600,000 – and he was tempted because a profit of £50,000 would have been a lot for just re-signing a deed and flying home again, but by then he was committed. Then Lloyd Webber asked if he could come in at the Old Vic as a partner. Looking back, Mirvish thought he would have made more money and had fewer problems that way. But he replied that he'd never had a partner, other than his family, and never would. He and his son David would run the Old Vic themselves. So it was settled. The deal was done. The Royal Victoria Hall Foundation removed its property from the theatre, leaving behind, as a gift to the new owner, an itemised list of goods, including:

> 4 chairs
> 1 kettle
> Gestetner duplicator and cabinet
> Safe
> 1 manual typewriter
> Several packets of Old Vic greetings cards

And that was the end of the Royal Victoria Hall Foundation's faithful stewardship of the Old Vic. The Foundation still exists today. After the sale of the theatre and the payment of all debts it was left with a capital sum, from the interest on which it makes twenty to thirty small grants a year, of up to £2,000 each, for small theatre projects in London. In 2012 it supported a promenade performance of *As You Like It* in the grounds of St Paul's Church, Covent Garden. The foundation also owns the archives of the Old Vic, which are on loan to the Bristol University Theatre Collection. As to Andrew Lloyd Webber, he went from strength to strength and, having failed to buy the Old Vic, acquired the Palace Theatre in Shaftesbury Avenue, which was perhaps more use to him since it was built, in 1891, as an opera house.

Back in 1982, it only remained for Mr Mirvish to restore the theatre he had bought. He had promised to spend a million. He did better than that. Having invited seven architectural firms to tender, he accepted the plans of Renton Howard Wood Levin, which were costed at £1.7 million. He was going to be lavish. Architects love theatres and their history. What they had, coldly looked at, was a once-elegant building that for 160 years had been sucessively run into the ground, neglected, bodged up, cut into two, bodged back into one, neglected again, patched up after the war, and then righteously vandalised by the National Theatre. Barry Pritchard, RHWL's project architect, found the backstage squalid and depressing, the basement liable to periodic flooding, and the auditorium a mixture of dark-green and grey-green, tired and run-down.

But the Old Vic is a theatre of character and some things about it were indestructible. The auditorium, mutilated though it was, still possessed its pillars and the fabric of its two circles. It was still essentially the grand house that Robinson the architect built in 1871 for Delatorre the impresario, who was convinced he was erecting a theatre to rival the Alhambra across the river. Delatorre had gone broke more than a century before but his grand vision was still there. The fabric of the proscenium had defied all efforts to destroy it and could be restored. The boxes had been hacked away but could be put back. The auditorium could still be splendid. As for the façade, it was a clumsy jumble, mostly dating from the necessary repairs of the 1920s when Miss Cons's coffee tavern was got rid of and the front of the building had threatened to collapse. But Cabanel's classical façade of 1818 could be reconstructed, with its elegant fenestration, its broken pediment, and even its coat of arms. All that could be done, and the rest could be updated, with wider foyers, more bars, and at last an entrance to the gallery through the main front doors and no longer up a dark and winding staircase at the side.

All this had to be done in a year. While the works were going on a banner was hung from the scaffolding, saying: 'Lilian Baylis, You're Going to Love This – Honest Ed'. She probably wouldn't. Her tastes did not lie in that direction, and she certainly would not have liked the three new bars. She would not have liked the cost either, which in the end came to £2 million, with the purchase price of £550,000 on top of that.

The gala reopening was on 31 October 1983, with the Queen Mother as the principal guest. Mr Mirvish was continuing the Old Vic's royal associations. He had wanted to outline the theatre in lights so that it looked like Harrods, but planning permission was refused. He made do with dazzling the audience with airport runway lights down the length of the Waterloo Road, and searchlights beaming from the theatre entrance.

The play was a musical called *Blondel*, but the critics mostly wrote about the building. Irving Wardle wrote in *The Times*: 'In the past we have always had to apologise for London's most loved theatre. The acoustics may have been perfect but it was incurably cramped, peeling, and dowdy; the penny-pinching ghost of Lilian Baylis still haunted the place. [Now] it emerges from its dusty old carapace as a superb compromise between Victorian restoration and modern open-plan design.' As for *Blondel*, it was not much of a plot, about a twelfth-century English wandering minstrel who attempted a Eurovision song contest hit in praise of Richard I and set off in pursuit of the crusading monarch. The one thing that could be claimed for the story, said Wardle, was that it never mentioned chastity belts.

The tone of the *Guardian* review was much the same. Gone, said Michael Billington, was the old Black Hole of Waterloo Road. Stalls boxes were decorated with gold and silver and there was an overall impression of cream and coral-pink lightness. All, he wrote, was hunky-dory. As to the play, it would be wonderful if the Old Vic had opened with a new hit but in plain truth the musical presented was not much more than revolving medieval wallpaper. 'All one can do is gaze happily at the restored ceiling, relish the comfort of the new seating, and rejoice in the fact that Canadian loot has restored to us London's most historic playhouse.'

Praise for the restoration was almost unanimous. Iain Mackintosh, historian of theatres, wrote that it had been magnificently achieved. 'A seat in the circle or even in the Lilian Baylis circle (the old gallery) above provides one of the finest architectural and theatrical experiences in London, second only to that of the Royal Opera House . . . Worth the entrance money alone are the superbly silvered capitals to the original cast iron pillars.'

For the first year Mirvish had promised six plays or musicals. After *Blondel* there would be *Masterclass*, a play about Stalin, with Timothy West, formerly of Prospect, coming back to play that part; then a production from Stratford, Ontario, of *The Mikado*; then Albert Finney in John Arden's *Serjeant Musgrave's Dance*; and to finish the season a revival of Sandy Wilson's 1920s musical comedy *The Boy Friend*. It sounded an attractive season, but it did not work. As in Toronto, Mirvish was offering visiting companies runs of four to six weeks, but this was too short a run for a production to break even. And he also imported from Canada the idea of selling subscription tickets for the season. This worked well in Toronto, but not in London where there was a choice of forty or even fifty West End shows at any one time. And in London, in any case, many playgoers were visitors, many of them from abroad and in town for only a week or two. So Mirvish never had nearly enough subscribers. In 1987 the Old Vic ceased to be a receiving house, taking in other people's plays, and Mirvish went into production himself, appointing Jonathan Miller as artistic director.

This was bold. Miller was a famous polymath, a writer, television presenter, director in London and New York, and physician. Almost the first play he ever saw, after the war, was *Henry V* at the Old Vic. He first made his name in revue with the Cambridge Footlights. When the National Theatre was at the Old Vic he had made a great reputation as an associate director under Olivier, whom he directed in *The Merchant of Venice*, his last Shakespearean role. He was also a director of opera, and was particularly known for his Mafia setting of *Rigoletto*. He thought the Mirvishes asked him because they were disappointed that the Vic was going nowhere, and realised they needed someone with an idea. For his part he wanted to bring the classics back to that theatre – which was how, under Miss Baylis, it had made its reputation – and above all he wanted to make the point that the English theatre had become insular and that there was a world elsewhere.

So he started with Racine's *Andromache*, Ostrovsky's *Too Clever by Half*, Corneille's *The Liar*, and Voltaire's *Candide*. He also did Chapman's *Bussy D'Ambois*, a revenge play not acted since 1604. And a *Tempest*, and a *Lear*. He won prizes, but lost money. Ed Mirvish thought one of the main reasons was that Miller preferred unknown actors and seldom used stars, and he (Mirvish), though he was proud of the prestige the plays brought, had been in the business long enough to know that stars fill seats. As he later said, he constantly told Miller, 'If you ever have the urge to make money, don't fight it. It's not all that bad.'

Miller didn't have the urge. The brave venture had been intended to last three years, but ended suddenly. Mirvish had given his son David responsibility for the Old Vic. In October 1990 two linked productions, *A Midsummer Night's Dream* and Botho Strauss's modern German version of that play, called *The Park*, had been in rehearsal for weeks. Twenty-three actors had been engaged for six months. David Mirvish happened to be in London, though to save money he no longer stayed at the Savoy. One Friday night he looked at the balance sheet, said the budgeted figures didn't add up, and cancelled both productions there and then. The Mirvishes had always been generous. They were generally supposed to have lost about £1 million a year on the Old Vic, and the actors were given a ten-week payoff. But to cancel shows so late was unheard-of. Miller walked out, saying he could not stay on after the actors had been dismissed. He foresaw that the theatre's policy would change. 'I suspect he [David] will bring in spuriously prestigious productions, like reproduction antiques . . . [but] it would be very, very ungracious to say he's been a villain. I think he's been quite courageous.' David Mirvish later responded by calling Miller a genius, and a renaissance man.

The general opinion was that the money, or the will to spend it, was running out. But the Mirvishes carried on, though their next production could have been called a reproduction if not antique. It was *Carmen Jones*, Oscar Hammerstein's musical of 1943 based on Bizet's *Carmen*, of 1875, with the action transferred to the American deep south in the Second World War. It was deep in the Old Vic tradition, since Miss Baylis, whose first love was always opera, had again and again presented the Bizet. And though it cost more than any previous production at the Vic, *Carmen Jones* ran for a whole season, made a profit, and won an Olivier award for best new musical – new to London, that is.

One big venture having succeeded, another was tried – a revival of *Hair*, the peace, love, and nudity hit of the 1960s. It was no longer daring. Cut-price vouchers were handed out at night clubs at 3 a.m., but even this sold few tickets. After a month the cast consented to a thirty-three per cent pay cut to save the show, but *Hair* never played to more than seventy-five per cent capacity and closed after two months, having lost £2 million.

The Mirvishes did not give up easily. In 1996 they made one last, bold try, bringing in Peter Hall for a proposed five years to run his own company, give ten performances a week, seven days a week, and put on both classics and new works, twelve plays in repertory over a forty-week season. He promised to be 'very lean and very noisy'. Hall, director of the Royal Shakespeare Company until 1968 and of the National Theatre from 1973 until 1988, was in effect taking on both, running a sort of mini-National, though the money this time would come not from the state but from the Mirvishes and Bill Kenwright, a West End producer. Hall said the Old Vic was a place for dreamers. David Mirvish, more practical, told him he could carry on as long as he broke even, but if he lost money he would be closed down. Hall announced a company that included Felicity Kendal, Geraldine McEwan, Ben Kingsley, and Alan Howard, and a season of plays including Beckett's *Waiting for Godot*, *The Seagull*, and *King Lear*. For six months it worked. *Waiting for Godot* was a surprising hit, playing to full houses. People were queueing for tickets on the day in August 1997 when the Mirvishes decided enough was enough. They were offering the Old Vic for sale. Hall's company could stay until December and then they would sell. Hall replied that a second year would have turned a profit, but he didn't want to knock the Mirvishes who, he said, had been very generous for fifteen years but had now decided to go home. Hall continued with his *Lear*, strangely the first he had ever directed. The notices were excellent, particularly for Alan Dobie's Fool. Its last performance was on 6 December.

In Toronto, Ed Mirvish said the Old Vic deserved a full-time owner. He used to go to London every two months or so, but it was a year since he last made the trip. In London, David Mirvish said his family's time there had been a privilege, and that they were after all only caretakers of the theatre.

The asking price for the Old Vic was £7.5 million. It was generally reckoned that the Mirvishes' caretaking, over the years, had cost them four times that amount.

17

Sally Greene and Kevin Spacey

So the Old Vic was for sale again. After the last performance of his *King Lear* in December 1997 Peter Hall came on stage and, with all the cast and backstage crew standing behind him, told the audience – and the *New York Times* reported he did so tearfully – that he feared no one would come forward to use the historic building as a theatre. He was afraid it might become an amusement park, an experience along the lines of the London Dungeon. That is a tourist attraction, mainly for children, which celebrates the Black Death, the Gunpowder Plot, and Sweeney Todd. Sweeney Todd at least would have been at home at the Vic, a melodrama of that name having played there often enough in the mid-nineteenth century. Hall hoped to heaven that nothing of the sort would happen but, he said, we were a daft country.

Others feared that the Old Vic could become a shopping mall or a bingo parlour or a lap-dancing club. But the great and the good were on the Old Vic's side. In February 1998 Chris Smith, Culture Secretary in the Labour government, made a speech at the Olivier Awards, at which the Mirvishes, father and son, were receiving a Special Award for their long stewardship of the theatre and for the investment they had made in its restoration and upkeep. Smith asked them not to rush to a sale, and to give time for some sort of showbusiness

bid to be put together so that the theatre could remain a theatre. He offered his own services to negotiate the delay.

It happened that in the audience was Sally Greene, a
woman of spirit who came from three generations of a theatrical family, was herself an impresario, and knew everybody.
A grandfather of hers had been an actor, not very successful,
who had absconded to Australia with his mistress. Her father
was a lawyer, on the board of many theatres and himself the
author of many plays, in some of which Sally was cast as
the heroine, but none was ever produced. Sally herself had
been educated at a convent school and then went to drama
school, but was convinced she would never be more than the
worst actress in the world and abandoned that career. Very
young, she was the girlfriend of Ron Dennis, part-owner of
the McLaren motor-racing team, now a billionaire – ' Sally',
she now says, 'maketh the man' – and went round the world
with him from Grand Prix to Grand Prix. Her father told her
she should stop just going from pit to pit and do something
gainful, and gave her the decayed Richmond Theatre to work
on. She raised money and camped in a tent outside while the
works were going on. Everyone called her 'the girl', the local
paper published a cartoon of her in pigtails saying 'Give me
the money,' and the Richmond Theatre got rebuilt. Later she
did up another theatre, the Criterion in the West End, which
dated from 1870 and was where Terence Rattigan's plays were
first presented in the 1930s. So in 1998 she knew her way
round building sites and had taken a liking to the Old Vic.
Not that it was love at first sight. The last time she'd seen it she
thought it 'a big, big, black box, massive, and desolate around
there: little fires burning in the side streets, guys on the pave-
ment out front, paper bags flying around'.

But after Chris Smith's speech she got together with Stephen Daldry, then artistic director of the Royal Court. They formed a trust, found trustees, and found a chairman in Alex Bernstein, chairman of the Granada Group, another man with showbusiness in the family. He was the son of Cecil Bernstein and the nephew of Sidney, brothers who had founded first the grand chain of Granada cinemas and then Granada Television. Sally, Daldry, and Bernstein pushed and pushed and pushed, and offered the Mirvishes £3.5 million. Now the asking price for the Old Vic had been £7 million. A would-be buyer can get ten per cent off by asking, twenty per cent if he is very good at it, but half off? If she is asked this, Sally Greene says she has a husband who is very good at that. He is Robert Bourne, a developer and entrepreneur with swathes of property in England and France. They have a house in Chelsea outside which they park two Aston Martins with the number plates 2 BE and NOT 2 B. So they pushed, and by July 1998 the Mirvishes, in a final act of generosity, not only accepted £3.5 million but demanded only £1.5 million down and gave the trust twenty-one months to raise the rest. At a news conference Daldry said that the trust would not be in the business of producing plays itself, but would ideally be a home for companies who could present a season of plays, rather than just single productions. He said they had to look at the long game. 'We've got to look at what might be there in twenty years' time, not tomorrow.'

But tomorrow would not look after itself. Sally Greene at first wanted Daldry as artistic director, but he was busy making the film of *Billy Elliot*, the now celebrated story of a northern boy, the son of a miner, who becomes a dancer. Then, if the Old Vic was looking for repertory, the most obvious candidate was Peter Hall, who had after all directed the last season at the Mirvishes' Old Vic. In the end the new Vic did open with a single production of his, *Amadeus*, which had been first staged at the National and then in the West End and on Broadway.

And, as it happened, one of the first productions at the Old Vic was *The Iceman Cometh* by Eugene O'Neill, four hours long and an American classic. This was going to change the whole history of the theatre. The play's run had started at the Almeida in Islington and did so well that it needed to transfer to a larger theatre. The principal part of Hickey the salesman was played by Kevin Spacey, then known in England as a film actor. He went to look at possible theatres himself, did not like any of the West End houses he saw, remembered the Old Vic from a visit as a boy, and asked if that was available. Everyone said, 'Yeah, well it's over on the South Bank, audiences can't find it, and you don't want to go there.' He replied that Americans found their way to Wembley for concerts, which was much further from the West End, and insisted on going to see the Vic. He remembers the moment. 'There was nothing playing there at the time and I walked on to the stage, looked out at the house, and I knew instantly that was where we should come.'

He had seen the theatre he wanted, and Sally Greene had seen him. She had watched *The Iceman Cometh*, listened to his long impassioned harangue in the last act, and thought he was amazing. 'He reminded me of Andy Murray when he won Wimbledon. [Here she imitates the savage facial expression.] Agh, agh. And when he came off stage you missed him.' This last sentence is one of the greatest compliments that can be paid to an actor. Later she observed him when he was gazing at the Old Vic, and thinks she guessed what was in his mind. The *Iceman* transferred there. She knew by then that she wanted Spacey on the board of the trust, and took him to lunch with Stephen Daldry. She reckoned she only had ten

minutes before the two of them became immersed in their
own theatrical talk, so she told Spacey she had taken on what
she called 'this scary theatre' and then straight out asked if he
would come on the board. He looked at her slowly and then
said, 'Yeah sure, sweetie.' She thereupon left the two of them
to their talk, and as she went Daldry called after her, 'Well
done, Sal.' That was it.

The cash had been raised to buy the theatre, but it remained
to raise the money to run it. This was done in a way new to
the London theatre. Men like Lord Lytton at the Old Vic in
the 1930s, and later Lord Chandos at the National, had traditionally given their services and advice to the theatre, the
opera, and the arts. They had much wisdom and influence to
offer. Chandos had been in the War Cabinet. But times had
changed, an American kind of philanthropy had crossed the
Atlantic, and board members were increasingly expected to
contribute more than their influence. Of the £3.5 million
originally needed, £1 million was either given outright or
made as an interest-free loan by Sally and Robert Bourne. Alex
Bernstein gave £100,000, and so did Michael Bloomberg, an
investment banker, the seventh richest man in America, and
since then three times Mayor of New York. There were of
course other contributions, including $1,180 from Lee's Sum-
mit High School, Missouri.

In 2000 the *Guardian* ran a full-page story, under the headline 'Board Games', which explained how things now worked.
'These days it is not enough [for the rich and famous] to have
a fast car and a country retreat – the ultimate celebrity acces-
sory is a place on the board of one of our great art institutions.'
Those who secured places on boards were then expected to
give generously. The article gave examples – Vivien Duffield
was with the South Bank Centre, and Madonna with the

ICA – and then came to this conclusion: 'When it comes to glittering line-ups it will always be hard to beat the Old Vic. Sally Greene, its chief executive, has even managed to lure Kevin Spacey into her boardroom, while Tina Brown, former editor of *Vanity Fair*, and John Malkovich are associate members.'

Sally Greene is candid about the way she set about recruiting her board.

> I put a dining table on the stage [of the Old Vic] to try and seduce people. And those I really wanted to seduce would be looking out towards the auditorium, because it's beautiful. All the lights up, and flowers and sweets on the table . . . I knew Elton [John] anyway. Elton's a very good business person. That's one of the reasons I put sweets on the table, because I know he likes sweets. Who else was there? Michael Bloomberg. He was there to teach me about the money too. Just the most amazing sort of people.

In these early years the Old Vic continued as a receiving house, taking in other people's productions, a *Merry Wives of Windsor* from the Royal Shakespeare Company, a *Tempest* from Sheffield, and a *Lear* from the English Touring Company. It even, one night in February 2000, took in the Tony Blair Show, when the Prime Minister, choosing not a party conference platform but a theatre stage to set out his policies, told a selected audience that New Labour should be immensely proud of what it had achieved. Of course, he said, no matter what they did, they would be attacked by their right-wing opponents. Not only that, it was also the fate of progressive parties to be attacked from within by parts of their own side who wanted a more leftist government. Mr Blair was and is a natural, who could have made a fortune on the halls.

Sally Greene and her board, meanwhile, were seeing more and more clearly that it was not enough just to have a theatre. A company was needed, and an artistic director, and the board was busy looking for one. At the same time Kevin Spacey was spending more and more time in London, so much so that the *Observer* wrote that no London party was complete without him. He also turned up, with ex-President Bill Clinton, at the Labour Party conference. And in that same year the Old Vic, needing a new chairman after the resignation of Alex Bernstein, found a new one in Elton John. As the *Guardian* put it, 'Gilt, glitter, mirrors, sweeping staircases, giant chandeliers, standing ovations – the choice of Sir Elton John seems dazzlingly obvious.' Richard Eyre, on the board and a former director of the National, retorted that the higher the profile the better.

Precisely when and how Kevin Spacey then became artistic director is, very properly, a matter of legend. Theatres thrive on legends. Spacey's own recollection is clear and circumstantial. He had from the beginning wanted to know where the Old Vic stood in the Pantheon of theatres, what had happened to it in the previous thirty years and why, and he had learned enough of its history to be able to state that Gielgud's performances there in the early 1930s had 'shaped the way Shakespeare was seen in this town'. He also knew, in 1999, that he did not want to spend another twelve years just doing films, and was asking himself, 'Now what?' Then it dawned on him.

In November that year he had been to another of the trust's board meetings, in the rehearsal room high up behind the Old Vic stage. They had talked as usual about artistic directors. Later he could not get to sleep so got up and walked in the fine

London rain – rain he remembers clearly – and then flagged down a taxi. When the cabbie asked where to, he didn't know: he'd just got in out of the rain. So he said the National Theatre, and, never minding what anyone might say of the architecture, stood looking at the building and thinking of its foundation and of its tradition and of Olivier. Then he walked the four or five blocks to the Old Vic, where the National had begun, and stood and looked at it, still in the fine rain, and then asked himself what he was doing. Wasn't it staring him in the face? The old place seemed to be speaking to him: 'You're on the board making these lists when in your heart of hearts what you have wanted to do since you were thirteen years old is run a theatre.'

Next day he phoned Sally and told her he was throwing his hat in the ring. He went back to America for Christmas and then, at the next board meeting in January offered himself and found he was knocking on an open door.

So he would be artistic director, but not yet. He had his commitments, particularly directing and acting in *Beyond the Sea*, a film on the life of Bobby Darin, a singer of the 1960s whom he had always admired. So he could not take over for another three years, and he insisted on secrecy. This was the most difficult condition he could have made. Secrets are rare in the theatre. But the secret was somehow kept, and when the formal announcement of his appointment was made, in February 2003, it still came as a surprise. Then, at a press conference, along with Lord [Dickie] Attenborough, Dame Judi Dench, Sir Elton John, Sally Greene, and Stephen Daldry, Spacey said he would take creative control of the Old Vic from the 2004 season. He would not give up film acting but he would stay with the Old Vic for ten years, and would come to live in London. He said his devotion to the theatre would echo that of previous performers such as John Gielgud, Peggy Ashcroft, and Richard Burton. His priorities would be to discover talent and subsidise cut-price seats for students. 'We actors', he said, 'tend to search for places where the effort of perform-ance is minimal but the reward immeasurable. Both of these realities exist within the walls of the Old Vic. Laurence Olivier identified the sweet spot where an actor can stand downstage centre and simply place their performance where they want it.' He said he intended to take Old Vic productions to the United States and bring American productions to London: most American actors worth their salt wanted to come to Lon-don and prove themselves.

Not everyone was convinced. *The Times*, in an editorial, was to say that when he promised to stay for a decade not many believed him; but that article appeared in 2013, by which time he had done just that.

As ever, money was needed. The Old Vic put on a concert with Sting, Sinéad O'Connor, Elvis Costello, and Lulu – to help raise £500,000 to patch up the most leak-prone roof in theatrical history.

18

High Wire, Ritual, and Bridge

The Old Vic since 2004 has been a London theatre like no other. It has not been a West End theatre run by its producers at a profit or a loss on its box-office takings and, if it should fortunately find a winner, running that play for ever. It has not been a theatre like the National, subsidised by millions of public money. It is a charity putting on four productions a year, raising its own money from corporate sponsorship and public generosity, attracting and entertaining the philanthropic, and by them enabled not only to survive and thrive but also to subsidise the general audience and attract the young. It has been Lilian Baylis's Old Vic with added glamour, without which it could not have survived. That essential glamour has come from Kevin Spacey.

When he took over the directorship he was of course seen as a film star, which he was, and is. His performance on the London stage in *The Iceman Cometh* was well remembered, but he was a man who had after all won two Oscars, one in 1995, in *The Usual Suspects*, for Best Supporting Actor, and the second in 1999, in *American Beauty*, for Best Actor. But before that he had done a long theatrical apprenticeship. He was brought up for the most part in California, in the San Fernando Valley, which is not, as the song might suggest, rolling countryside but a city in greater Los Angeles. There he attended Chatsworth

High School, a school traditionally so strong on drama that it is known as Shakespeare High, and acted from the age of eleven. In his senior year, he was cast in the role of Captain Georg von Trapp in the school production of *The Sound of Music*. From there he went to study drama at the celebrated Juilliard School in New York – a huge leap – but dropped out after two years because he reckoned he had learned what he went there to learn, was ambitious, and was anxious to work as a professional. But he had, as he now admits, no prospects, no agent, no money, nothing. He auditioned for the Shakespeare Festival in Central Park, and landed the part of a messenger in *Henry VI Part One*. He had six lines. It paid $120 a week.

After that he took what he could get. He worked as a stand-up comic. He sang. He played parts in Molière's *Le Misanthrope* in Seattle, *The Mousetrap* in Abingdon, Virginia, and Chekhov's *The Seagull* in Washington DC. To make a living he worked as a hat-check man in a restaurant, and as a caretaker in an apartment building. Then he approached Joe Papp, director of the New York Public Theatre, who gave him an office job which at least paid the rent. While working there Spacey was cast as the lead in an off-Broadway production called *The Robbers*. This got him his first New York review, in the *Village Voice*, and very flattering it was, since it compared him to Marlon Brando. Joe Papp saw the show one night, called Spacey in the next day, and fired him. The bewildered Spacey asked why, at which Papp replied: 'I saw an *actor* last night on stage, and you've become too comfortable here.' Spacey now says Papp did him the greatest favour in the world by showing him the door, *making* him act. Four months later he made his Broadway debut in Ibsen's *Ghosts*, with Liv Ullmann.

His great break came in 1986 when he finagled his way into a Broadway production of Eugene O'Neill's *Long Day's*

Journey into Night. The principal role of Tyrone was to be played by Jack Lemmon. The director was Jonathan Miller, who while he was still casting the other parts gave a lecture at the Juilliard. Spacey filched an invitation to the drinks party afterwards, stood around nervously drinking cocktails, and then, seizing the moment, slipped into the chair next to Miller, which Kurt Vonnegut had just vacated. Miller remembered the moment:

> This rather truculent young man accosted me and said I ought to audition him [for the part of Tyrone's son James]. He was very insistent and something about him made me think, 'Oh, I'll have to concede . . .' He came along first thing the next morning and, within five minutes, I said, 'Well, it seems you've got the part.' He was so outstanding.

That was his real start, and Spacey has ever afterwards been grateful to Jack Lemmon for his encouragement in the run of that play. To this day he thinks it an actor's duty, when he has achieved eminence, to 'send the elevator back down'. This was Lemmon's phrase, which Spacey has stolen and frequently uses.

So the year was 1986, there was Spacey about to break into the big time, as a stage actor, and the point is that he had at the time never made a film. It was only that same year that he had his first film part, as a subway thief who mugs Meryl Streep, in *Heartburn*. By 2003, when he took over the Old Vic, he had made thirty films, but he had been well on the way to establishing himself in the theatre before he made a single movie. As he said when he came to the Old Vic: 'I've always been a theatre rat, and ended up having a film career that surprised

45 (*Above*) Ed Mirvish outside his other theatre, the Royal Alexandra in Toronto. He was the unexpected, and last minute, buyer of the Old Vic in 1982, where he spent millions rebuilding the Georgian façade and restoring the gilded auditorium

46 (*Left*) The tatty Old Vic as Ed Mirvish renovated it at a cost of £2 million, gilded and restored to the glories of its 1871 design

47 Sally Greene, impresario, and Kevin Spacey, Artistic Director

48 Ian McKellen as Widow Twankey in *Aladdin*, 2005, a role he insisted he had always wanted to play

49 Jennifer Ehle as Tracy Lord in Philip Barry's *Philadelphia Story*, 2005, which ended Spacey's first season

50 Diana Rigg in the
2007 world premiere
of an English adap-
tation of Almodóvar's
All About My Mother

51 The Somme. A re-enactment of the battle of 1916 produced with a cast of a hundred children and local residents at the Imperial War Museum, near the Old Vic

52 Kevin Spacey and Jeff Goldblum directed by Matthew Warchus in David Mamet's *Speed-the-Plow*, a satire on the Hollywood movie business, 2008

53 Sinead Cusack as Ranevskaya in the Bridge Project's *Cherry Orchard*, 2009

54 Simon Russell Beale as Leontes in the Bridge Project's *Winter's Tale*, 2009

55 Robert Lindsay as Archie Rice in
John Osborne's *The Entertainer*, 2007

56 Anne-Marie Duff in a revival of
Terence Rattigan's *Cause Célèbre*, 2010

57 The Old Vic reconfigured in 2008 as a theatre in the round for a revival of Alan
Ayckbourn's trilogy of *The Norman Conquests* and for Brian Friel's *Dancing at Lughnasa*

58 Kevin Spacey as Richard III, a role he played 198 times in a world tour

59 Sheridan Smith as a demonic Hedda, with Daniel Lapaine as Eilert in an adaptation by Brian Friel of Ibsen's *Hedda Gabler*, 2012

60 (*Right*) Clive Rowe
and David Burt as the
two gangsters in Trevor
Nunn's production of
Cole Porter's classic,
Kiss Me Kate, 2012

61 (*Below*) Eve Best as
the duchess in
John Webster's
Duchess of Malfi, 2011

62 Kim Cattrall and Seth
Numrich in Tennessee
Williams's *Sweet Bird of
Youth*, 2013

63 Iain Glen as the hanger-on and Lucy Briggs-Owen
as his daughter in *Fortune's Fool*, a little-known play by
Turgenev that was the find of the 2013–14 season, and
the unluckiest, losing two leading men during its run

64 Matthew Warchus, who in May
2014 was appointed to succeed Spacey
as artistic director in 2015

65 Kevin Spacey as Clarence Darrow in
his one-man show which sold out all performances in the summer of 2014

me, so I just decided that I didn't want to spend the next ten
years making movie after movie after movie and occasionally
trying to fit a play in, so I thought I'd rather do it the other way
round.'

Spacey's first season began in September 2004, and not
with Shakespeare or O'Neill or Chekhov, but with an unknown
Dutch play called *Cloaca*, about the condition of middle age
and the fragility of long friendships. The critics, if not some
of the audience, knew that the title in Latin meant sewer,
and their notices were mixed. The kindest was probably the
Times Literary Supplement's, which said that there was a super-
abundance of talent in the cast, and moments in the play that
were far better than the play as a whole: there were indica-
tions in *Cloaca* of a determination to fashion theatre that was
imaginative, brave, and novel, and in one way it was a good
thing that Spacey had not begun with a huge success. 'Now he
has a chance to build, and London's audiences – far more generous and appreciative than its press – will be happy to see him
succeed.' In another way, it might be said that first seasons had
begun like this before. Back in 1962 Olivier, opening the new
Chichester theatre, had begun with two forgotten seventeenth-
century plays, one by the Duke of Buckingham. That season
had been saved only by a famous production of *Uncle Vanya*,
with Olivier, Michael Redgrave, Joan Plowright, Joan Green-
wood, Sybil Thorndike, and Lewis Casson.

Spacey to this day insists that he would still do *Cloaca*. Look,
he says, the critics are always complaining that too few new
plays are presented, and that no management will put on
European plays, and then when you do both you are damned
for it. Still, he continued his first season with a safe production, though it may not have seemed safe to him since it was
a pantomime – something that with its cross-dressing baffles

Americans. He had never even seen one himself, but he had asked Ian McKellen what he had always longed to play, and he had replied Widow Twankey, so McKellen appeared in *Aladdin* at the Old Vic, playing to full Christmas audiences. Then came Spacey himself in *National Anthems*, a satire on the 'greed is good' culture of late 1990s America. Spacey got good reviews but the play did not. Charles Spencer of the *Telegraph* wrote that he hated putting the boot in twice, for Spacey's project was a noble one – 'but let's see him in Shakespeare and American classics'. Both came along. The American classic comedy was *The Philadelphia Story*. Few at the Old Vic can have seen the play since it had, astonishingly, never been presented in London, but everyone knew the film of 1940 with Katharine Hepburn, James Stewart, and Cary Grant. At the Vic Jennifer Ehle played Hepburn's part and Spacey played Cary Grant's, and it was a delight. Spacey did take several weeks off in the middle of the run to film *Superman Returns* – and that did not help the box office. But then ever since the 1930s, as Harcourt Williams once lamented, the Vic had occasionally lost its best actors to the movies, and at the last moment.

The Shakespeare came next with *Richard II*, in modern dress. Michael Billington of the *Guardian* wrote that Trevor Nunn, as director, had released the Shakespearean inside Spacey and shown that he had the kingly authority to command the Old Vic stage. The *New York Times* saw him as a Tony Blair-like king, stalking the sleek corridors of contemporary English realpolitik. Reviews this good are in a way ironic, since Spacey insists that he never reads them. It is a pity if he did not, because with those two plays he established himself at the Old Vic. There would be the odd dud play, and the odd financial crisis, but nobody from then on would doubt his authority.

So why then, after *Richard II*, had he not gone on to play Iago, or Astrov in *Uncle Vanya*, as everyone expected? He doesn't give a direct answer to this. He has, though, said that he has ceased to *covet* roles, and that he didn't want his tenure to be all about the roles he played but about the company, even if he was its leading actor. But it was just as well he had so established himself, because, after another *Aladdin* and a new version of Stravinsky's *Soldier's Tale*, the last play of the second season was one of those duds, and a disaster for the theatre. It should not have been. *Resurrection Blues* was the last play of Arthur Miller, a great playwright. It was directed by Robert Altman, the celebrated film director of *MASH*, with a string of awards to his credit, and starred Maximilian Schell, the leading man in fifty films. None of those names saved it. The critics called the direction inept, Schell could not speak or even remember his lines and had to be constantly prompted through an earpiece, and the show closed two weeks early. 'It was', says Spacey, 'a good idea on paper. You can bring the best people in the world together and still produce a turkey. It happens. It was a disaster.' At the time he declined to get into a fight with the Press, telling the *New York Times* – which continued to cover the Old Vic in a way it covered no other London theatre except the National – that it was not Us against Them, but that to some degree the press took advantage of his being a well-known actor and used his name to sell papers. In other words, as he had told the London papers before, he knew he was a Big Target.

Resurrection Blues was a low, but it was the turning point. The third season, 2006–7, began with Eugene O'Neill's *Moon for the Misbegotten*, with Spacey and Eve Best and directed by Howard Davies. This made friends of the London critics – the Old Vic was said to be at last aiming at mountain peaks – and transferred to Broadway. There followed two all-male

Shakespeares directed by Edward Hall, Peter's son, and then a fiftieth-anniversary production of John Osborne's *The Entertainer*, and all was well.

Spacey is more than 'a well-known actor' as he puts it, and more than a Hollywood star – a term he declines to recognise, pointing out that he does not live in Hollywood, that he is a character actor, and that his first love is the stage. As he puts it, in the movies you can do scenes on your own, or in bits and pieces, and hardly meet the other actors, whereas in the theatre there is the ritual of rehearsing together, the discovery of the play together, and you're learning with your fellow actors and may fall flat on your face in front of them. But maybe, if you're lucky, the company becomes a family.

And then the danger of every performance? 'Then you walk on the high wire every night. I just happen to love the thrill of it – the high-wire act of it and the ritual of it.'

Spacey has the same gift of anonymity that was famously possessed by Olivier and by Alec Guinness, both of whom were unmistakable on stage but could be near invisible in the street, in a restaurant, or even in a theatre foyer. They would have made wonderful spies, seeing but never being seen. Spacey too, in a flat cap and jeans, goes unrecognised in the streets around the Old Vic. 'That quality,' he says. 'We love being looked at when we're working, but not otherwise.'

And he becomes as it were a blank sheet on which his part for the moment is imprinted? 'Yes, and I give myself over to a role in a way that I couldn't possibly give myself over to another person.'

But invisible though he may be at times, the fact is that as a public figure he is recognised well beyond both the stage and the screen. The American ambassador in London gave a lunch for Spacey at his residence in Regent's Park. Paul McCartney sang for the Old Vic at Battersea Power Station on an evening when pictures given by Tracey Emin and Peter Blake were auctioned. Spacey is also a friend of ex-President Clinton, and has been since Clinton was Governor of Arkansas, back before 1992. He campaigned for Clinton and for the late Ted Kennedy. He and Clinton have watched the tennis at Wimbledon together, and Spacey was compère at the charity auction at Clinton's sixtieth birthday party. And at the first-night party for *Moon* in New York, at which the American Associates of the Old Vic paid $500 a plate to dine at Planet Hollywood in Times Square, invitations were sent out in the names of 'William Jefferson Clinton, Kevin Spacey, and Sally Greene'. Clinton worked the room, the guests stood in line to shake his hand, and then he made a speech on behalf of the Old Vic.

And because Spacey has to be a fundraiser for his own theatre he has benefited mightily from seeing such naturals as Kennedy and Clinton at work. And, he says, Mandela.

Nelson Mandela? 'To this day he stands out as one of the finest fundraisers I've ever met. Because to some degree he knew that some people thought he was a saint, and he wouldn't let you leave the room until you'd written the cheque.'

And did Spacey himself have some of this gift? 'I am not afraid to say what I have come to ask for.'

In the same season as Spacey did his *Richard II* the Old Vic put on a show of quite another kind in London, and not at the theatre but at the Imperial War Museum, half a mile away. Lilian Baylis always believed that the Old Vic should also entertain and involve the local residents. The Old Vic has continued this tradition, perhaps most vividly in its recreation at the museum of the Battle of the Somme. More than a hundred residents of Lambeth and Southwark, aged from thirteen to sixty-five, helped by a professional director, stage manager,

and actors, produced a spectacle to commemorate the nine-
tieth anniversary of the battle. The young soldiers were urged
on by King George V, in a voice-over by Spacey, whose English was as kingly, and as uncannily *English*, without a trace of
American, as it had been in his *Richard II*.

This community theatre is part of Old Vic New Voices,
another of whose purposes is to give new talent a chance,
and sometimes to bring on young people who would otherwise never have gone near a theatre. A distinctive feature of
OVNV has been the 24 Hour Plays where, each year, thirty
young people selected at auditions from as many as three
thousand applicants conceive, write, and present six short
plays – all this done in twenty-four hours, from scratch. The
plays are then presented on the Old Vic's stage to capacity
audiences. Two young people have also been sent to Whitgift
School, Croydon, on drama scholarships. Each year several
young companies have been sent to the Edinburgh Festival
fringe. Under the T. S. Eliot US/UK exchange scheme five
new plays and their young casts are brought from America to
the Old Vic, and performances given in the main rehearsal
room, converted for the occasion into a studio theatre.

In the fifth season the Old Vic was utterly changed, and
the auditorium with its proscenium made into a theatre in the
round. The plays presented were Alan Ayckbourn's 1970s trilogy of *The Norman Conquests* – modern English country-house
satirical comedies in which Norman, who believes it is his mission to make women happy, ineptly tries to seduce his wife,
his wife's sister, and his sister-in-law. Spacey wanted all things
new; Ayckbourn's plays had been traditionally presented in the
round at Scarborough, the director Matthew Warchus wanted
to bring them to London, and Michael Hintze, the Australian hedge-fund manager and philanthropist, gave £250,000

towards reconstructing the auditorium. This has been one of the many generosities of the Michael and Dorothy Hintze Foundation to the Old Vic. Hintze had previously restored Michelangelo's frescos in the Pauline chapel at the Vatican, made great gifts to the National Gallery and the Victoria and Albert Museum, and was knighted in the 2013 Birthday Honours for services to the arts. His gift was in a grand tradition, taking the mind back to the £30,000 given to the Old Vic by the impresario George Dance in the 1920s.

One of the most ambitious of the theatre's ventures has been the Bridge Project. For three years from 2009 productions originating either at the Old Vic or at the Brooklyn Academy of Music (BAM), with half-English and half-American casts and all directed by Sam Mendes, played in both New York and London and toured worldwide. In the first year *The Cherry Orchard* and *The Winter's Tale* went as far as Singapore and Auckland. In the second, *As You Like It* and *The Tempest* toured just as ambitiously. By then Spacey had given his *Richard III* at the Old Vic, the single role for which he is probably best remembered. So in the third year of Bridge *Richard III* toured on its own, having begun in London, then taking in the Gulf, Sydney, Beijing, and San Francisco before ending with a gala in New York. In two of those years the company also played in the great Greek amphitheatre of Epidaurus, before audiences of up to fourteen thousand.

That performance of *Richard III* ended memorably with Spacey hung upside down by the feet – just as Mussolini was in 1945 after his summary execution by partisans. That was the idea of the director, Sam Mendes. For Spacey it was one of his favourite moments of the evening. After three hours of his legs being restrained and crunched up by a brace, to simulate Richard's deformity, he was at last able to stretch out.

In 2010 Spacey was appointed an honorary Commander of the Order of the British Empire for services to drama. For an American this is a rare honour. Back in London, the eighth season of the Spacey–Greene Old Vic, that of 2011–12, continued triumphantly and most profitably with Michael Frayn's *Noises Off* transferring from the Old Vic to the West End, to be followed by Eve Best in Webster's *Duchess of Malfi*. In the previous nine months Spacey had given 198 consecutive performances of *Richard III* round the world – compared with Olivier's celebrated 155 performances in that part, from 1944 to 1949. The *New York Times* said Spacey had performed with 'all-conquering audacity', and that as to the mixed Anglo-American companies, the stars centre-stage had usually been British but between British and American there had been no jagged faultlines in technique. Charles Isherwood ended one *New York Times* article with this paragraph:

> It took two major theatre luminaries [Spacey and Sam Mendes] four years to achieve the seemingly modest goal of mounting five classical productions with mixed American and British casts. It doesn't sound so very challenging, does it? But then most of us don't really think much about the engineering and labour involved in its construction when we drive across the Brooklyn Bridge.

The Old Vic has been seen to be as much Spacey's theatre as it was once Lilian Baylis's. He feels the presence of ghosts – 'ghosts of actors, good ghosts; they urge you on; I've never felt they want to chase you out of the building'. Spacey is a Big Beast, a Large Target, however you like to put it. Directors, actors, and audiences have come to the Waterloo Road because he is there. No actor–director has received such consistent publicity as he has over his time in London, not even Olivier in his day. This is partly because there is now much more acreage of space in newspapers and infinitely more time on television, not to mention the Internet, but the coverage has still been extraordinary. When a portrait of Spacey is exhibited at the National Portrait Gallery it commands a whole page in the London *Evening Standard*. When on a visit to Boston he adopts a new dog, he and the dog are pictured in newspapers on both sides of the Atlantic. American tourists in London tweet about a glimpse of him in the Old Vic bar after a performance. He has had notoriety thrust upon him, and for the theatre it has become a necessary notoriety. He did a series of television commercials for American Airlines, which became indirect advertisements for the theatre. 'People often ask me what's the best seat in the house,' he would say, as the camera showed him first sitting in the Old Vic's red plush stalls and then reclining in American Airlines' business class. It was part of his bargain with the airline that during the Bridge seasons it should fly the company's actors across the Atlantic free. It is a long way from Lilian Baylis scrounging cast-off evening dresses from her better-off patrons, to be used as costumes. Just as the tours were a long way from the Old Vic's 1938 *Hamlet* at Elsinore, in the rain or in a hotel lobby, but the spirit was the same. Spacey loved it all. Of his performance in *Richard III*, betraying all around him on his murderous way to the throne, he said: 'Looking into the eyes of your audience and making them your co-conspirators, seeing the glee, it was delicious.'

Behind Spacey is his staff. When he began at the Old Vic his producer was David Liddiment, formerly Head of Entertainment at the BBC, and then Director of Programmes at ITV. He left when he became a member of the BBC Trust in 2006 and was succeeded by the duo of Kate Pakenham and John Richardson. She had previously been head of Old Vic New Voices. He had spent six years producing in the West End, on Broadway, and on tour. They were co-producers for five years until she went to the Donmar Theatre as executive producer. Richardson then took over on his own.

The three branches of Old Vic New Voices were run until 2013 by Steve Winter, an actor and teacher who came to the Old Vic in 2004 by way of the Tricycle Theatre. One branch, OVNV Talent, does what its title says and looks for budding actors, directors, and theatre people. OVNV Education gives free tickets to forty schools, and training sessions at those schools. OVNV Community has offered tickets, backstage tours, and encouragement to eleven thousand local residents and workers.

The time was when the business side of a theatre was run by one man and a dog, or in the Old Vic's case by one woman, her secretary and someone to look after the box office. But the Old Vic now has a staff of seventy-five, and has to comply with ever-increasing regulations and employment laws of one sort or another, so its business affairs are managed by Kate Varah, a solicitor formerly with the City firm of Linklaters. Her grandfather, Chad Varah, founded the Samaritans. She read Theology at Oxford but does not choose to emulate Lilian Baylis by wearing her Master's cap and gown on first nights.

By 2011 Spacey had extended his stay at the Old Vic from the promised ten years to twelve, until 2015. Early in 2013 he also starred in an American adaptation of the British political television series *House of Cards*, a twenty-six-part drama in which the action is transferred from Westminster to Washington and in which he plays the part of a villainous and conniving Congressman. The red-carpet world premiere was in London, in Leicester Square, in aid of the Old Vic. The unique selling proposition was that the series was not to be seen on television proper but on Netflix, over the Internet, and that the viewer could watch one programme or, if he wished, download a whole series and watch the episodes straight away, one after another. This was something quite new, was reported in more acres of newsprint, and once again Spacey's fame rubbed off on the theatre. That was the occasion when *The Times* carried an editorial saying that when he had first promised to stay in London for a decade not many had believed him, but that now, thousands of performances later, he was 'rapidly becoming an adopted British national treasure'.

It is undoubtedly true that the Old Vic has presented a variety of plays offered by no other London theatre, or only by the National and its three auditoriums and lavish state grants. The Old Vic has presented a repertory in several broad classical traditions. The plays presented have included six of Shakespeare's – with Spacey himself in *Richard II* and *Richard III*; Chekhov's *Three Sisters* and *The Cherry Orchard*; Ibsen's *Hedda Gabler*; eight plays from the classical American tradition – *The Philadelphia Story, Speed-the-Plow, Inherit the Wind*, and *Sweet Bird of Youth* among them; eight modern English classics – Shaw, Coward, Rattigan, Osborne, Ayckbourn, Stoppard, and Frayn; two Irish masterpieces in *Playboy of the Western World* and *Dancing at Lughnasa*; two pantomimes, and the musical *Kiss Me, Kate*. Kim Cattrall, Jennifer Ehle, Eve Best, Diana Rigg, Vanessa Redgrave, Kristin Scott Thomas, Ian McKellen, Robert Lindsay, Jeff Goldblum, David Suchet, and Simon Russell Beale have appeared on stage. Sam Mendes, Peter Hall, Trevor Nunn, Richard Eyre, Anthony Page, Matthew Warchus, Marianne Elliott, Anna Mackmin, Thea Sharrock, Lindsay Posner, and Spacey have directed. Seventy-five performances of *Hedda Gabler* were seen by

51,314 people; 103 of *Sweet Bird* by an audience of 75,253.

So it is predominantly a classical theatre. But from 2009 on the Old Vic did also run the Tunnels, thirty thousand square feet of them, across the road from the theatre under Waterloo Station. In these disused Victorian railway arches the Punchdrunk company put on its version of Fritz Lang's *Metropolis*, encouraging the audience to roam. A film by the graffiti artist Banksy was given its premiere. The American rap singer Azealia Banks gave a gig. And Bill Clinton turned up at a fundraiser. The Tunnels were popular but bled money the theatre could not afford, and had to close in 2013.

Not since 1963, when Michael Elliott's company vacated the theatre to make place for the National Theatre, has the Old Vic ever received a regular state grant. It has always had to earn its own living. By 2013 it needed to raise £3 million a year on its own just to keep the theatre going – to pay its seventy-five permanent staff, produce four plays a year, and maintain a building which in parts dates back nearly two hundred years. In that year Arts Council England did give the theatre not a grant but a conditional promise of £5 million if it were itself able to raise £15 million – the whole £20 million then going towards an endowment fund whose income would go towards the day-to-day running of the theatre. Spacey, with the example of Clinton and Mandela in mind, and with his constant optimism, is aiming to raise £75 million for that endowment.

At the same time, aiming even higher, the Old Vic is launching a separate appeal for £30 million to be spent on the building. In the 1970s and 1980s the Mirvishes spent lavishly on the fabric, and the auditorium remains glorious. But Cabanel's famous roof of 1818, though miraculously surviving, is still leaking, and the theatre backstage is chaotic – the result of two hundred years of bricking up, knocking through, and botching. The stone staircase to the only rehearsal room is a three-storey precipitous climb, the ancient lift breaks down, the dressing rooms could kindly be described as squalid if not prison-like, and there is not and never has been a green room for the actors. Front of house, the foyers and staircases are hot, crowded and in places dark where the old long windows on both sides were bricked up in the 1920s. These will be opened up and the whole place lightened. Apart from this, the building immediately behind the theatre, to the south, has already been bought and will be converted into a new studio auditorium seating eighty to a hundred.

These audacious plans are overseen by the Old Vic Theatre Trust and a separate Endowment Trust, and their success will depend as ever on the small generosities of the many and the larger generosities of the few – encouraged by Vivien Wallace, the Old Vic's director of fundraising who has been with Spacey since 2004. Before that she was with the Royal Opera House, and then worked with four artistic directors of the National Theatre from Peter Hall to Nicholas Hytner. In television's golden time in the 1980s she ran Granada's New York office, was on the Granada Board, and as chief executive of Granada Television International raised millions for TV co-productions worldwide. Now she and her team have other millions to raise.

And the Old Vic needs as many millions as it can raise in whatever way. Show business is rarely steady business. Success and failure are unforeseeable, and there are few better illus-trations of that than the Old Vic's seasons of 2012–13 and 2013–14.

The season of 2012 began with Brian Friel's version of Ibsen's *Hedda Gabler*, with Sheridan Smith; continued with Trevor Nunn directing the musical of *Kiss Me, Kate*; then

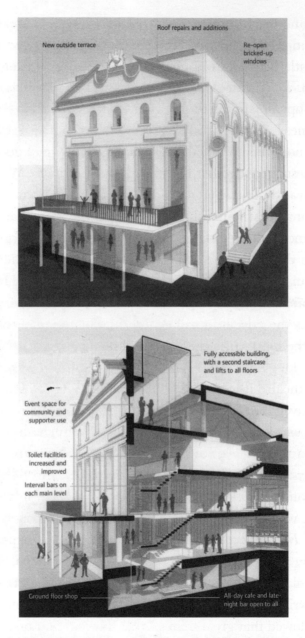

Above, Architects' plans for a re-working of the façade. A new balcony, right across the front, is proposed to open out from the present circle bar. *Below*, the plans of the theatre, seen from Waterloo Road, showing a lift, new bars and a café

offered another Rattigan, *The Winslow Boy*, with Henry Good-man; and concluded with Tennessee Williams's *Sweet Bird of Youth*, with Kim Cattrall. The notices and the takings were splendid. The theatre was riding high, and there was moreover a starry opening to the next season to look forward to – no less than James Earl Jones and Vanessa Redgrave in *Much Ado About Nothing*, both memorable actors commanding great good will, who had starred together in *Driving Miss Daisy* in the West End. But he was 81 and she 75, and their casting as Shakespeare's young, or at least youngish, Benedick and Beatrice never began to convince. The setting of the play in a Second World War England did not come off either, especially since the young American airmen supposedly based there were played by Eng-lish actors, and it showed. Michael Billington of the *Guardian*, who likes the adventurous and the boldly eccentric, called it one of the most senseless Shakespearean productions he had seen in a long time. *The Times* called it a sad fiasco. In the com-mercial theatre it would have been off in a week. At the Old Vic it played for almost three months to scanty audiences.

And what was to follow? Next came the uncertain attrac-tion of a rarely presented play by Turgenev, as a playwright generally known only for *A Month in the Country*, which has itself prompted unkind critics to wish it were only a fortnight. So what was to be expected of his lesser-known tragicomedy, *Fortune's Fool?* Everything that happened was then perverse. The play was written in 1848, and not performed in Eng-land until at Chichester. But it turned out to be a great find. It was written fifty years before Chekhov, and in some ways foreshadowed that great man's work. The adaptation by Mike Poulton, directed at the Old Vic by Lucy Bailey, was by turns hilarious, vicious, and most moving. In particular Iain Glen, known mostly for his television work, was touching as the fortune's fool of the title, the hanger-on in a country house, the poor relation who has precariously hung on for years. The scene in which he is made recklessly drunk and betrays his one deadly secret, and the later interview between him and his daughter, were moving and memorable. First night audiences, being made up in large part of friends of the theatre and friends and family of the cast, are traditionally enthusiastic and indulgent, but many of that first night audience were genuinely astonished, a rare thing in the theatre. The applause was different. The notices were splendid. Libby Purves, writing online, called it a quintessentially Russian mixture of comedy and pathos, dignity and humiliation. Charles Spencer of the *Telegraph* found it strangely addictive, melancholy, absurd, and surprising to the end. It was, he said, good to find the Old Vic back to the top of its game.

So against all the odds a quite unexpected success seemed assured. Then, a few days into the run, Glen was taken ill and withdrew. This could be overcome, perhaps. A replacement was rehearsed for two weeks, came into the play, and then himself withdrew. The result was that the understudy appeared on stage for most of the run. Bookings fell off. On some nights the circle was closed so that the theatre should not appear too empty. It was foul luck for a most distinguished play, and for the theatre.

The Old Vic put a brave face on it. At a celebrity auction at Christie's, London, in February 2014, to raise money for the theatre, Spacey stated his familiar confident aim of raising £50 million, and then asked: 'Is that a great deal to ask? Yes and no. Six years ago Christie's, our co-hosts, sold one painting by Monet for $80 million. And four years ago Picasso's *Nude with Green Leaves* beat that and fetched $100 million. So look at it this way – it can be done.'

The auction was a good start. Of the works given for auction by their artists, a ballerina by Banksy, the graffiti painter and political activist, fetched £175,000; two neons by Tracey Emin fetched £165,000; a portrait of Spacey to be painted by Jonathan Yeo, creator of the portrait of Spacey as Richard III exhibited in the National Portrait Gallery, made £100,000. The sixteen lots altogether realised more than £900,000 which Christie's, with a gift of £100,000, rounded up to more than a million.

After *Fortune's Fool* the Old Vic was again recast as a theatre in the round, as it had been in 2008, and once again it was a gift of £250,000 by Michael Hintze – bringing his donations to the Old Vic over the years to £1 million – that made this possible. This generous man, whose interest in the arts began when he was eleven and heard Joan Sutherland sing at the Sydney Opera House, runs the asset management firm of CQS, which is why the theatre in the round is known as the CQS space.

To put the Space in place meant dismantling the stalls, modifying the stage, removing the great chandelier and the bow-fronts of the boxes, and took thirty men two weeks, along with 26,000 screws and 960 metres of new carpet. This radical change transforms, and yet does not jar with, the high-Victorian gilt and glitter of the auditorium. As it happened, and as the *Guardian* put it, the new theatre in the round turned out to be 'perfect for the vicious family circle' of the next play. This was Jon Robin Baitz's *Other Desert Cities*, the desert being that of California, that of the Republican Right-wing, and that of a political family whose daughter is hell-bent on publishing her memoirs and thereby betraying her parents. Martha Plimpton as the daughter was the one American in the cast and was the expected star, and yet the performances that also remained in the mind were those of Sinead Cusack as the icy

Nancy Reagan-like figure of the mother, and Peter Eagan's portrayal of the thoroughly decent, Reagan-like father.

The new theatre in the round promised much and would continue to the next season, but the cold fact was that the Old Vic in 2013–14, what with losses on the Tunnels and on the stage, must in a year have spent much of its reserves.

One Sunday in May 2014 saw one of the more remarkable events in the modern history of the Old Vic. It was not a play but a memorial celebration of Peter Seamus O'Toole, who had died the previous December. He is perhaps best remembered for his performance in David Lean's film *Lawrence of Arabia*, but he was first a much-loved stage actor. It was he who opened the National Theatre's first season at the Old Vic in 1963 with a performance of *Hamlet* in which, on the first night, he notoriously ignored Olivier's direction and pleased himself. He was also the man who in 1980, again at the Old Vic, played an outrageously bloody and hilarious Macbeth so unanimously condemned by the critics that everyone wanted to see it, with the happy result that O'Toole played to full houses for months, made £200,000, and achieved a *succès de scandale* that almost but not quite saved the Prospect Theatre Company from bankruptcy.

The theatre was packed for his memorial. Michael D. Higgins, poet and author, a friend of forty-four years and also President of Ireland – last seen in London on a state visit to the Queen a month before – gave an address in which he remembered his friend O'Toole as a man of grace and charm, to be in whose company was not an experience of the raising of hell – as some tabloids would have it – but to be a witness of great talent, mischief, and genius too. 'May his soul,' said the president, 'always loiter on the right hand of his chosen god.'

Omar Sharif, O'Toole's co-star from *Lawrence of Arabia*, was there. Kevin Spacey read 'Fear no more the heat of the sun' from *Cymbeline*. Tall stories having been told about O'Toole's swordsmanship in *Hamlet* and his love of rugby football, students from the Bristol Old Vic presented a swashbuckling O'Toole-style swordfight on stage, and then eight rugger internationals and a choir sang 'Swing low, sweet chariot'. Albert Finney, to whom the house rose, began by remembering how he and O'Toole had spent their first day at RADA together; and then he wept.

O'Toole's daughter Kate spoke a eulogy, and said her father's ashes would be scattered later in the year in County Galway, a place he always loved, but that in the meantime they were in the safe keeping of President Higgins. Very much an O'Toole touch, that. Then the celebration ended with the singing of a traditional Irish air, 'The Parting Glass,' of which the last verse ran:

> So fill to me the parting glass
> And drink a health where're we fall
> Then gently rise and softly call.
> Goodnight and joy be with you all,
> Goodnight and joy be with you all.

The Old Vic season continued with Spacey in *Clarence Darrow*, a two-act one-man play by David W. Rintels. Spacey had played Darrow before on the Old Vic stage in *Inherit the Wind*, a dramatisation of the Scopes monkey trial of 1925, but Rintels's play is a one-man *tour de force* in which the only actor remembers and re-enacts great moments of Darrow's career, from Ohio country lawyer to the monkey trial and his famous defence in 1924 of Leopold and Loeb, charged with the killing of a fourteen-year-old-boy for thrills. To make up the early losses of the season Spacey packed in as many performances as

233

he could. He played both evenings and matinées on Saturdays and Sundays. His name sold out the house every night, each batch of tickets selling as soon as it was released. The notices were splendid. Michael Billington of the *Guardian* called it a mighty performance. Charles Spencer of the *Telegraph* said you had to take your hat off to Spacey; when the going had got rough, as it had with several spectacular flops, he had refused to quit; he had been chilled and thrilled in the past by Spacey, who now also revealed a vulnerability and warmth that were very special indeed. And Libby Purves in her online notice wrote: 'America has lent us, these past eleven years, a magnificent throwback to the days of the great actor–managers.'

The last night, a Sunday, was a gala where, after the play, the audience went on to Annabel's night club in Berkeley Square. Tickets for that were £500, but throughout the run, in the Old Vic tradition, twenty tickets had been sold on the day, for each performance, at £10. The adventurous season then ended with Yaël Farber's powerful version of *The Crucible* by Arthur Miller. This play was famously directed by Laurence Olivier in 1964 when the National Theatre was at the Old Vic. Yaël Farber's production is likely to be as well remembered. Her new version was three and a half hours long, a length audiences don't traditionally welcome. But the critics of five London papers gave it five stars, variously describing it as mesmerising, as ferocious, and as doing honour both to Miller and to the Old Vic. Ticket sales took off, and altogether the production became one of the Old Vic's most successful.

It was announced that the next season would start with Kristin Scott Thomas in Sophocles' *Electra*, directed by Ian Rickson. That season would still be under the direction of Kevin Spacey but then, having completed his promised ten years in London – or rather the promised ten and the two more he had volunteered – he would hand over to a new artistic director. The theatre board, under its new chairman Nick Clarry, searched for a successor, but in the end that successor, like Spacey in 1999, threw his hat in the ring and offered himself. This was Matthew Warchus, whose appointment was announced in May 2014.

He was already an associate director at the Old Vic. He directed the trilogy of Ayckbourn's *Norman Conquests* there in 2008, and it was he who insisted it should be done in the round, as Ayckbourn himself presents his plays in Scarborough. Warchus is eclectic. Among more than seventy productions he has directed *Hamlet* and *Volpone*, but also the 1960s bedroom farce of *Boeing-Boeing*. He directed the musical *Matilda*, first at the Royal Shakespeare Company and then in the West End and on Broadway. And in 2009 he won a Tony for his direction of Yasmina Reza's *God of Carnage*, also in New York. In other words he is at home with the subsidised and the commercial theatre, and in both London and New York. He has a great range. He has also done some opera and directed in the cinema. At the time of his appointment he was about to open his film *Pride* at the Cannes Film Festival.

He is the son of a vicar – a distinction he shares with Laurence Olivier. He was born in Rochester, Kent, in 1966, but by the 1980s was living in the Yorkshire village of Drax, which was dominated by the largest coal-fired power station in Britain and by the pit. It was there, at the time of the miners' strike, that he observed the miners who appear in *Pride*. And as to the theatre, he says that at the time his greatest treat was to go and see *Evita* in Manchester, and that he gravitated to Andrew Lloyd Webber long before he heard of Brecht. After Drax, he studied music and drama at Bristol University.

New directors are not always unanimously welcomed. With Warchus there was hardly a dissenting voice. Spacey saw him as a man who loved the Old Vic, and was delighted. Sarah Crompton in the *Telegraph* said theatres usually got the directors they deserved, and that at the Old Vic, which had never been quite establishment, Warchus felt like a perfect piece of casting. Michael Coveney in the online *What's On Stage* said that under Warchus the Old Vic had a real chance of becoming the home of the best British actors in the finest international repertoire, stealing a march on the National.

AFTERWORD

The Lucky Theatre

That is where the Old Vic now stands, and this book has traced its history. Above all it is and has been a theatre of character. It is what the inelegant language of the marketing man would call a 'brand'. Old Vic is a name instantly recognised not only in England but worldwide, and particularly in America. There are other historic London theatres: Covent Garden, Drury Lane, and the Haymarket come to mind. But Covent Garden is the third theatre on its site and since the 1890s has been predominantly an opera house, and the others, though beautiful, have no long-fixed traditions.

Above all the Old Vic has been lucky. Other nineteenth-century theatres were built south of the Thames, transpontine theatres in the Latinate jargon of the time, theatres across the bridge. None of the others has survived, not Astley's near Westminster Bridge, and not the Surrey, for long the Old Vic's rival, half a mile further south; that decayed into a cinema and was demolished in 1934.

The Old Vic's luck might be disputed by the thirteen lessees or managements which have over the years since 1818 gone bankrupt. And not all them were as fortunate as Joseph Glossop who in 1823 fled an arrest warrant and his creditors and took himself off to run La Scala, Milan, then the biggest theatre in the world. Poor Daniel Egerton, a classical actor who became the third bankrupt, told the insolvency court that he had lost the entire earnings of a frugal, industrious life; and then he died soon after. And thirty years later another bankrupt was reduced to taking out a pitiful small ad offering dancing lessons.

So impresarios came and went but the theatre survived, though falling more and more into decrepitude, until in 1871 there came along the most extraordinary and most irrational stroke of luck. For years the neighbourhood had got rougher and rougher and yet a grandiloquently brave man with the splendid name of Romaine Delatorre, deludedly certain that he could replicate south of the river the great success of the Alhambra music hall in Leicester Square, bought the wreck of the Victoria, gutted it, and in twelve weeks rebuilt within the walls an auditorium of great splendour. In that district at that time it was crazy. He was bankrupt in three years and was sold up, protesting, for a pitiful £820 – but he left the auditorium that has lasted to this day.

Then came Miss Cons who, just because she wanted not a theatre but a temperance hall, was able to preserve the building by her Christian licence constantly to beg funds in a charitable cause. And then, after Miss Cons died in 1912, strokes of luck came in droves. Lilian Baylis, unlike her aunt, did want to put on shows, though opera rather than the drama was her first love. Shakespeare came to the rescue. But it was Rosina Filippi, a fading actress but a woman of bold ambition, who brought Shakespeare to the Vic, and incidentally cast her sixteen-year-old daughter as Juliet. Both Miss Filippi and Shakespeare were quite unasked for and at first unwelcome to Miss Baylis. But Shakespeare caught on. And in 1914 war broke out, and even the war was a stroke of luck since actors, unwanted in the depressed West End just because of the war, were willing to work for the pittance offered at the Vic. And then one evening, quite unexpectedly, came Ben Greet, an English actor-manager who had been tatting Shakespeare companies round the United States for years; he came from a naval family, offered to work for nothing as his contribution to the war effort, and it was he more than anyone else who established the Shakespeare seasons for which the Old Vic became famous. Shakespeare, as it were, became the Old Vic's brand.

It was lucky too that the kind of Shakespeare production by then acceptable, even fashionable, was not at all in the elaborate style that Henry Irving had adopted in his seasons at the Lyceum in the 1880s, but in the simpler, 'purer' manner of William Poel. Greet had hardly any direct connection with the Old Vic. True, he had been manager there for two years in Emma Cons's time but had never produced a play because Miss Cons did not want plays. For her he never put on more than an evening of Shakespeare songs, and had to go elsewhere to present his Shakespeare plays, but by 1914 his bare style, with an open stage and little or no scenery, was the done thing. This was lucky for the Old Vic because it had no scenery, and no means of getting sets on and off stage even if it had any, because at the time it had lost the entire backstage to Morley College.

Lilian Baylis's long rule was of course the greatest good fortune. West End impresarios might belittle her, saying as they did that it was easy enough for her to put on season after season of plays when she had a licence to beg and that in any case the charitable governors of the Old Vic owned the freehold and she therefore did not even have any rent to pay. That was true enough, but still, without her saintly monomania, the theatre would have come to nothing, and monomania is rare and lucky.

And – more good fortune – once Shakespeare was established there the Old Vic could attract, for ten or fifteen pounds a week, already successful West End actors who came because they could there as nowhere else play a whole season of Shakespeare, making a new reputation in the great parts. What luck that already eminent actors should think they hadn't made it until they'd played Shakespeare. But it was and is so. The day came when the young Gielgud, the young Ashcroft, the Richardsons and the Oliviers – the greatest of their generation – offered themselves to the Old Vic. Luck begets luck.

The more recent strokes of good fortune are fresh in the memory. The newly formed National Theatre went there in 1963 – reluctantly as it happened because the new National wanted and expected a new theatre and did not at all welcome the venerable wreck which was all that was on offer. It was expected to be only a short stay, but lasted thirteen years, and this long tenancy of the National preserved and increased the Old Vic's prestige. After the National left, Ed Mirvish appeared in 1982, from Toronto – having heard only by chance and only just in time that the theatre was for sale – and it was his millions and his generosity that restored Delatorre's grand fabric of 1871.

And then in 1998 Sally Greene appeared, and in 2003 Kevin Spacey – and all that is why the Old Vic is where it is today.

Acknowledgements

It is my happy duty to thank all who have helped in the writing, illustration, and publishing of this book.

I thank the Royal Victoria Hall Foundation, the trust that owned the Old Vic for the century from 1880 to 1981 (and still makes grants to small theatre projects in London) and particularly its clerk, Carol Cooper. Historically the Foundation, through its governors and trustees, did its utmost to preserve and maintain the theatre. The foundation still owns the archives of the Old Vic, and has since 1981 left them on permanent loan at the University of Bristol Theatre Collection, where they now form an important part of a great collection, and are cherished and air-conditioned. At Bristol I thank Jo Elsworth, Director of the Collection, Laura Gardner, archivist, and Jill Sullivan for their kindness and help; and also Biddy Hayward at ArenaPAL.

The London Borough of Lambeth, in which the Old Vic lies, has its own collection of archives at the Minet Library, and there I thank Len Reilly, Archive and Library Manager, and Philip Norman. I'm also indebted to the Islington Local History Centre at Finsbury Library which because of its connection with Sadler's Wells theatre has a rich collection of Vic-Wells memorabilia, and a happily surprising amount of material from the early Old Vic.

Now a great debt. The collections of the Victoria and Albert Museum are famously splendid, and I am grateful to the Director, Professor Martin Roth, for his generosity in waiving all reproduction fees. I thank Claire Hudson, Head of Collection Management at the V&A, and Amy King, Assistant Curator, for taking all sorts of trouble, showing me prints and photographs, finding others, and telling me whom else I should approach. I'm grateful to Thomas Messel for permission to use his uncle Oliver Messel's atmospheric painting of the Old Vic in 1938, and to the Topolski Studio for allowing me to reproduce two sketches by Feliks Topolski.

The Old Vic, both the Theatre Trust and the theatre company, have few objects of any age. The historical archive, up to 1981, belonged to the Foundation which wisely took it away to preserve it, since working theatres have no inclination to bother with the past. Laurence Olivier when Director of the National Theatre at the Old Vic declined as 'fearsome clobber' an offer to the theatre of the bells from Henry Irving's famous play of that name. But people do occasionally walk in with gifts from the past, which are zealously looked after by Deano McCullagh, manager of the backstage acres, and which are occasionally hung on office walls. I reproduce in this book an original print in fine condition of Arthur Moreland's sketch of the Vic in 1929. There is also a signed photograph of Ben Greet, full of history but now too faded to reproduce, with the names handwritten below it in ink, on the mount, of the thirty-four plays he produced at the Vic in the war years of 1914–18.

The Old Vic may have few objects, but its people have been generous in all sorts of ways. I thank Kevin Spacey and Sally Greene, Kate Varah, Nicola Howson, Natasha Harris, Catrin John, Fiona English, Rebecca Pepper, and the photographers who most generously allowed me to use their handsome images of the shows put on since 2004: Manuel Harlan, Johan Persson, Ellis Parrinder and Matt Humphrey. And Vivien Wallace, the Old Vic's director of fundraising and also my wife, without whose constant encouragement I should not have written this book.

I thank also my agents of many years at Peters Fraser & Dunlop, Michael Sissons and Fiona Petheram. And Dinah Wood, formerly of the National Theatre and now Editorial Director, Drama, at Faber and Faber, who has commissioned this book. Also at Faber I am indebted to Anne Owen, Managing Editor, and to James Rose, Project Editor, who designed and set this book.

And I make this small gesture of gratitude to Ben Challacombe, late Royal Artillery, for his art and humanity – beyond the call.

Illustrations

1 Opening night at the Royal Coburg, 1818. Originally published 1 January 1819 after a drawing by Robert Schnebbelie dated 11 May 1818, the original of which is in the Victoria and Albert Museum. (This print by kind permission of Lambeth Archives)

2 The Coburg by evening, c.1820, by Daniel Havell. (Lambeth Archives)

3 Playbill for the first night's melodrama. (Old Vic Theatre Trust)

4 The Coburg's glass curtain. Print published by G. Humphrey, London, 20 March 1822. (Wikimedia Commons)

5 Junius Brutus Booth as Richard III, drawn by C. Shoosmith, 1817. (V&A Theatre and Performance)

6 Sarah Egerton, as Madge Wildfire in Scott's *Heart of Midlothian*. (V&A Theatre and Performance)

7 Edmund Kean as Othello. (Author's collection)

8 Eliza Vincent. (From *Theatrical Times*, 13 February 1847)

9 *The Sea*, a melodrama of the 1840s. (From *The Old Old Vic* by Edwin Fagg, 1936)

10 T. P. Cooke as the innocent sailor William in *Black Ey'd Susan*. (V&A Theatre and Performance)

11 The Victoria Palace in the mid-1870s. Woodcut after Percy William Justyne, from *Old and New London*, 1873–8, with hand colouring. (Author's collection)

12 A packed gallery on Saturday night. (From *The Graphic*, October 1872, by Godefroy Durand)

13 Temperance menu offered by Miss Cons. (*Illustrated London News*, 1883)

14 The Victoria Coffee House as Miss Cons built it. (*Illustrated London News*, 22 February 1890)

15 Emma Cons, *c.*1895. (From *The Old Vic* by Cicely Hamilton and Lilian Baylis, 1926)

16 Packed gallery at a Victoria Coffee Hall's penny matinée. (From *The Graphic*, 1882)

17 Royal visit to the Vic, 1910. (Mander and Mitchenson/ University of Bristol/ArenaPAL)

18 Charles Corri conducting opera at the Old Vic. (Sketch by Harry Powell Lloyd)

19 1923 Old Vic programme. (Lambeth Archives)

20 Ben Greet, actor-manager at the Old Vic. (Old Vic Theatre Trust)

21 Miss Baylis with eight producers, from an Old Vic programme, 1933. (Lambeth Archives)

22 Tyrone Guthrie. (From *A Life in the Theatre* by Tyrone Guthrie, 1940.)

23 Charles Laughton. Woodcut by unknown artist. (V&A Theatre and Performance.)

24 Lilian Baylis's office, after the 1928 modernisation. (Old Vic Theatre Trust)

25 Diana Wynyard as Eliza Doolittle in Shaw's *Pygmalion*, 1937. (From *Vic-Wells*, ed. Harcourt Williams, 1938)

26 Peggy Ashcroft as Rosalind in *As You Like It*, sketched by Walter Sickert. (Reproduced from Harcourt Williams's *Four Years at the Old Vic*, 1935)

27 Old Vic audience arriving for the evening performance. (Mander and Mitchenson/University of Bristol/ArenaPAL)

28 Laurence Olivier and Vivien Leigh as Hamlet and Ophelia at Elsinore in May 1937. (Author's collection)

29 Lilian Baylis wearing the insignia of a Companion of Honour, 1937. (Photo Gordon Anthony, © V&A Theatre and Performance)

30 The Old Vic auditorium, 1938. Oil painting by Oliver Messel. (Courtesy Thomas Messel, his nephew, and V&A Theatre and Performance.)

31 Judith Anderson as Lady Macbeth, 1937. (Chalk drawing by unknown artist.)

32 John Gielgud as Lear, 1940. Costume design and sketch by Roger Furse. (V&A Theatre and Performance)

33 Alec Guinness as Hamlet, 1938. (Old Vic Theatre Trust)

34 The Old Vic after an air raid. Painting by Roger Furse, 1942. The theatre did not reopen until 1950. (From *A Theatre for Everybody* by Edward J. Dent, 1945)

35 Richard Burton and Claire Bloom as Hamlet and Ophelia, 1953. (Photo Angus McBean/Mander and Mitchenson/University of Bristol/ArenaPAL)

36 Eileen Atkins as Miranda and Alastair Sim as Prospero in *The Tempest*, 1954. (Lambeth Archives)

37 The Queen after a performance of *Henry VIII* in 1953, with Paul Rogers as the king and Leo Genn as the Duke of Buckingham. (Mander and Michenson/University of Bristol/ArenaPAL)

38 John Stride and Judi Dench in Zeffirelli's *Romeo and Juliet*, 1960. (Houston Rogers/V&A Theatre and Performance)

39 Laurence Olivier as Othello and Maggie Smith as Desdemona, 1964. (Author's collection)

40 Geraldine McEwan in Somerset Maugham's *Home and Beauty*, 1968. Poster design by Ken Briggs. (Royal National Theatre Archive.)

41 A sketch by Feliks Topolski of Tony Harrison's version of Molière's *Le Misanthrope* at the Old Vic, 1975. (Topolski Studio, V&A Theatre and Performance)

42 John Stride and Edward Petherbridge in Tom Stoppard's *Rosencrantz and Guildenstern Are Dead*, 1967. (Photo Anthony Crickmay, © V&A Theatre and Performance)

43 John Gielgud and Ralph Richardson in Pinter's *No Man's Land*, 1975. (Photo Douglas H. Jeffery, © V&A Theatre and Performance)

44 Sing-song in the Old Vic rehearsal room after Olivier's last performance there or on any stage, 21 March 1974. (Author's collection)

45 Ed Mirvish outside the Royal Alexandra Theatre, Toronto. (Courtesy Mirvish Enterprises)

46 The auditorium after its restoration, 1981. (Old Vic Theatre Trust)

47 Sally Greene and Kevin Spacey. (Photo Richard Young)

48. Ian McKellen as Widow Twankey in *Aladdin*, 2005. (Photo Manuel Harlan)

49 Jennifer Ehle in Philip Barry's *Philadelphia Story*, 2005. (Photo Manuel Harlan)

50 Diana Rigg in Almodóvar's *All About My Mother*, 2007. (Photo Manuel Harlan)

51 Re-enactment of the battle of the Somme in *On the Middle Day*, at the Imperial War Museum, near the Old Vic, 2006. (Old Vic Theatre Trust)

52 Kevin Spacey and Jeff Goldblum in *Speed-the-Plow*, 2008. (Photo Ellis Parrinder)

53 Sinead Cusack in the Bridge Project's *Cherry Orchard*, 2009. (Photo Joan Marcus, Brooklyn Academy of Music)

54 Simon Russell Beale as Leontes in the Bridge Project's *Winter's Tale*, 2009. (Photo Joan Marcus, Brooklyn Academy of Music)

55 Robert Lindsay in John Osborne's *The Entertainer*, 2007. (Photo Manuel Harlan)

56 Anne-Marie Duff in Terence Rattigan's *Cause Célèbre*, 2010. (Photo Johan Persson)

57 The Old Vic as a theatre in the round, 2008, called the CQS Space, after its sponsor. (Photo Matt Humphrey)

OTHER ILLUSTRATIONS, IN THE TEXT

Western elevation of Delatorre's new Royal Victoria Palace, 1871. (National Archives) *p. 52*

A crowded Royal Victoria Hall (above) and coffee tavern (below). (From *The Graphic*, 20 August 1881) *p. 63*

Poster for Miss Cons's coffee tavern and hall, 1884. Lithograph by Miss Duncan. (V&A Theatre and Performance) *p. 65*

Opera queue for the Old Vic gallery. (Old Vic Theatre Trust, probably from annual report of the Royal Victoria Hall Foundation, *c.*1912) *p. 73*

Old Vic green slip advertising the 1914–15 season. (Author's collection) *p. 79*

Old Vic appeal for money. (*Old Vic Magazine,*1922) *p. 88*

The Old Vic, 1928 or 1929. Sketch by Arthur Moreland. (Old Vic Theatre Trust) *p. 94*

Laurence Olivier as the captain in Strindberg's *Dance of Death*. Pen-and-ink drawing by Claude Marks, signed by Olivier. (Author's collection) *p. 164*

Peter Hall rehearsing John Gielgud in Pinter's *No Man's Land* at the Old Vic, 1975. Drawing by Feliks Topolski. (Topolski Studio, V&A Theatre and Performance) *p. 175*

Architects' plans for the Old Vic. (*Courtesy of Bennetts Associates, Architects*, 2014) *p. 228*

The author and publishers have made every effort to trace the copyright to illustrations 32 and 34, by Roger Furse, in the V&A Theatre and Performance Collections, and would be glad to hear from the holder.

Sources and Bibliography

This list intends to be a brief selection. Many actors and directors have written memoirs, those who worked at the Old Vic always mention it, and I have listed only those I think the most informative, or revealing, or elegant, or amusing.

I have throughout quoted from the newspapers of the time. I do not assert the too-literal truth of the quotation from Lord Macaulay that used to appear on the title page of the quarterly index to *The Times*, in which he stated: 'The only true history of a country is to be found in its newspapers.' But I do believe newspapers are often the best guide to what happened when, and that they have the priceless merit of giving an account of events before the participants can begin to fashion legends out of them. And certainly, before Emma Cons arrives in 1880, newspapers are often the only way of knowing what was happening at the Coburg and then the Victoria. So it is fortunate that a whole swathe of nineteenth-century newspapers are now online – not just the likes of *The Times* and the *Pall Mall Gazette* but also the *Era*, which specialised in news of the theatre and the licensed trade, and sixty or so others. After 1900, I have continued to use newspapers as a prime source, along with memoirs, biographies, and autobiographies.

After 1880 there are also the archives of the Royal Victoria Hall Foundation, the charitable trust that owned the Old Vic until 1981. These are now in the University of Bristol Theatre Collection. There are also the *Old Vic Magazine*, 1919–30, and the *Old Vic and Sadler's Wells Magazine*, 1931–9, published mostly bi-monthly by the theatre and full of information found nowhere else. Bristol University, the London Borough of Lambeth at the Minet Library, and the Borough of Islington at the Finsbury Library, have runs of these magazines.

GENERAL HISTORIES

The Old Vic Theatre: A History, by George Rowell, Cambridge 1993. A scholarly work by a former Reader in Theatre History at Bristol University.

The Old Vic Story, by Peter Roberts, 1976. By a former editor of *Plays and Players* magazine.

The Old Old Vic, by Edwin Fagg, 1936. An entertaining mishmash of the theatre's history up to 1880, with some prints. Published by the Vic-Wells Association and sold at the Old Vic for ninepence.

The Old Vic: a Century of Theatrical History, by John Booth, 1917. Briefly takes the story up to 1916.

The Old Vic, by Cicely Hamilton and Lilian Baylis, 1926. A book in two parts. The shorter and much the better part, only thirty-six pages, is by Miss Baylis herself and is the most comprehensive account of Emma Cons's life that we have.

The National Theatre Story, by Daniel Rosenthal, 2013. Covers National Theatre productions and politics at the Old Vic, 1963–76, in great detail.

ON LILIAN BAYLIS

Lilian Baylis, by Sybil and Russell Thorndike, 1938. Hagiography with anecdotes.

Lilian Baylis: the Lady of the Old Vic, by Richard Findlater, 1975. The author knew the London theatre well and had the advantage of knowing Miss Baylis's personal secretary.

Lilian Baylis: A Biography, by [Professor] Elizabeth Schafer, 2006. The standard biography, sympathetic, impeccably researched from the archives, strong on Miss Baylis's inner life.

OTHER BIOGRAPHIES, AUTOBIOGRAPHIES, MEMOIRS, AND LETTERS

(Listed sometimes under the author's name, sometimes under the subject's, whichever seems the more useful.)

[Ashcroft] *Peggy Ashcroft*, by Michael Billington, 1988.

Bloom, Claire, *Leaving a Doll's House*, 1996.

Dent, Edward J., *A Theatre for Everybody*, 1945.

Gielgud, John, *Early Stages*, 1939.

Gielgud, The Authorised Biography, by Sheridan Morley, 2002, who knew his subject well.

Gielgud's Letters, ed. Richard Mangan, 2004. Splendid stuff.

Gielgud: A Theatrical Life, by Jonathan Croall, 2001.

[Greet] *Ben Greet and the Old Vic*, by Winifred Isaac, 1964. Essential for early Baylis days.

Guinness, Alec, *Blessings in Disguise*, 1985, and *My Name Escapes Me*, 1995. Always charming, sometimes candid.

Guthrie, Tyrone, *A Life in the Theatre*, 1940. By one of the great men of the Vic, and essential for the 1930s.

Hunt, Hugh, *Old Vic Prefaces*, 1954.

[Miller] *Jonathan Miller: In Two Minds, a Biography*, by Kate Bassett, 2012.

[Mirvish] *Honest Ed Mirvish*, Toronto, 1993. Lively tales from the saviour of the Vic.

Olivier, Laurence, *Confessions of an Actor*, 1982. Wildly inaccurate, full of life.

Olivier, The Authorised Biography, by Terry Coleman, 2005.

Olivier, by Philip Ziegler, 2013.

Quayle, Anthony, *A Time to Speak*, 1990.

[Thorndike] *Sybil Thorndike, A Star of Life*, by Jonathan Croall, 2008.

Valois, Ninette de, *Come Dance With Me*, 1957. Memoir by a woman as strong as Lilian Baylis, and who was also there.

West, Timothy, *A Moment Towards the End of the Play*, 2001. On the Prospect period.

Williams, Harcourt, *Four Years at the Old Vic*, 1935, after his time as producer.

Williams, Harcourt, *Old Vic Saga*, 1949. Well illustrated and, like Dent (above), full of post-war hope.

Williamson, Audrey, *Old Vic Drama 1934–47*, 1948, and *Old Vic Drama 2, 1947–57*, 1957. More drama criticism than history, as the author intended, but full of details not found elsewhere.

MISCELLANEOUS

The Report of the House of Commons Select Committee on Dramatic Literature, 1832, heard evidence on the Coburg [paragraphs 119 to 1405] from its proprietor, George Bolwell Davidge.

Plans for Robinson's 1871 rebuilding of the Victoria, and some correspondence with impresario, manager, and architect can be found in the Lord Chamberlain's papers, National Archives, Kew, LC 1/47, 1/248, and 1/249.

The Old Vic Refurbished, by D. F. Cheshire, Sean McCarthy, and Hilary Norris, 1983, gives a summary of the theatre's early history, together with an account of the Mirvish reconstruction, with many illustrations.

The Bulletin of the Association for Preservation Technology, Vol. 17, 1985, has a long article, 'Upon Reflection: the Architect's Account of the Restoration of the Old Vic Theatre' by Barry Pritchard, the project architect for Renton Howard Wood Levin partnership, which gives details of the 1982 works and of previous alterations.

Dramatic School, by Patricia Don Young, 1954. Innocent memoir by an unknown young actress, good on the atmosphere at the Old Vic and of The Cut, 1936–8.

Index

Numbers in *italics* show pages with line illustrations in the text. Illustrations in the four-colour plate sections, numbered 1 to 65, are listed, also in italics, as '*plate 1*' and so on.

The Old Vic entry starts from the time that Lilian Baylis received a theatre licence in 1912. For earlier entries, *see* Royal Coburg Theatre, Royal Victoria Theatre, Victoria Theatre, Royal Victoria Palace, Royal Victoria Hall.